Helen Mar Kimball

AUTHOR & DEFENDER OF THE
RESTORATION

JOSEPH SMITH'S PLURAL WIVES
VOLUME 1

JOSEPH SMITH®
FOUNDATION

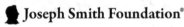
Joseph Smith Foundation®

Joseph Smith Foundation is an organization focused on supporting and contributing to projects founded in the words of Jesus Christ. Those contributing to *Joseph Smith Foundation* projects are members of The Church of Jesus Christ of Latter-day Saints, but the foundation is not sponsored by the Church. *Joseph Smith Foundation* projects include documentary films, Latter-day Answers, ZionTube, InspiraWiki, FAQs, Papers, Audio, Ebooks and much more.
www.JosephSmithFoundation.org

Published by:
Joseph Smith Foundation®
Salem, UT, USA

1st printing

Interior Design: Leah M. Stoddard, Isaiah M. Stoddard

Cover Design: Leah M. Stoddard, James F. Stoddard III

Thanks & Contribution: Jim F. & Margaret J. Stoddard, Russell H. & Heidi S. Barlow, Cameron & Kimberly W. Smith, Ephraim J., Mary D., & Ezra B. Stoddard, Julie A. & Natalie Smith, Jeff & RaeLyn Stoddard, Jared & Kaylene Stoddard, John & Meredith Stoddard

Library of Congress Control Number: 2022900312
ISBN: 978-163752341-4

Printed in the USA

The editors have preserved the original spelling and grammar of the quotations—particularly the diaries, letters and historical documents—featured in this book.

Helen Mar Kimball

JOSEPH SMITH'S PLURAL WIVES

VOLUME 1

L. Hannah Stoddard
James F. Stoddard III

*To my dearest sisters (Leah, Mary, & Eliza), my future
daughters, and all women in Zion: may you discover renewed
hope—a victorious vision of womanhood by walking in
the faithful footsteps of the heroines of the Restoration.*

Russell H. Barlow . . . . Assistant Writer, Senior Editor

Leah M. Stoddard . . . . Citation Editor

Kimberly W. Smith . . . . Senior Researcher

Jill Limburg Korajac. . . . . Senior Editor

Emma Katherine Korajac . . . . Senior Editor

Margaret J. Stoddard . . . . Editor, Researcher

Rebecca Connolly . . . . Researcher

Threesa L. Cummings . . . . . Researcher & Assistant Editor

Isaiah M. Stoddard. . . . . Layout Editor

Marinda R. Cummings . . . . Assistant Citation Editor

Luke William Korajac. . . . . Assistant Citation Editor

Benjamin G. Mulder. . . . . Assistant Citation Editor

Beverly J. Arbon . . . . Editor

Joseph Smith Foundation®

Thanks & Acknowledgment
FOR RESEARCH & REVIEW

Heidi S. Barlow	Emily Dayley
Amber E. Schmidt	S. Dawnyka Peterson
Elizabeth G. Vidrine	Rachel B. Barlow
Ephraim J. Stoddard	Mary D. Stoddard
Tyler S. Croall	Iris V. Mathias
RaeLyn Stoddard	Alexis P. Dollar
L. William Utsch	Sariah N. Jackson
Sasha L. Silvaz	Sarah B. Nash
Stryder W. Smith	Elowen E. Schmidt
Sorena Marble	Esther B. Schmidt

This work details the life and experiences of Helen Mar Kimball, one of the plural wives of the Prophet Joseph Smith. Helen's marriage—an eternal sealing—to Joseph is used repeatedly by critics of the Prophet to attack Joseph Smith's character, honor, and integrity. The purpose of the work is to present an accurate history of Joseph and Helen's relationship in regard to Celestial plural marriage, as well as an examination of Helen's personal feelings and testimony, and a general account of her life and legacy—a story that should be of great worth to Latter-day Saint women today. This book seeks to look candidly at plural marriage as it factored into the lives of the early Saints. We acknowledge the fact that The Church of Jesus Christ of Latter-day Saints does not currently practice plural marriage, as reflected in Official Declaration 1, contained in the Doctrine and Covenants, available at ChurchofJesusChrist.org.

CONTENTS

In Memoriam of our Dad
JAMES F. STODDARD III

This volume was begun in 2020 with our father, James F. Stoddard III. Sadly, Dad passed away on the morning of September 6, 2021, in faith and peace, after a courageous battle with stage 4 lung cancer. Even during the painful last months of his life, he worked steadily on this book and other projects, intensely driven to help as many members as he could to strengthen their testimony of the Gospel. Dad's life was defined by an unparalleled love for his children, an unshakeable witness of the Son of God, Jesus Christ, and the Prophet Joseph Smith, as well as an unwavering devotion to the Gospel. We remember well how whenever parting, our Dad would bid goodbye by calling out, "Keep the faith!" Dad used the Gospel to transform our home, and he pled with us to share that hope with others! Living gospel principles, consecrating our time and talents, raising our standards, and following in the footsteps of our Master, Jesus Christ, has filled our home with joy—even in the midst of suffering and pain. It is our desire to continue the legacy our father began—to share that hope with the world! To learn more about his life and legacy, visit:

www.JosephSmithFoundation.org/Memorial

PREFACE

'Polygamy' was never on my radar as a controversy I anticipated addressing in the public square. With so many causes to engage in and passions to pursue, studying and defending Celestial plural marriage just wasn't on my bucket list. But that began to shift as I came face to face with hundreds of women throughout the Church who were struggling—even hurting—due to a fundamental *misunderstanding* of this eternal principle.

While speaking with my father at conferences, expos, and firesides throughout the years, I began to notice a recurring theme when questioning an audience with: "What 'tough issue' do you want to talk about?" During 'Answers to Faith Crisis' presentations, we typically presented a list of topics, including: The Book of Abraham, multiple First Vision accounts, DNA and the Book of Mormon, science and religion, etc.—but over and over again, the nearly universal response came: "Polygamy. We want to know about polygamy!" Really??

Although we sometimes joked about this during our speaking engagements, in the back of my mind, I realized: "There is a real need here—a need often beset with worries, questions, doubts, and nearly tangible *fear*."

During one 2018 presentation, I casually mentioned I could share resources with women who were wrestling with plural marriage— history from our past that could bring peace and understanding amidst the turbulent controversy. I apparently didn't realize what I was getting myself into. For several hours after my presentation, I was caught behind our booth as women gathered and brought in chairs, sitting anxiously on the edge of their seats and hoping for answers. Looking into their eyes, I saw agony etched in their faces, and the realization struck me again: "There is a serious need here." That night, I walked away determined that *something* needed to be done. As I continued searching, I discovered that the only professional materials available were written primarily by progressive historians and, with a sinking feeling, I began encountering member after member whose testimony had been shattered by these publications. What could be done? What could I do?

My personal search for understanding had begun four years earlier as a 19-year-old woman. Even as a child, I had always been insistent on finding *answers*—never being content with ignorance, the unknown, or letting my questions accumulate on a gospel 'shelf.' Driven by a desire to know more, I felt compelled to claim my own grounding— my own *informed* testimony. As a member of The Church of Jesus Christ of Latter-day Saints, currently participating in the practice of plural marriage was never a personal consideration,[1] but as a film producer and speaker, I recognized the serious implications of the doctrine and its history as it pertains to the character and viability of Joseph Smith's work. Was this doctrine a black mark on our past? Do we need to apologize? Or was this among the *crowning principles* of the Celestial kingdom, as Joseph Smith taught—and can we find credible, faith-inspiring answers to complete our understanding?

At the time, I was researching original documents on women's rights—including first, second, and third wave feminism, suffrage in the Church, the patriarchal order, and temple covenants—when I happened to stumble across the forgotten writings of a woman who would forever change my life—a woman who has unfortunately been stigmatized as the infamous 14-year-old plural wife of Joseph Smith: Helen Mar Kimball. I later returned to this study with a team of researchers and writers in the spring of 2020—and before long, Helen had become a kindred spirit whose life and struggles resonated deeply. We were absolutely fascinated with this compassionate, independent, and resolute woman. As we poured over her diaries, letters, and published articles, we discovered a wife and mother who employed voice and pen to defend the Gospel and the Prophet Joseph Smith. We learned that while a younger Helen had initially felt serious reservations in regard to Celestial plural marriage, she had walked through her own shadowed valley of doubt, wrestling for truth before emerging with a searing and steadfast testimony. Helen would publicly and passionately uphold Celestial plural marriage until the day she died. Her pamphlet, *Why We Practice Plural Marriage*, was the impetus behind gaining my own witness of the doctrine and Joseph Smith's practice of plural marriage.

---

1   The Church of Jesus Christ of Latter-day Saints does not currently practice plural marriage. See the revelation on this subject: Official Declaration 1, ChurchofJesusChrist.org

As I have pondered my many conversations with troubled women over the years, one recurring question has continually come to my mind: *Could Helen help my troubled sisters in the faith?* Was Helen Mar Kimball's life and legacy an answer to this plague of doubt?

A Woman's Voice for Our Time

We live in an age of controversy. Conflicting narratives, shaken faith, and decades of progressivism have challenged the traditionalist foundations of the Restoration, leaving Joseph Smith's revelation on Celestial Marriage (Doctrine and Covenants 132) all but hanging by a thread. On one hand, we hear allegations that the Prophet Joseph Smith was guilty of hidden sins. Some say he was an adulterer, a womanizer—even a pedophile! On the other hand, we see the foul resurrection of a revisionist movement based on a century-old claim that Joseph Smith never practiced plural marriage. Some of those behind this dark narrative are actually claiming that the death of the Prophet Joseph Smith was plotted by Brigham Young. Consequently, temple covenants, priesthood blessings, family sealings, and more, are suddenly left null and void. In an age of ignorance, naivety, and widespread unfamiliarity with true history and doctrine, thousands continue to find themselves unintentionally seduced by the voices coming from either camp. *Where is the truth?*

In the midst of this war of words and tumult of opinions, a woman steps forward—a woman with a story and a testimony borne of perseverance and firsthand experience, a woman whose voice and pen has the potential to shatter the attacks on both the Prophet Joseph Smith and his rightful successor, Brigham Young. Ironically, this woman is also the oft-maligned icon of the Restoration's harshest critics who attempt to hijack her story for their own destructive purposes. That woman is Helen Mar Kimball.

Helen's character has endured the excoriation of historians and critics who famously—infamously to some—refer to her as the 14-year-old girl sealed to Joseph Smith in 1843. Although many who are antagonistic toward the Church love to cite her name disparagingly, they also bury her complete story, silencing her words within their context. Why? Because her words vindicate Joseph and the Gospel he restored.

Today we live in an age when the characters of Joseph Smith and Brigham Young are under attack. I believe it is the responsibility and covenant duty of every member of the Church to become informed, and to stand in defense of the Restoration with real facts, real data, and *real history*.

Women have a central role in this latter-day struggle. Throughout history, generations have looked for inspiration from women who shaped destiny—Esther, Joan of Arc, Abigail Adams, Florence Nightingale, and many others. Sadly, the heroines of the Restoration have largely been forgotten, reconstructed, or taken out of context, despite—or perhaps, because of—the preeminent significance of their leadership and bountiful contributions. Women have a special place in the Restoration—an extraordinarily unique place of influence and testimony. I personally believe the legacy of righteous women in the Church has too long been undermined, silenced, and hidden by opposing forces. The story of the women needs to be told—it *must* be told—and so we begin by resurrecting a compelling heroine of the Restoration—Helen Mar Kimball.

Behind nearly every great man is a great woman. And behind the Prophet Joseph Smith stood a remarkable cohort of stalwart queens in Zion whose lives and testimonies changed the course of history forever. Ironically the most-often slandered of all Joseph's wives—the one who began with her own struggles, doubts, and fears as a young woman—Helen would become one of the most significant female defenders of Celestial plural marriage—past, present, and even future. Helen's life signifies that she was raised up by the Lord to exonerate Joseph's character in both her day and ours. Her legacy speaks to her calling—her mission to articulate and preserve Joseph's teachings. The dynamics of her life story are a compelling template and model for Latter-day Saints in our contemporary quest for Zion.

In a day fraught with confusion, Helen's voice has the potential, I believe, to set the record straight, and blaze a trail for succeeding Saints to tread in taking on the mantle and securing the Restoration. Helen knew the Prophet. She lived difficult doctrines. She laid down her life to preserve the Gospel of Jesus Christ. This is her story.

L. Hannah Stoddard, 2022

CHAPTER 1

Daughter of Destiny

"Helen, would you believe me if I told you that it was right for married men to take other wives?"[1]

Helen Mar Kimball, not quite fifteen, was unprepared for the sudden, spontaneous question. It was a summer morning in Nauvoo, Illinois in the year 1843. Heber C. Kimball, a member of the Quorum of the Twelve Apostles, had gently pulled aside his beloved daughter to approach a sensitive, but vitally important, principle—and a potentially dangerous subject. Helen was stunned. Her father's startling question triggered "a similar effect to the sudden shock of a small earthquake."[2] Her "first impulse was anger" because she thought her father was "test[ing her] virtue."[3] How could he question her integrity?

"No, I wouldn't!" she cried out emphatically. Helen and her father shared a strong relationship of trust and respect that was seasoned with moments of humor and jest. Now—for the first time—she had "openly manifested anger"[4] to her father.

The enemies of the Church and of the Prophet Joseph Smith were in a constant state of excitement. Like many, Helen had heard rumors of 'polygamy' and 'spiritual wifery' in Nauvoo—lurid tales published by former friends-turned-apostate, including John C. Bennett and the Higbees—but she regarded such scandals as nothing more

---

1   Helen Mar Kimball Whitney, "Scenes and Incidents in Nauvoo," *Woman's Exponent* 11, no. 5 (August 1, 1882): 39.

2   Helen Mar Kimball Whitney, "Scenes in Nauvoo After the Martyrdom of the Prophet and Patriarch," *Woman's Exponent* 11, no. 19 (March 1, 1883): 146.

3   Helen Mar Kimball Whitney, "Scenes and Incidents in Nauvoo," *Woman's Exponent* 11, no. 5 (August 1, 1882): 39.

4   Ibid.

than baseless gossip. Now, she thought her father must certainly be questioning her loyalty and "test[ing *her*] virtue":[5]

// My sensibilities were painfully touched. I felt such a sense of personal injury and displeasure; for to mention such a thing to me I thought altogether unworthy of my father, and as quick as he spoke, I replied to him, short and emphatically, *No, I wouldn't!* I had always been taught to believe it a heinous crime, improper and unnatural, and I indignantly resented it.[6]

Helen's ancestry included stalwart English reformers—men and women who risked life and limb to worship their true King, the Lord Jesus Christ, according to the dictates of their own conscience.[7] The Kimballs' ancestors had become refugees, fleeing persecution and threats of imprisonment—eventually establishing roots in the untamed wilderness of the New World. Virtue and chastity—both characteristics of valor—were revered and strictly observed. Honor had defined their bloodline through the generations.

Helen was a true daughter of these righteous forebears, sharing her ancestral passion for purity. What seemed like a challenge of her integrity provoked an irritable and heated response. However, instead of annoyance, her sharp answer drew a "rather pleased"[8] expression from her father's face. With tender sobriety, he began to gently expound the principle of plural marriage—disclosing the practice as a necessary part of the "Restoration of all things."[9] According to Helen's account in 1882, her father introduced the

---

5   Ibid.

6   Ibid; emphasis in original.

7   Augusta Joyce Crocheron, *Representative Women of Deseret* (Salt Lake City: J. C. Graham & Co.), 109.

8   Helen Mar Kimball Whitney, "Scenes and Incidents in Nauvoo," *Woman's Exponent* 11, no. 5 (August 1, 1882): 39.

9   Prophets, both ancient and modern, have testified that this dispensation is the greatest of all gospel dispensations. The Prophet Joseph Smith also taught that the greatest prophets, priests, and kings all looked down through time to this age with joy and delight, including Peter (Acts 3:21), Paul (Ephesians 1:10), Alma (Alma 41), Isaiah, John the Beloved, and others. Joseph Smith also explained: "The dispensation of the fulness of times will bring to light the things that have been revealed in all former dispensations, also other things that have not been before revealed. . . . " Joseph Smith, History, 1838–1856, volume C-1 [2 November 1838–31 July 1842], p. 1230, The Joseph Smith Papers.

Heber C. Kimball home, Nauvoo, Illinois

doctrines and principles associated with the institution, but may not have intimated that anyone had already engaged in plural marriage.[10]

For the next 24 hours, Helen's mind raced as "thoughts, fears and temptations"[11] flashed like lightning in a flurry of emotion. *Polygamy?* The thought was so foreign—so new and incongruent with tradition that she struggled to fathom the very idea:

Also, "... all the ordinances and duties that ever have been required by the Priesthood under the directions and commandments of the Almighty in any of the dispensations, shall all be had in the last dispensation—Therefore all things had under the authority of the Priesthood at any former period shall be had again, bringing to pass the restoration spoken of by the mouth of all the Holy Prophets ..." Joseph Smith, History, 1838–1856, volume C-1 [2 November 1838–31 July 1842], p. 18 [addenda], The Joseph Smith Papers.

Heber C. Kimball would later teach that this last dispensation is the greatest dispensation, and that Joseph and Hyrum Smith have the responsibility to rise up and confer power upon every other dispensation. Heber C. Kimball, "The Latter-Day Kingdom—Men not to Be Governed By Their Wives—Love to God Manifested By Love to His Servants," in *Journal of Discourses*, vol. 5 (London: Asa Calkin, 1858), 28. Discourse given on July 12, 1857.

10   Helen's 1881 autobiographical letter written as a mother's last words for her children seems to suggest that Helen was asked by her father to marry the Prophet Joseph Smith during their first conversation. However, in her 1882 *Woman's Exponent* account, Helen explains that during this discussion, her father "did not tell me then that any one had yet practiced it ..." Helen Mar Kimball Whitney, "Scenes and Incidents in Nauvoo," *Woman's Exponent* 11, no. 5 (August 1, 1882): 39.

11   Ibid.

❙❙ I was filled with various and conflicting ideas. . . . I was skeptical—
one minute believed, then doubted. I thought of the love and
tenderness that [my father] felt for his only daughter, and I
knew that he would not cast her off, and this was the only
convincing proof that I had of its being right. I knew that he
loved me too well to teach me anything that was not strictly
pure, virtuous and exalting in its tendencies; and no one else
could have influenced me at that time or brought me to accept
of a doctrine so utterly repugnant and so contrary to all of our
former ideas and traditions.[12]

Around this time, Helen's father approached her, inviting her to
share her feelings concerning a special opportunity. Would she not
only accept plural marriage as a sacred doctrine, but also choose to
unite herself under a sacred covenant sealing to the Prophet Joseph
Smith? Of all the men in the world, with their varying characters and
personalities, would she accept the Prophet's vision by uniting with
his family to build up the kingdom for the glory of God? As Helen
waded through overwhelming thoughts and feelings—grasping for
new understanding—her mind seemed to return again and again to
an examination of her own father's character.

Taking a Step of Faith

As a committed Christian and devoted follower of God, Heber C.
Kimball and his wife, Vilate, had already forged their way through
many faith-demanding experiences as they embraced each new
principle revealed from the heavens. The restoration of temple
ordinances, the call to build Zion in the settlements of Kirtland,
Missouri, and Nauvoo, the bestowal of priesthood power, the
revelation of the three degrees of glory, and so forth, had truly
stretched their faith. And then came plural and Celestial Marriage.
Helen was unaware that her mother had previously faced the
inevitable consequences of this new doctrine,[13] having received

---

12   Ibid.

13   The confidentiality of many plural marriages in Nauvoo was required due to
dangerous legal and societal consequences should the practice become publicized.
Bigamy was illegal in Illinois and the already heated persecution against the Latter-
day Saints, as well as the historical precedent for forced expulsion and mobbings,
required prudence and secrecy to avoid adding additional fuel to the flame.

*Painting of Heber C. and Vilate Kimball with
two of their children, ca. 1851-1852*

her own personal communication and witness from God. In fact, unbeknownst to Helen, her father and mother had already accepted a second wife.[14]

---

14 Heber was led through a series of tests to try his loyalty, much like the Lord had done with Abraham. First, Heber was asked to give his wife, Vilate, to Joseph Smith as one of his plural wives. "Three days he [Heber] fasted and wept and prayed. Then, with a broken and a bleeding heart, but with soul self-mastered for the sacrifice, he led his darling wife to the Prophet's house and presented her to Joseph. . . . Joseph wept at this proof of devotion, and embracing Heber told him that was all that the Lord required. He had proved him, as a child of Abraham, that he would 'do the works of Abraham,' holding back nothing, but laying all upon the altar for God's glory.

"The Prophet joined the hands of the heroic and devoted pair, and then and there, by virtue of the sealing power and authority of the Holy Priesthood, Heber and Vilate Kimball were made husband and wife for all eternity." Orson F. Whitney, *Life of Heber C. Kimball* (Salt Lake City: Kimball Family, 1888), 334-335.

The next test came when Heber was asked to enter plural marriage himself—without telling his wife Vilate, for fear she would reject and expose the practice—leading to treacherous attacks on the Saints. Heber was asked to marry Sarah Noon, a recent convert who had fled an abusive marriage—forced to abandon her drunken husband—leaving her family destitute. Heber was in agony over his inability to confide in his wife, and Vilate noticed his distress. Turning to the Lord in prayer, Vilate was given a vision of Celestial marriage, in which she had the principle

Nauvoo Remembered, by Jon McNaughton

Heber and Vilate were driven by necessity to live their newfound testimony in secret due to the doctrine's sacred nature, the legal prohibitions in Illinois, and the guaranteed criticism that would beset them from all sides—friends and strangers alike—who had not been taught this order of Celestial Marriage in its proper context. Many members were struggling to understand even the most basic concepts of eternal marriage and family sealings; *plural* marriage was a step too far for the Church at large.

Bigamy[15] was illegal in the state of Illinois. If caught, Helen's father would face imprisonment and heavy fines, the Kimball family would be separated, and knowledge of the practice might contribute to a repeat of the horrors in Missouri. The price was steep, and Heber and Vilate knew well the cost.

However, these committed Saints firmly maintained that personal revelation had communicated—without doubt—the glorious

---

explained and taught to her in its fullness. Immediately following the vision, Vilate rushed to her husband "with a countenance beaming with joy, for she was filled with the Spirit of God," and told him, "'Heber, what you kept from me the Lord has shown me.' . . . She covenanted to stand by him and honor the principle, which covenant she faithfully kept, and though her trials were often heavy and grievous to bear, she knew that father was also being tried, and her integrity was unflinching to the end. She gave my father many wives, and they always found in my mother a faithful friend." Ibid., 338.

15   Defined by Webster's 1828 Dictionary as, "The crime of having two wives at once. But the term is ordinarily used as synonymous with Polygamy, and may be more justly defined, the crime of having a plurality of wives." Noah Webster, *An American Dictionary of the English Language* (New York: S. Converse, 1828), 261.

eternal blessings this familial decision would bring. Heber and Vilate did not practice plural marriage because of Joseph Smith—but rather, because of conviction born through direct inspiration from their Father in Heaven. Having walked through their own fiery furnace, Heber and Vilate felt that the time had arrived for their precious daughter to wrestle with this eternal principle—a 'blessing' she could not be sheltered from.[16] However, she would ultimately be left to choose for herself; the final decision had to rest firmly with Helen.

> *The final decision had to rest firmly with Helen*

The day following Heber's conversation with Helen, the Prophet Joseph Smith called to visit with the family. Vilate watched as her daughter quietly listened to the Prophet teach "the principle and explain it more fully."[17] Joseph respectfully turned to Vilate and asked her permission—was she comfortable with her daughter being approached? Although Heber had previously introduced the thought to Helen, the Prophet felt it was essential to show respect to her mother. Vilate replied, "If Helen is willing I have nothing more to say." Vilate's heart bled with emotion,[18] but her feelings were not unlike the wisdom of a parent who allows their child to stumble when learning to walk. Despite the certain difficulty that would follow, Vilate knew her consent would ultimately open the door for Helen to gain greater growth and happiness.

---

16   Although standards of maturity in 19th-century children were unquestionably superior to those of our day, Helen was still young. In spite of her youth, however, Heber clearly felt impressed to introduce the subject at this time. The Prophet's unexpected, violent death just a year later, in 1844, may explain why Heber felt impressed by the Lord to approach his daughter and to entrust her with this sensitive knowledge at that time.

17   Helen Mar Kimball Whitney, "Scenes and Incidents in Nauvoo," *Woman's Exponent* 11, no. 5 (August 1, 1882): 39.

18   "None but God & his angels could see my mother's bleeding heart—when Joseph asked her if she was willing, she replied 'If Helen is willing I have nothing more to say.' She had witnessed the sufferings of others, who were older & who better understood the step they were taking, & to see her child, who had scarcely seen her fifteenth summer, following in the same thorny path, in her mind she saw the misery which was as sure to come as the sun was to rise and set; but it was all hidden from me." Helen Mar Kimball Whitney, Helen M. Kimball Whitney papers, 1881-1882, Autobiography, March 30, 1881, https://catalog.churchofjesuschrist.org/assets/2c0cb6bb-493b-417a-8bd5-dce48180827f/1/3.

Throughout her life, Helen exhibited the tenacity of an independent, freethinking woman. Although her parents had taught her to respect the Prophet and President of the Church, Helen noted that Joseph Smith's introduction of the principle was *not* the determining factor in her decision to accept this new teaching. Helen poetically explained:

/ / I'd been taught to revere the Prophet of God

And receive every word as the word of the Lord.[19]

But had this not come through my dear father's mouth,

I should ne'r have received it as God's sacred truth.[20]

Deep stirrings within her heart moved Helen to take a step of faith—to choose to believe. Of one matter she was certain: she was unshakably confident that her father was a man of honor and integrity who possessed no ulterior motives. With particular intent, she exercised a careful observation of her father throughout her entire life, and she knew "he loved me too tenderly to introduce anything that was not strictly pure and exalting in its tendencies . . . I could have sooner believed that he would slay me, than teach me an impure principle."[21] Why did Helen exhibit such enduring trust in her father? Perhaps a better question might be: *Was her father worthy of Helen's confidence?*

---

19   Note that the Prophet Joseph Smith adamantly taught against yielding blind obedience to any man or leader. He reproached the Relief Society in Nauvoo for having "darkened" minds because they were "depending on the prophet." The Prophet taught that true, inspired leaders teach correct principles and let the people govern themselves, and was himself frequently unafraid to acknowledge shortcomings and mistakes in ecclesiastical leadership—even placing himself and the First Presidency on trial before the people in 1843! Throughout his life, the Prophet abhorred priestcraft and the dangerous practice of 'leader worship.' President Brigham Young would later teach that no man is capable of entering the Celestial Kingdom who follows his leaders blindly. For sources and additional historical documentation, see "10 Largely Forgotten, but Timeless Principles, in Sustaining Leaders," Joseph Smith Foundation, https://josephsmithfoundation.org/10-largely-forgotten-but-timeless-principles-in-sustaining-leaders/.

20   Helen Mar Kimball Whitney Autobiography, March 30, 1881. Located within the "Helen M. Kimball Whitney papers, 1881-1882," Church History Library, https://catalog.churchofjesuschrist.org/assets?id=2c0cb6bb-493b-417a-8bd5-dce48180827f&crate=1&index=4.

21   Augusta Joyce Crocheron, *Representative Women of Deseret* (Salt Lake City: J. C. Graham & Co.), 110.

CHAPTER 2

A Vermont Boy's Search for Truth

⤛⤜

Truth was a long-sought pearl for Heber Chase Kimball, even while a young lad roaming the forested hillsides of Vermont. One day, nine-year-old Heber was lying on his bed when his mind opened to a vision of the future—an unveiling of events destined to occur later in his life.[1] Age was not a factor for the Lord—when Heber pondered and asked for wisdom with a sincere heart, the Lord always answered.

The gift of revelation Heber experienced as a youth would continue with him throughout his life. Reflecting on her father's character, Helen recorded, "He had a natural reverence for the Supreme Being, and I have often heard him, when relating his experience, say that when a little child he loved to be alone and reflect upon what his mother had told him about heaven . . ."[2]

Heber's young mind often pondered uncommon things, and as a twelve-year-old boy, he wrestled with "many serious thoughts and strong desires to obtain a knowledge of salvation." Like his future friend, Joseph Smith, Heber struggled with the apparent widespread dearth of truth and, as a young teen, despaired at "not finding anyone who could teach me the things of God." Over the years, he frequented neighborhood revivals, sought out and investigated religious sect after religious sect, and often sat with desperate anticipation "upon the anxious bench to seek relief from the 'bands of sin and death.'"[3]

---

1   Heber C. Kimball, "Forbearance to Each Other," in *Journal of Discourses*, vol. 12 (Liverpool: Albert Carrington, 1869), 190. Discourse given on April 12, 1868.

2   Helen Mar Kimball Whitney, "Life Incidents," *Woman's Exponent* 9, no. 18 (February 15, 1881): 138.

3   Orson F. Whitney, *Life of Heber C. Kimball* (Salt Lake City: Kimball Family, 1888), 30.

During his early 20s, while working as a blacksmith and potter, Heber met Vilate Murray, a woman of uncommon valor, and a true match in his zeal for truth. For Heber, the encounter was love at first sight[4]—and indeed for both of them, their union was destined for eternity. They married and settled down in Mendon, New York.

Many future Latter-day Saints would hail from the Mendon area, then a hotbed of men and women thirsting for truth. During the night of September 22, 1827,[5] the Kimballs were awakened by the persistent knocking of their neighbor, John P. Greene, who anxiously beckoned them to come out and witness a spiritual drama that played for hours across the midnight sky. Visionary armies

---

4   Heber C. Kimball's biography records Heber and Vilate's first meeting as follows:

"In one of his [Heber's] rides he chanced to pass, one warm summer day, through the little town of Victor, in the neighboring County of Ontario. Being thirsty, he drew rein near a house where a gentleman was at work in the yard, whom he asked for a drink of water. As the one addressed went to the well for a fresh bucketful of the cooling liquid, he called to his daughter Vilate, to fetch a glass from the house, which he filled and sent by her to the young stranger.

"Heber was deeply impressed with the beauty and refined modesty of the young girl, whose name he understood to be 'Milaty,' and who was the flower and pet of her father's family. Lingering as long as propriety would permit, or the glass of water would hold out, he murmured his thanks and rode reluctantly away.... It was not long before he again had 'business' in Victor, and again became thirsty (?) just opposite the house where the young lady lived. Seeing the same gentleman in the yard whom he had accosted before, he hailed him and asked him for a cup of water. This time the owner of the premises offered to wait upon him in person, but Heber, with the blunt candor for which he was noted, nearly took the old gentleman's breath by saying, 'if you please, sir, I'd rather My-Laty would bring it to me.'

"'Laty,' as she was called in the house, accordingly appeared and did the honors as before, and returned blushing to meet the merriment and good-natured badinage of her sister and brothers. She, however, was quite as favorably impressed with the handsome young stranger, as he with her. More visits followed, acquaintance ripened into love, and on the 7th of November, 1822, they were married." Ibid., 24-25.

5   "Joseph Smith received the golden plates on the Israelite Day of Remembrance (or Rosh ha-Shanah [Feast of Trumpets]). Biblical references and interpretation by Jewish sages through the centuries set this day as the day God would remember his covenants with Israel to bring them back from exile. Also called the Feast of Trumpets, this day features ritual trumpet blasts to signify the issuance of revelation and a call for Israel to gather for God's word of redemption. The day, which is set at the time of Israel's final agricultural harvest, also symbolizes the Lord's final harvest of souls. Furthermore, it initiates the completion of the Lord's time periods, the Days of Awe, and signifies the last time to prepare for final judgment and the Messianic Age. The coming forth of the Book of Mormon is literally fulfilling such prophecies of the day." Lenet Hadley Read, "Joseph Smith's Receipt of the Plates and the Israelite Feast of Trumpets," *Journal of Book of Mormon Studies* 2, no. 2 (July 31, 1993): 110.

marched from horizon to horizon, engaging in a tremendous battle, complete with the sounds of combat ringing in their ears. Years later, Heber would discover that this vision had taken place on the very night that young Joseph Smith was venturing to the Hill Cumorah under cover of darkness to finally obtain the Nephite record.[6] From that night, as mobs lay in wait to ambush Joseph in hopes of stealing the gold plates, the battle to bring forth the Book of Mormon would become a furious contest between the forces of light and darkness. Heber would soon discover that the controversy beginning with the delivery of the plates would extend far beyond the translation of that record, and would require all the courage, strength, and fortitude he and his family could muster. It would eventually prove to be a controversy that would continue on into our own day—a battle yet un-won.

Helen Mar, the Kimball's third child and only surviving daughter, was born the following year. Three years later, five Latter-day Saint elders visited the Mendon, New York area with a resonating message,

---

6   Heber described the vision as follows:

"It was one of the most beautiful starlight nights so clear we could see to pick up a pin. We looked to the eastern horizon, and beheld a white smoke arise towards the heavens. As it ascended, it formed into a belt, and made a noise like the rushing wind, and continued southwest, forming a regular bow, dipping in the western horizon.

"After the bow had formed, it began to widen out, growing transparent, of a bluish cast. It grew wide enough to contain twelve men abreast. In this bow an army moved, commencing from the east and marching to the west. They continued moving until they reached the western horizon. They moved in platoons, and walked so close the rear ranks trod in the steps of their file leaders, until the whole bow was literally crowded with soldiers.

"We could distinctly see the muskets, bayonets and knapsacks of the men, who wore caps and feathers like those used by the American soldiers in the last war with Great Britain. We also saw their officers with their swords and equipage, and heard the clashing and jingling of their instruments of war, and could discern the form and features of the men. The most profound order existed throughout the entire army. When the foremost man stepped, every man stepped at the same time. We could hear their steps.

"When the front rank reached the western horizon, a battle ensued, as we could hear the report of the arms, and the rush.

"None can judge of our feelings as we beheld this army of spirits as plainly as ever armies of men were seen in the flesh. Every hair of our heads seemed alive.

"We gazed upon this scenery for hours, until it began to disappear.

"... The next night a similar scene was beheld in the west, by the neighbors, representing armies of men engaged in battle." Orson F. Whitney, *Life of Heber C. Kimball* (Salt Lake City: Kimball Family, 1888), 31-32.

Heber C. Kimball

and Heber C. Kimball enthusiastically accepted the Gospel taught by these emissaries. Here at last was the truth, the light—the hope he had spent his life in search of!

The experiences of the Mendon Saints were of no small consequence. One day, while Heber was cutting wood with his close friend, Brigham Young, Brigham's father and brother joined them, sharing their joy regarding this new restoration of truth. Suddenly, the chopping of their axes was interrupted by a glorious vision:

／／ While we were thus engaged we were pondering upon those things which had been told us by the Elders, and upon the saints gathering to Zion, when the glory of God shone upon us, and we saw the gathering of the saints to Zion, and the glory that would rest upon them; and many more things connected with that great event, such as the sufferings and persecutions that would come upon the people of God, and the calamities and judgments that would come upon the world.

These things caused such great joy to spring up in our bosoms that we were hardly able to contain ourselves, and we did shout aloud "Hosannah to God and the Lamb."[7]

Heber soon turned to share his joy and elation with those among his father's household—but one by one, the message was refused. Heber, formerly the "favorite brother," was abandoned by his father's family and left to accept the Gospel alone. His oldest sister "was rich and proud, and although she loved him, she felt so humiliated that she said she never wanted to see his face again." His brother Solomon felt a desire to join, but because of the "bitter opposition" from their mother, he did not. In spite of the rejection, Heber exhibited the strength of character that would be a hallmark of righteousness throughout his life. Helen recorded that "when convinced of the truth of it, [he] went forward and obeyed its requirements," even before "knowing whether [his wife, Vilate] would receive it or not."[8] Heber fasted and prayed for Vilate to unite with him in his new faith. Thankfully, his dear wife became one of his strongest supporters. Heber shared the following during a sermon in 1868:

// Soon after I was baptized, brother Orson Pratt came to my house. I was standing in the door yard when he came, and at the time I felt much of the holy Spirit upon me. I was then a potter at my wheel. While brother Pratt was talking with me a voice spake to him and said "Orson, my son, that man will one day become one of my apostles." I did not know this till afterwards. A voice also spoke to me and told me my lineage, and I told my wife Vilate that she was of the same lineage, and she believed it. I told her also that we would never be separated.[9]

A determined Heber pressed forward, following Joseph Smith to Kirtland, and then on to Missouri. He weathered the Zion's Camp expedition, and was among the first elders commissioned to open the

---

7   Ibid., 35.

8   Helen Mar Kimball Whitney, "Life Incidents," *Woman's Exponent* 9, no. 18 (February 15, 1881): 138.

9   Heber C. Kimball, "Forbearance to Each Other—Necessity of Reading the Bible and Book of Mormon—Counsel to the Young Brethren," in *Journal of Discourses*, vol. 12 (Liverpool: Albert Carrington, 1869), 190-191. Discourse given on April 12, 1868.

door for missionary work in the British Isles. During the Kirtland apostasy, many leaders and members fell away from the Church, with dissenters threatening mortal harm toward the Prophet. Throughout those dark days, Heber was one of *only two* from the original Quorum of the Twelve who never wavered in his loyalty to, and support of, the Prophet Joseph. The other was his faithful friend, Brigham Young. "Of the first Twelve Apostles chosen in Kirtland and ordained under the hands of Oliver Cowdery, David Whitmer, and myself," Joseph remembered, "there have been but two, but what have lifted their heel against me, namely Brigham Young and Heber C. Kimball."[10] Heber's daughter, Helen, likewise observed, ". . . the love and reverence [my father] felt for the Prophet was so great that he would rather have laid down his own life than have betrayed him."[11]

In addition to possessing stalwart faith and an unshakeable testimony, Heber and his wife, Vilate, were renowned for their gifts of sincere charity and compassion. Many years later, during the 1856 famine in Utah, Heber and Vilate Kimball opened their doors to relieve "hundreds of the poor of Salt Lake City":

// Many are the acts of mercy and charity related of President Kimball and his family, especially his noble and unselfish partner, Vilate, during this time of sore distress. They kept an open house, and fed from twenty-five to one hundred poor people at their table, daily, besides making presents innumerable of bread, flour and other necessaries, which were then literally worth their weight in gold. . . .

While thus feeding the poor on the best that her larder afforded, Vilate would send her own children into the fields to dig roots (artichokes) which she would cook for them. This, with coarse corn bread, while her guests were served with wheaten bread, potatoes and boiled beef, was the frequent diet of the Kimball family during the famine of "fifty-six."[12]

---

10   Joseph Smith, History, 1838–1856, volume D-1, p. 1563, The Joseph Smith Papers, https://www.josephsmithpapers.org/paper-summary/history-1838-1856-volume-d-1-1-august-1842-1-july-1843/206.

11   Helen Mar Kimball Whitney, "Scenes and Incidents in Nauvoo," *Woman's Exponent* 10, no. 10 (October 15, 1881): 74.

12   Orson F. Whitney, *Life of Heber C. Kimball* (Salt Lake City: Kimball Family, 1888), 414-415.

Heber's selfless, sacrificial lifestyle led him to receive remarkable prophetic gifts from the Lord. One of Heber's sons remembered that "President Brigham Young on more than one occasion said: 'Heber is my prophet, and I love to hear him prophesy.'"[13] Orson F. Whitney, Heber's grandson through Helen, wrote:

> **"** It is related that, during this famine [1856 Utah famine], a brother, sorely in need of bread, came to President Kimball for counsel how to procure it.
>
> "Go and marry a wife," was Heber's terse reply, after relieving the immediate wants of the applicant.
>
> Thunderstruck at receiving such an answer at such a time, when he could hardly provide food for himself, the man went his way, dazed and bewildered, thinking that President Kimball must be out of his mind. But the more he thought of the prophetic character and calling of the one who had given him this strange advice, the less he felt like ignoring it. Finally he resolved to obey counsel, let the consequences be what they might. But where was the woman who would marry him? was the next problem. Bethinking himself of a widow with several children, who he thought might be induced to share her lot with him, he mustered up courage, proposed and was accepted.
>
> In that widow's house was laid up a six months' store of provisions!
>
> Meeting President Kimball shortly afterwards, the now prosperous man of family exclaimed:
>
> "Well, Brother Heber, I followed your advice—"
>
> "Yes," said the man of God, "and you found bread."[14]

On another occasion, Heber was speaking with fellow Church member George Nebeker when he broke forth with a prophecy that the day would come when Brother Nebeker "would live to see the kings and great ones of the earth pass by his door." Mere reason

---

13   J. Golden Kimball, *Conference Report*, October 1930, 59.

14   Orson F. Whitney, *Life of Heber C. Kimball* (Salt Lake City: Kimball Family, 1888), 415.

would have dismissed such an unexpected prediction as impossible. However, Heber's grandson, Orson F. Whitney recalled:

> Brother Nebeker resided in the nineteenth ward. The railway at that time was not thought of in Utah. But the iron horse now rushes along the street immediately in front of Brother Nebeker's family residence, and he himself lived to see such celebrities as President Grant, the Emperor of Brazil and other royal and great ones literally pass by his door.[15]

Heber's prophetic gifts were borne of faith and refined by his impeccable character. Like his daughter, Helen, he depended on his Maker for daily support, exhibiting a simple faith in God through service to his fellow man. His giving nature required his reliance on miracles to supply the means necessary to perform his acts of devotion—resources the Lord amply provided:

> One day President Young made a call upon father for $1,000., for some public purpose, and not having the ready cash, he was at a loss to know where to get it. At his suggestion we went down in the garden and bowed ourselves in prayer, father calling upon the Lord to direct him in the matter. We then arose and started down the street, and he remarked that the Lord would answer our prayer and direct him aright. When even with Godbe's corner, William Godbe came out of his store and told him that, in looking through his safe, he had come across about $1,000 in gold-dust, belonging to him, which his son Heber P. had left there for him some time before, though father until then knew nothing about it.[16]

Heber's consistent track record of fulfilled prophecy was no accident, nor was it the result of winning a 'spiritual lottery.' Heber lived with confidence because his life was in harmony with God's will, and his obedience had proven, time and time again, the Lord's support and guidance.[17] Following Heber's death,

---

15   Ibid., 447.

16   Ibid., 439.

17   *Lectures on Faith*, a series of lessons likely contributed to and approved by the Prophet Joseph Smith, defines true 'faith' as follows: "Let us here observe, that three

George Q. Cannon spoke of the magnanimity of his friend and fellow member of the Quorum of the Twelve:

▟▌ No man, perhaps, Joseph Smith excepted, who has belonged to the Church in this generation, ever possessed the gift of prophecy to a greater degree than Brother Kimball.[18]

Heber was great because he was good. But with all his gifts, he did not become prideful—he always exhibited enduring charity and compassion. Elder Cannon added:

▟▌ Heber Chase Kimball was one of the greatest men of this age. . . .

He was fearless and powerful in rebuking the wrong-doer, but kind, benevolent and fatherly to the deserving. He possessed such wonderful control over the passions of men, combined with such wisdom and diplomacy that the Prophet Joseph Smith called him "the peace-maker."[19]

Helen remembered that her father's reputation as a "peace-maker" came from his remarkable gift to settle marital disputes between the Prophet Joseph and his wife, Emma. Heber's united empathy and wisdom earned him respect, allowing him to heal broken relationships:

▟▌ I know of . . . [my parent's] daily associations with him [Joseph Smith] and his wife Emma. When he [Joseph] could do nothing with her he would send for my father, for whom she had such love and unbounded respect that he could always make peace

---

things are necessary, in order that any rational and intelligent being may exercise faith in God unto life and salvation. First, The idea that he actually exists. Secondly, A *correct* idea of his character, perfections, and attributes. Thirdly, An actual knowledge that the course of life which he is pursuing, is according to his will.— For without an acquaintance with these three important facts, the faith of every rational being must be imperfect and unproductive . . ." *Lectures on Faith*, Lecture Three, found in Doctrine and Covenants, 1835, p. 36, The Joseph Smith Papers; italicized in original.

18   Orson F. Whitney, *Life of Heber C. Kimball* (Salt Lake City: Kimball Family, 1888), 465.

19   Heber C. Kimball, *President Heber C. Kimball's Journal* (Salt Lake City: Juvenile Instructor Office, 1882), iii.

between them, and this was how he received the appellation of the "peace-maker."[20]

Throughout her childhood, Helen observed her father living by faith. This family tradition, carried on by Helen's children, is reflected in her son's nostalgia of his grandfather—memories of family prayer held each morning and evening:

/ / Family prayer was an institution in the Kimball household. Morning and evening the members were called in to surround the family altar and offer up praise and petitions to the Throne of Grace. It is a common remark to this day that such prayers are seldom heard as were wont to issue from the heart and lips of Heber C. Kimball.[21]

The Kimball family's devotion was natural and authentic. Heber approached prayer with innocent ease and humble confidence, for God was his friend—the exalted Father he desired to emulate. One humorous story is retold by a family member as follows:

/ / On one occasion, while offering up an earnest appeal in behalf of certain of his fellow-creatures, he startled the kneeling circle by bursting into a loud laugh in the very midst of his prayer. Quickly regaining his composure and solemn address, he remarked, apologetically: "Lord, it makes me laugh to pray about some people."[22]

Helen had been born and raised in a home of devotion, selfless sacrifice, and love. The Kimball family's consistent history of unyielding honor, integrity, and virtue softened Helen's heart and opened her mind to the new and everlasting doctrine embraced by her father Heber—as well as her righteous Hebraic forefathers from ancient days. Abraham, Isaac, Jacob, Joseph, Moses, and many other prophets had lived this marital institution—and now the time for restoration had come. Helen *knew* her father; she *knew* his motives and intentions—and she knew they were nothing but pure.

---

20   Helen Mar Whitney, *Plural Marriage as Taught by the Prophet Joseph* (Salt Lake City: Juvenile Instructor Office, 1882), 14.

21   Orson F. Whitney, *Life of Heber C. Kimball* (Salt Lake City: Kimball Family, 1888), 437.

22   Ibid., 437-438.

Sealed to the Prophet Joseph Smith

The gospel nourished the spiritual lifeblood of the Kimball family, shaping both the motivations of the parents, as well as their love for Helen Mar. For the world—who denied life after death—the Saints' hopes, dreams, and expectations were mocked as childish fantasies— the empty dreams of deluded men and women. For the Kimballs and other early Saints, however, they *knew* through personal revelation and a witness born of the Spirit that every worthy decision made in mortality would serve to bring greater happiness, joy, and reward in the next life—a life when all losses would be made up, and all injustices set aright.

According to Helen, around the time of her introduction to the principle of plural marriage, her father approached Joseph Smith for a special favor—a request Helen later explained in her autobiography:

// Just previous to my father's starting upon his last mission but one, to the Eastern States, he taught me the principle of Celestial marriage, & having a great desire to be connected with the Prophet, Joseph, he offered me to him; this I afterwards learned from the Prophet's own mouth. My father had but one Ewe Lamb, but willingly laid her upon the alter[23] . . . I will pass over the temptations which I had during the twenty four hours after my father introduced to me this principle & asked me if I would be sealed to Joseph, who came next morning & with my parents I heard him teach & explain the principle of Celestial marr[i]age—after which he said to me, "If you will take this step, it will ensure your eternal salvation and exaltation & that of your father's household & all of your kindred.["][24]

Was the Prophet coercing Helen into a plural marriage sealing by intimating that her family's entire salvation rested solely on her acceptance of the proposal? No. Such claims contradict the

---

23   The editors have preserved the original spelling and grammar of all quotations— particularly of the diaries, letters, and historical documents—featured in this book.

24   Helen Mar Kimball Whitney Autobiography, March 30, 1881, p. 3-4. Located within the "Helen M. Kimball Whitney papers, 1881-1882," Church History Library, https://catalog.churchofjesuschrist.org/assets/2c0cb6bb-493b-417a-8bd5-dce48180827f/1/2.

clear teachings of Joseph Smith throughout his life. The Prophet repeatedly taught that salvation is an *individual* affair.[25] None can enter any degree of glory by riding on the shoulders of another—or by piggybacking or sponging off a fellow Saint. When each child of God comes to stand before the judgment seat, one's salvation will come through personal accountability between them and the Lord.

Helen's sealing alone would not save even her. Instead, the full context of her statement, in addition to other writings throughout her life, clarifies that the "step" was her willingness to live Celestial laws, embrace consecration, develop a fullness of love for one's fellow man, practice perfect integrity, and to honor sealings to family members enduring beyond death. All of these are essential characteristics of true Celestial marriage. Whenever the Prophet taught a new principle, he always explained the purpose, and provided depth behind the reason *why*. His conversation with the Kimball family opened a discussion on the true nature of heaven, the influence of the premortal life on mortality, and the Father's exalted lifestyle. Helen's sealing to Joseph in and of itself was not the deciding factor in their salvation: the deciding factor was the Kimball family's obedience to *all* commandments from God. Mention of these doctrines and principles are scattered throughout the Kimball family's writings and teachings.

Based on available historical sources, Helen Mar Kimball's sealing was not consummated as a marriage in mortality. Helen did not live as a wife with the Prophet Joseph Smith,[26] but continued with her family.

---

25   For example, the Prophet Joseph Smith taught the Relief Society in 1842: ". . . you will be responsible for your own sins. It is an honor to save yourselves— all are responsible to save themselves." Joseph Smith, Nauvoo Relief Society Minute Book, p. 39, The Joseph Smith Papers. See footnote 20 in Chapter 1 for additional sources.

26   See "Appendix 1: Why did Joseph Smith marry a 14-year-old?" for an examination of Helen's age, and cultural context. Although there is no evidence that Helen's marriage was consummated, some still feel uncomfortable with her age at the time of her sealing. An examination of the historical context, as well as Biblical precedent, can help to alleviate this concern.

It should also be noted when discussing her marriage to the Prophet that as far as we are aware, Helen never referred to her age as a concern or source of doubt; she, apparently, did not consider it an issue. It also appears that she did not feel the need to explain or justify her youth, nor the gap in age between her and the Prophet. Throughout her life, Helen was often requested to talk with curious visitors who wanted to hear about her experience with plural marriage in Nauvoo. It is also of note that at the time of Helen's sealing to the Prophet, another nonmember family was

Helen's sealing was made in view of future maturity, and of eternal life, which extended far beyond the bounds of this mortal sphere.

Although they never lived together as husband and wife, the Prophet appeared to have been conscientious and prompt in arranging for the security of the young woman who may have been seen as having claim upon him as a provider. On June 7, 1843, Joseph Smith deeded to Helen, as well as her "heirs and assigns forever," a parcel of land in Nauvoo.[27] By signing the property directly to Helen alone, the teenage girl became an independent landowner.

Years later, Helen would reflect upon her sealing to the Prophet Joseph Smith, and her desire to lay claim to the promises she received that day:

> I have long since learned to leave all with Him, who knoweth better than ourselves what will make us happy. I am thankful that He has brought me through the furnace of affliction & that He has condesended to show me that the promises made to me the morning that I was sealed to the Prophet of God will not fail & I would not have the chain broken for I have had a view of the principle of eternal salvation & the perfect union which this sealing power will bring to the human family & with the help of our Heavenly Father I am determined to so live that I can claim those promises.[28]

Helen took a step of faith—believing, as Paul taught the Hebrews, in the assurance of things not seen,[29] that her sacrifices would bear fruitful blessings in this life, and in the next. She trusted her father's

---

attempting, with "sly hints," to promote an attachment between Helen and their own son. Concerns with Helen's age stem more from modernist convention and current cultural trends, rather than timeless principles of honor, integrity, and virtue. Again, to clarify, no credible historical evidence exists to indicate that Helen's marriage with the Prophet was consummated.

27   Nauvoo Registry of Deeds, Book B, p. 346, Church History Library, https://www.josephsmithpapers.org/paper-summary/deed-to-helen-mar-kimball-7-june-1843/1.

28   Helen Mar Kimball Whitney Autobiography, March 30, 1881, p. 5. Located within the "Helen M. Kimball Whitney papers, 1881-1882," Church History Library, https://catalog.churchofjesuschrist.org/assets?id=2c0cb6bb-493b-417a-8bd5-dce48180827f&crate=1&index=4.

29   Hebrews 11:1.

wisdom and the promises bestowed upon her, well expressed in a blessing she received in 1843:

// Let thy mind be diligent in study and no one shall excel thee. Be upright, be pure, and whatsoever covenant thou shalt enter into let it be a view of eternity, that thou mayest look upon thy father and thy mother and thou wilt then see their anxiety which they have had for thee.[30]

Despite the testimony and the affirmations that accompanied her at the time, Helen confessed that within her heart, a great battle waged—a struggle between "the allurements of the world ... and [a] desire to be saved. The germ was there but it took time and patient care and much watering from the pure fountain before it gave evidence that it had taken root or would spring forth to bear fruit."[31] As Vilate's only daughter, Helen had always been protective of her mother. After learning of plural marriage, she noted her mother's sacrifices to live this sacred, but refining, principle. The practice embodied an individual family's ability to live the law of consecration—and consecration required *sacrifice*. At times, Helen "felt to rebel. I hated polygamy in my heart." She believed plural marriage was commanded by God—but *why*? The wrestle within her soul was of no small consequence as she faced the daunting questions: Did plural marriage bring joy or pain? Why would God require this sacrifice of His sons and daughters? What path would Helen choose? With faith, Helen adopted the prayer: "give me patience to wait until I can understand it for myself."

---

30   Blessing given to Helen Mar Kimball by her father, Heber C. Kimball on May 28, 1843. Helen Mar Kimball Whitney papers, 1843, 1868, p.1, located in the Heber C. Kimball family collection, 1840-1890, Church History Library, https://catalog.churchofjesuschrist.org/assets?id=355f1771-8adb-439e-aba0-81a614be6bfa&crate=0&index=0.

31   Helen Mar Kimball Whitney, "Retrospection," *Woman's Exponent* 10, no. 3 (July 1, 1881): 17.

CHAPTER 3

Childlike Faith

Helen's mortal journey began August 22, 1828 as the only surviving daughter born to Heber and Vilate Kimball. The doting love and compassion embodied within the hearts of these two young parents would find its object in her. Close friends likewise lavished her with affection, including Brigham Young's sister, Fanny,[1] who claimed the honor of christening the newborn babe.

Known as a "great reader," Fanny would gather the children around her in the evening to read animated tales of Scottish adventure. Inspired by the courageous heroine of the historical fiction work, *The Scottish Chiefs*, she drew the name 'Helen Mar' from the wife of the Scottish martyr, Sir William Wallace.[2] Thus, Heber and Vilate's newborn became Helen Mar Kimball. Prophetic in a sense, this name would foreshadow her mortal life, and echo her standing in eternity. Little Helen entered this world as the daughter of passionate defenders of liberty, and would later choose to be sealed to the "greatest advocate of the Constitution,"[3] and a man willing to shed his lifeblood on the altar of liberty—the Prophet Joseph Smith.

During Helen's early years, the Kimball and Young families lived near one another in Mendon, New York, becoming more family than mere friends. "... Fanny Young was living with my parents

---

1 Fanny Young would later become a plural wife of the Prophet Joseph Smith, sealed November 2, 1843.

2 Helen Mar Kimball Whitney, "Life Incidents," *Woman's Exponent* 9, no. 6 (August 15, 1880): 42.

3 "It is one of the first principles of my life, and one that I have cultivated from my childhood, having been taught it of my father, to allow everyone the liberty of conscience. I am the greatest advocate of the Constitution of the United States there is on the earth." Joseph Smith, October 15, 1843. History, 1838–1856, volume E-1, p. 1754, The Joseph Smith Papers.

when I was born," Helen later wrote. "[She] took care of me, and she was always ready to defend me if necessary."[4] As the sole daughter of Heber and Vilate, Helen received the attention and spoils of an 'only girl,' especially from Fanny's brothers who vied for her favor, frequently asking:

// ... which I [Helen] loved the best, Pa, Uncle Brigham or Uncle Joseph;[5] I would never give but one answer, 'I love you all at once.' If I had a leaning towards one more than another it was Uncle Joseph, as he was without any family, and I was the first to expect and to receive his sugar plums and kisses.[6]

The Kimball family was both aware and proud of their New England heritage—Separatist Pilgrims who settled Massachusetts.[7] According to Augusta Joyce Crocheron, in her 1883 biographical sketch of Helen Mar:

// [The Kimball] ancestors were among the Pilgrims and her kindred prided themselves that they were descended from a noble stock. Though they cared little for nobility and rank, they were proud to know that their grandsires who would not submit to tyranny and oppression, helped to gain them independence, and that their descendants were noble, hard working, self-sacrificing and conscientious people, who believed in rising by their own merits. Many of her ancestors died fighting for the liberty which is denied to some of their children, by men who have usurped authority and become oppressors.[8]

---

4   Helen Mar Kimball Whitney, "Life Incidents," *Woman's Exponent* 9, no. 5 (August 1, 1880): 38.

5   Joseph Young, the elder brother of Brigham Young, was present during many famous events in early Latter-day Saint history, such as the dedication of the Kirtland Temple, the massacre at Haun's Mill, and the founding of the Council of Fifty, as well as being one of the first to receive his endowment under the hand of the Prophet Joseph Smith. By the time of his death in 1881, Joseph Young had served either as a general authority or missionary for the Church for nearly 50 years.

6   Helen Mar Kimball Whitney, "Life Incidents," *Woman's Exponent* 9, no. 5 (August 1, 1880): 38.

7   Helen Mar Kimball Whitney, "Life Incidents," *Woman's Exponent* 9, no. 18 (February 15, 1881): 138; Helen Mar Kimball Whitney, "Life Incidents," *Woman's Exponent* 9, no. 20 (March 15, 1881): 154; Augusta Joyce Crocheron, *Representative Women of Deseret* (Salt Lake City: J. C. Graham & Co.), 109.

8   Augusta Joyce Crocheron, *Representative Women of Deseret* (Salt Lake City: J. C. Graham & Co.), 109.

Helen's ancestral culture and identity strongly influenced her outlook on life. She knew where her forebears had stood, and in many ways, felt she was born to carry on that legacy.

While she carried the blood of Pilgrim reformers and revolutionary patriots, Helen's genetic lineage also stemmed from the ancient patriarchs: Abraham, Isaac, Jacob, and Joseph. According to a blessing preserved in the Church History Library and given originally by her father, Helen was also prophetically pronounced to be a daughter of Judah: "Thou art of the seed of Judah[9] and thou shall be blest and crowned with his blessings."[10] In an interesting parallel, another wife of Joseph Smith, Eliza R. Snow Smith, was likewise given a blessing by the Prophet which revealed her lineage as "a daughter of Judah's royal house."[11]

Early Training in Faith

As a child, Helen was admonished by her parents to reverence God with humility and soberness. Writing of one experience when around five years of age, she remembered:

---

9   Jeremiah 3:18 prophesied that in the latter days, the tribes of Judah and Joseph would be found in the land of the 'North.' "In those days the house of Judah shall walk with the house of Israel, and they shall come together out of the land of the north to the land that I have given for an inheritance unto your fathers." The land of the north has been identified by latter-day prophets as northern Europe.

Historical and archeological evidence for the blood of Judah being scattered throughout northern Europe can be found in resources such as Hidden Bloodlines: The Grail & The Lost Tribes in the Lands of the North (DVD: Joseph Smith Foundation), Israel's Lost Empires (Book: Steven M. Collins), and Israel's Tribes Today (Book: Steven M. Collins). One fascinating observation includes that Judah's blessing likens him to an old lion as well as a young cub. In Scottish and English heraldry, we often find a large lion depicted, accompanied by what are called "lioncels" or young, small lions.

In 1872, President Brigham Young commissioned Elder George A. Smith (cousin to the Prophet Joseph) to return and essentially rededicate the land of Palestine. Sister Eliza R. Snow Smith (plural wife of Joseph Smith) and her brother Lorenzo Snow accompanied him to the Holy Land. These brothers and sisters had a particular bloodline that gave them the legal right to dedicate the land and initiate the return of their people to Old Jerusalem.

10   Heber C. Kimball blessing to Helen Marr Kimball, undated, p. 3, Church History Library, https://catalog.churchofjesuschrist.org/assets/005e0b00-3470-4553-83ed-e69b99603907/0/2. Another copy of this blessing has the line, "Thou art of the seed of Joseph {the same seed with thy brother}."

11   Edward W. Tullidge, The Women of Mormondom (New York: 1877), 32.

▌▌ . . . a terrible thunderstorm coming up and our parents telling us we must sit quiet and not talk, for the Lord was speaking. I was hardly five years old but their words with the awful thunder and lightning made so strong an impression upon my mind that I have always felt that we should keep silent when the Lord was speaking.[12]

The Kimball home exuded a passionate love for God and scripture, yet Heber and Vilate struggled to find a denomination that aligned with the Bible. Years of searching led them to finally join the Baptist faith in 1831. Only three weeks later, five elders from the Church of Christ (later renamed by the Prophet Joseph Smith as the Church of Jesus Christ of Latter-day Saints) knocked at the home of Phineas Young, the brother of Heber's closest friend, Brigham. When Heber heard of these guests, he visited them out of curiosity, and "for the first time I heard the fullness of the everlasting gospel."[13] Within a short period of time, both he and the Youngs gained powerful testimonies.[14]

Helen was only about three and a half years old at the time, but her conversion began when she was five, after an unidentified event led her to consider herself "within the fold of Christ." She later

---

12   Helen Mar Kimball Whitney, "Life Incidents," *Woman's Exponent* 9, no. 22 (April 15, 1881): 170.

13   Orson F. Whitney, *Life of Heber C. Kimball* (Salt Lake City: Kimball Family, 1888), 34.

14   "At their meetings Brigham and Heber saw the manifestations of the spirit and heard the gift of speaking and singing in tongues. They were constrained by the spirit to bear testimony to the truth, and when they did this the power of God rested upon them.

"Desiring to hear more of the saints, in January, 1832, Heber took his horses and sleigh and started for Columbia, Bradford county, Penn., a distance of one hundred and twenty-five miles. Brigham and Phineas Young and their wives went with him.

"They stayed with the church about six days, saw the power of God manifested and heard the gift of tongues, and then returned rejoicing, bearing testimony to the people by the way. They were not baptized, however, until the following spring. Brigham was baptized on Sunday, April 14th, 1832, by Eleazer Miller, and Heber C. Kimball was baptized the next day.

"Just two weeks from that time I was baptized by Joseph Young, with several others.

"The Holy Ghost fell upon Heber so greatly, that he said it was like a consuming fire. He felt as though he was clothed in his right mind and sat at the feet of Jesus; but the people called him crazy. He continued thus for months, till it seemed his flesh would consume away. The Scriptures were unfolded to his mind in such a wonderful manner by the spirit of revelation that he said it seemed he had formerly been familiar with them." Edward W. Tullidge, *The Women of Mormondom* (New York: 1877), 105-106.

recorded in her journal as a 65-year-old widow that, "from my 5th year [I] have been kept within the fold of Christ, and blessed with what is of more worth than all else besides—a perfect knowledge of the truth of 'Mormonism'—the gospel of salvation as taught by the Savior of the world."[15] Helen's faith only continued to grow from that very young age.

The Kimballs moved to Kirtland in 1833, and then, three years later, eight-year-old Helen was baptized by "Uncle Brigham" during the chill of winter.[16] Her father started out ahead of the others to chop an opening in the frigid ice of the Chagrin River, into which Helen excitedly waded. She had "longed for this privilege," and even her cold walk home in soaking wet clothes could not abate the joy of this precocious child, who exclaimed that she "felt no cold or inconvenience from it."[17]

Even when young, Helen "had perfect faith and confidence to ask of God." Her childlike faith is illustrated in a tender story Heber shared with the Prophet:

// My wife, one day when going out to make a call, gave my little daughter, Helen Mar, a charge not to touch the dishes which she had left standing on the table, as, if she broke any during her absence she would give her a whipping when she returned. While my wife was absent, my daughter broke a number by letting the table leaf fall; and then she went out under an apple tree and prayed that her mother's heart might be softened, that when she returned she might not whip her. Although her mother was very punctual when she made a promise to her children to fulfil it, yet when she returned she had no disposition to chastise

---

15 "Tues. 22nd. Sixty five years ago this morning I entered this probationary state, & from my 5th year have been kept within the fold of Christ, and blessed with what is of more worth than all else besides—a perfect knowledge of the truth of 'Mormonism'—the gospel of salvation as taught by the Savior of the world." Charles M. Hatch and Todd M. Compton, *A Widow's Tale: 1884-1896 Diary of Helen Mar Kimball Whitney* (Logan: Utah State University Press, 2003), 562.

16 Helen Mar Kimball Whitney Autobiography, March 30, 1881. Located within the "Helen M. Kimball Whitney papers, 1881-1882," p. 1, Church History Library, https://catalog.churchofjesuschrist.org/assets?id=2c0cb6bb-493b-417a-8bd5-dce48180827f&crate=1&index=2.

17 Helen Mar Kimball Whitney, "Life Incidents," *Woman's Exponent* 9, no. 22 (April 15, 1881): 170.

the child. Afterwards the child told her mother that she had prayed to God that she might not whip her.

"Joseph wept like a child on hearing this simple narrative and its application, and said it was well timed."[18]

Experience continued to mold the life of this intrepid Latter-day Saint, who, years later as a 52-year-old mother, would remember the experience and its outcome: "I had been taught that there was a higher power, and I went and cried to God to forgive me and to soften my mother's heart, that she might not punish me; and that simple prayer was heard and answered, which greatly increased my faith in Him."[19]

Helen saw the power of faith and healing manifested repeatedly in her home. When she was ten years old, she witnessed her four-year-old brother miraculously healed after being burned with hot coals:

 ❙❙ . . . I had a severe attack of fever, and a heavy storm coming on, the weather was quite cold, and not having a fire-place in the room, mother placed a kettle of live coals in the center of the apartment. Just as she stepped out into the other room, my little brother, aged about four years, came in and accidentally fell into the kettle, and burned him badly. I was so frightened that I was upon the point of leaping out of bed when mother heard him scream, but he sprang out before she got into the room and cried for her to anoint him with the consecrated oil. She immediately administered it,[20] and was silently praying, when he cried, "P[r]ay loud." She obeyed him, and in a few minutes he was sound asleep. He never cried from the burn after the oil was administered, and it was healed from that moment. What a pity we cannot always have faith like a little child . . .[21]

---

18   Helen Mar Kimball Whitney, "Life Incidents," *Woman's Exponent* 9, no. 12 (November 15, 1880): 90.

19   Helen Mar Kimball Whitney, "Life Incidents," *Woman's Exponent* 9, no. 13 (December 1, 1880): 98.

20   See Chapter 14, "Rolling Waters & Power from Heaven" for a discussion on women giving blessings of healing in the early days of the Church.

21   Helen Mar Kimball Whitney, "Life Incidents," *Woman's Exponent* 9, no. 3 (July 1, 1880): 18.

Pioneer Girl, by Ken Corbett

For the early Latter-day Saints, miracles and healing were not irrelevant relics only spoken of in the Primitive Church. These were the fruits of the Restoration; all of the spiritual gifts that were present anciently were being restored in this new dispensation, and Helen experienced these blessings firsthand.

"Dear Old Kirtland"

Helen fondly remembered the happiest days of her childhood "in and around dear old Kirtland." She recalled gathering nuts, berries, and flowers as she wandered over "the lovely meadows, where we used to gather the white and also the gaily dressed lilies," while walking through "wintergreen which grew thickly under our feet":

❙❙ . . . in early spring I used to go with hymn or story book and sit alone and sing, or listen to the little birds chirping and warbling as it seemed their sweet songs of praise for the beautiful spring, and I would feel perfectly happy . . .[22]

Helen attended a school taught by Eliza R. Snow where the Book of Mormon served as part of the curriculum. She wrote, "the Book of Mormon was one of our school books."[23] While attending Sunday School, Helen memorized entire chapters of the New Testament:

❙❙ . . . among other pleasing recollections were our Sunday Schools, where I used to love to go and recite verses and whole chapters from the New Testament, and we received rewards in primers, etc., which I think were more highly appreciated in those days than they are at the present time. At ten o'clock we would form in line and march with our teachers up to the temple.[24]

Her father likewise improved his own literacy by attending the School of the Prophets and other classes for men, organized under the direction of the Prophet Joseph Smith. Among the many opportunities the Saints were given to excel intellectually, Helen remembered a time when the Quorum of the Twelve met at her home to study the Hebrew language:

---

22   Helen Mar Kimball Whitney, "Life Incidents," *Woman's Exponent* 9, no. 6 (August 15, 1880): 42.

23   Helen Mar Kimball Whitney, "Life Incidents," *Woman's Exponent* 9, no. 22 (April 15, 1881): 170.

Helen's account also adds the following note regarding Eliza R. Snow: "I never knew Sister Eliza intimately until after our expulsion from Nauvoo and we had quartered for the winter in what is now Florence, Iowa. There I made her acquaintance under peculiar and trying circumstances. The first time I remember of meeting her there she was lying sick with a fever in a poorly covered wagon, with the blazing sun beating down upon it. Many more were in a similar condition and had no other shelter, until after the heavy rains was on us and the nights had become cold and frosty, which made matters still worse, but in the midst of these trials, with trusting faith in the Almighty the Saints were sustained and comforted. His power was made manifest many times to our perfect astonishment. Before starting from Winter Quarters Sister Eliza was able to go around and administer to her sisters in affliction. For many years she had helped to comfort those who stood in need, and in blessing she has been blessed."

24   Helen Mar Kimball Whitney, "Life Incidents," *Woman's Exponent* 9, no. 6 (August 15, 1880): 42.

❒❒ President Thomas B. Marsh I can remember, with others, seated around the table studying, and they would frequently practice talking Hebrew, which afforded us children considerable amusement, and often they would burst out laughing at their own awkward mistakes. They were all young men, and as humble as little children. I often heard my parents speak of those days and how their hearts were bound together as one. They were willing to go without purse or scrip to the nations to preach the gospel, the spirit and power of their mission resting down upon them. If they had always cultivated that humility, nothing could have destroyed their union.[25]

The bustling Kimball home also kept Helen busy making "luscious maple sugar," and gathering nuts and apples for winter. At his potter's wheel, her father handcrafted a variety of "cunning little dishes and toys"—gifts she "generously divided with [her] mates who were less fortunate." She and her siblings would:

❒❒ ... stand and watch and wonder how he ever learned to manage the clay so skilfully as to turn out the numerous and curiously shaped jars and dishes of all sorts and sizes. . . . We never wanted for any comfort as long as he worked at his trade which was a very profitable one, and previous to hearing "Mormonism" he was carrying on a flourishing business in that part of the country where he lived and was in comfortable circumstances and highly respected by the community, but when this gospel saluted the ears of my parents they gladly embraced it and sacrificed their good name and all they had for the sake of everlasting riches. Some wept over them and others treated them with scorn.[26]

Accepting the Gospel would disrupt the Kimball family's economic prosperity as Heber and Vilate literally consecrated all of their finances and assets. When Helen's family abandoned their worldly wealth to preach the Gospel, some neighbors could not comprehend this seemingly radical decision, and often mocked the family for their poverty. Helen remembered one experience as a young child:

25   Helen Mar Kimball Whitney, "Life Incidents," *Woman's Exponent* 9, no. 17 (February 1, 1881): 131.

26   Helen Mar Kimball Whitney, "Life Incidents," *Woman's Exponent* 9, no. 6 (August 15, 1880): 42.

Kirtland temple, by Jon McNaughton

❝ School was out for noon and I having an apple one of my mates
asked me for a piece of it when I handed her the apple, as she
was biting it another girl some five years our senior whose
parents were well off and had not as yet been called to leave
their home or sacrifice any property, with a proud look said—"*I
wouldn't touch her apple*"; one of her companions asked why?
When she said why "*her father's poor*," the other laughingly
replied "I'm sure he don't look very poor," meaning in flesh.
Having a proud and sensitive nature her words stung me and
though I said nothing I remembered it.[27]

The societal deference given to men and women with wealth
and economic superiority confused Helen as a young girl, and she
struggled to understand the purpose and value of sacrifice. Years
later, she would plead with Latter-day Saints to purge all materialistic
prejudice, defining it as a stumbling block to the weak:

❝ There were times when I wondered if religion by some other
name would not do just as well. I thought of the contrast
between our circumstances and those of our kindred who were
enjoying wealth and worldly homes while we were not only
enduring privation but were looked down upon and despised by

27   Helen Mar Kimball Whitney, "Retrospection," *Woman's Exponent* 10, no. 3
(July 1, 1881): 18; italicized in original.

the most of them and the people at large, and I saw a difference even in our own midst; those who could dress the finest were the ones who were most respected and admired, and they in turn looked upon those that did not dress and make as fine an appearance as themselves ...

I am very sorry to have it to say that there is too much of this spirit manifested among us now, not only in the hearts of some of the children but older ones are guilty who bear the name of Latter-day Saints and should be more exemplary but instead are stumbling blocks to the weak, as well as a reproach to the cause which we have espoused.[28]

Helen's father was frequently away from home serving missions across the United States.[29] In the midst of growing apostasy in Kirtland, a majority of the Twelve, as well as many of the members, abandoned the Prophet Joseph Smith. Joseph later recalled, "God revealed to me that something new must be done for the salvation of his church."[30] That "something new" consisted, at least in part, of the Lord calling Heber on a mission to "go to England and proclaim my Gospel, and open the door of salvation to that nation." The Lord foresaw that gathering Israel from the lands of the North would provide fresh recruits to eventually take the places of apostate members who had rejected His Gospel in America. Heber was overwhelmed by the calling, but he:

❝ ... felt a determination to go at all hazards, believing that He would support me by His almighty power, and endow me with every qualification that I needed; and although my family was dear to me, and I should have to leave them

---

28 Ibid., 17-18.

29 Although the Kimballs were sober and reverent in spiritual matters, Heber was also cheerful and enjoyed moments of wholesome laughter. His journal in 1835 records that while on a mission in 1835, he received word that Vilate had given birth to a son and for some time, Heber delighted in telling the brethren around him with a twinkle in his eye, "I have three children now, and have not seen one of them. This was a great puzzle to them until I unraveled it—one of them I had not seen." Helen Mar Kimball Whitney, "Life Incidents," *Woman's Exponent* 9, no. 14 (December 15, 1880): 111; emphasis in original. See also, Orson F. Whitney, *Life of Heber C. Kimball* (Salt Lake City: Kimball Family, 1888), 94; emphasis in original.

30 Joseph Smith, History, 1838–1856, volume B-1, June 1837, p. 761, The Joseph Smith Papers.

almost destitute, I felt that the cause of truth, the Gospel of Christ, outweighed every other consideration.[31]

Heber returned home from Great Britain in 1838, only to discover that the Prophet Joseph and "almost all the members who had any faith in Mormonism" had already abandoned Ohio and relocated to Missouri. Helen was, by this time, nine years old. Without delay, the ever-faithful Heber packed his belongings and left with his family to join the Saints in Missouri, arriving in July of that year. He later recalled:

// During our journey from Kirtland to Missouri, the weather was extremely warm, in consequence of which I [Heber] suffered very much, my body being weakened by sickness, and I continued very feeble for a considerable length of time.

Sunday, July 20th, I met Joseph, Sidney and Hyrum on the public square, as they started for Adam-Ondi-Ahman. Joseph requested me to preach to the Saints and give them a history of my mission, saying, "It will revive their spirits and do them good," which I did, although I was scarcely able to stand. I related many things respecting my mission and travels, which were gladly received by them, whose hearts were cheered by the recital, while many of the Elders were stirred up to diligence, and expressed a great desire to accompany me when I should return to England.[32]

The fertile Missouri wilderness had been set apart for the building up of Zion and the long-foretold city of peace, the New Jerusalem. Here Adam once walked, and Enoch cried repentance. Here ancient Nephites built their cities, and their prophets received glorious revelations concerning an eventual marvelous work and wonder. And now—after centuries of apostasy and darkness— Latter-day Israel was eagerly preparing to repair the breach and to build up the waste places once again. But as it grew, so grew the antagonism that began to surface among their new neighbors, stirring up conflict to yet again haunt the emigrating Saints.

---

31   Orson F. Whitney, *Life of Heber C. Kimball* (Salt Lake City: Kimball Family, 1888), 116-117.

32   Ibid., 217.

CHAPTER 4

Endurance, Healing & Forgiveness

⌒⌒

The intriguing prospect of change! Helen looked upon her family's move from Kirtland with excited anticipation for new scenery and novel adventure. Her 'castles in the sky' were soon dashed to pieces, however, with a rude awakening to the fierce reality of *persecution* in the life of a faithful Latter-day Saint.

The Kimball family relocated to Missouri just as conflict between the local mobs and members of the Church was reaching a boiling point. In the fall of 1838, growing peril forced the Kimballs to abandon their home and flee with other Saints to the town of Far West for safety. Helen's father was appointed a captain of fifty in the Saints' militia. They watched as thousands of mobocrats, their faces concealed with Indian warpaint, hijacked and abused their position as state militia to surround the city, thirsting for blood and plunder. Ironically on Halloween day, Colonel George Hinkle, a pretended friend of the Saints and member of the Church, returned to Far West after engaging an audience with the mob. The treacherous Hinckle offered the Saints a false hope, claiming that the so-called 'militia' had requested a peaceable audience with Joseph Smith and other listed brethren to consider a possible resolution. Joseph Fielding Smith, in *Essentials in Church History*, records:

❝ As they approached the camp in compliance with this order, General Lucas, with a guard of several hundred men, rode up, and with a haughty air ordered his men to surround the brethren. Colonel Hinkle was heard to say: "General, these are the prisoners I agreed to deliver up."[1]

Like Judas of old, Hinkle turned traitor by handing Joseph and the other brethren over as hostages, in exchange for a secret bargain with General Lucas:

> Then the mob force was let loose. They entered the city without restraint, on pretext of searching the homes for additional arms. They tore up floors; ruined furniture; destroyed property; whipped the men and forced them to sign deeds to their property at the point of the bayonet; and violated the chastity of women, until their victims died.[2]

With the eruption of the hate-filled violence surrounding the city, Helen's mother, Vilate, fled with her children to the home of Mary Fielding Smith—wife of Hyrum Smith, who was preparing to give birth to her first son—a child born in the fire of adversity, who would later be called to lead the Saints as a president of the Church—Joseph F. Smith. Helen recalled the alarming events of that period:

> I well remember the night that the Prophet and others of the brethren gave themselves up to save the rest of us from being massacred, which the mob, numbering about 7,000, had threatened to do. After the brethren had delivered up their weapons, the mob surrounded the city and commenced plundering, and committing horrible outrages upon some of the helpless women, the brethren being prisoners. Our house being on the outskirts, my mother took her children and went into the heart of the city to stay all night with Sister Mary Smith, who was lying sick, but previous to going there we called on the widow of David Patten, who had been killed but a few days before. I can never forget her fearless and determined look. Around her waist was a belt to which was attached a large bowie-knife. She had a fire in her stove and a large iron kettle full of boiling water

---

1   Joseph Fielding Smith, *Essentials in Church History* (Deseret Book Company, 1972), 200.

2   Ibid., 201.

Saints Driven from Jackson County Missouri, by C. C. A. Christensen

and a big tin dipper in her hand intending, she said, to fight if any of the demons came there.[3]

As mobs descended upon the city, women prepared to struggle—to the death, if necessary—for their lives and the lives of their children. Helen recorded that the mob included not only non-member Missourians, but traitors whom the Kimball family had formerly considered friends—men who had once stood by the Prophet, such as David Whitmer and William E. McLellin.[4] These now-darkened

---

3   Helen Mar Kimball Whitney, "Early Reminiscences," *Woman's Exponent* 8, no. 24 (May 15, 1880): 188.

4   William E. McLellin was originally a member of the Quorum of the Twelve, but was excommunicated on May 11, 1838. While Joseph was in prison, McLellin "went into Brother Josephs house and comenced searching over his things and Sister Emma asked him why he done so for and his answer was becaus he could he took all the julery out of Josephs box and took a lot of bed clothes and in fact, plundered the house and took the things off and while Brother Joseph was in prison he suffered with the cold and he sent home to his wife Emma to send him some quilts or bed cloths for they had no fire there and he had to have something to keep him from the cold it was in the dead of winter My wife [wife of John L. Butler] was up there when the word came and she said that Sister Emma cried and said that they had taken all of her bed clothes except one quilt and blanket and what could she do . . ." John L. Butler autobiography, circa 1859; Autobiography, circa 1859, p. 26, Church History Library, https://catalog.lds.org/assets/8e634e8e-51e5-4db2-b2e6-1b20a56d034a/0/54.

Note this account taken from "History of Brigham Young": "McLellin also took part in persecuting the Latter-day Saints in Missouri. "While Joseph was in prison at Richmond, Missouri, McLellin, who was a large and active man, went to the

souls "piloted the mobs into the city" to begin pillaging homes, raping women, torturing children, slaughtering animals, and massacring the Saints at will. McLellin took special delight in taunting Heber C. Kimball:

❝ Among the mob who surrounded the brethren were men who had once professed to be beloved brethren. They had piloted the mobs into the city, two of the first Twelve Apostles and two of the witnesses to the Book of Mormon and many others were led by Neil Gillium, a white man who was painted and styled himself the "Delaware Chief." A portion of the troops were also painted like Indians. They pointed their guns upon the brethren and swore they would blow out their brains, although they were disarmed and helpless. William E. McClellen wanted to know where Heber C. Kimball was, when someone pointed him out as he was sitting on the ground. He came up to him and said: "Brother Heber, what do you think of Joseph Smith the fallen prophet now? Has he not led you blindfolded long enough; look and see yourself, poor, your family stripped and robbed and your brethren in the same fix, are you satisfied with Joseph?" He replied, "Yes, I am more satisfied with him, a hundredfold, than ever I was before, for I see you in the very position that he foretold you would be in; a Judas to betray your brethren, if you did not forsake your adultery, lying and abominations. Where are you and Hinkle and scores of others; have you not betrayed Joseph and his brethren into the hands of the mob, as Judas did Jesus? Yes, verily you have; I tell you Mormonism is true, and Joseph is a true prophet of the living God, and you with all others who turn therefrom will be d—d and go to h—l and Judas will rule over you."[5]

Joseph and Heber's bitterest opposition always came from false friends—defectors whose aggression far exceeded those who had

---

sheriff and asked for the privilege of flogging the Prophet. Permission was granted on condition that Joseph would fight. The sheriff made known to Joseph McLellin's earnest request, to which Joseph consented, if his irons were taken off. McLellin then refused to fight unless he could have a club, to which Joseph was perfectly willing; but the sheriff would not allow them to fight on such unequal terms." "History of Brigham Young," *Millennial Star* 26 (December 17, 1864): 808.

5   Helen Mar Kimball Whitney, "Early Reminiscences," *Woman's Exponent* 9, no. 1 (June 1, 1880): 5.

never embraced the Gospel. The Son of God spoke of this principle during the Sermon on the Mount, when he proclaimed, "If therefore the light that is in thee be darkness, how great is that darkness!"[6]

Escaping Missouri

The Saints were driven from the state, while their leaders were incarcerated on trumped-up charges. Helen's father, Heber, was released, but he chose to linger behind in order to assist the more impoverished members as they tried to escape the inhumane treatment. Heber sent Vilate and her children ahead to flee Missouri with Brigham Young's family in the freezing winter weather of February 1839.[7] Vilate soon discovered that many Missourians they encountered along the way were "bitterly opposed to the 'Mormons.'" In an attempt to avoid danger, Vilate and Brigham's wife, Mary Ann, along with their children, disguised their identity by pretending to act as nonmembers. Helen recalled:

/ / The day we started the weather was terrible, and my mother and Sister Young, with their children, stopped at a house and asked the privilege of warming themselves. There were no men, only women there, but they began talking about the horrible "Mormons" and eyed us very closely. Sister Young and my mother appeared to believe all they said, and looked horrified, and we children imitated them. We found some who were more humane and we were allowed the privilege of staying all night, at other times we were obliged to content ourselves with a fire by the roadside. Our bedroom was one little wagon, which contained all we had left.

One day in particular I remember was so cold we were obliged to walk to keep from freezing. My oldest brother, who drove our cow, had gone ahead, and becoming very sleepy in consequence of the cold, got off from his horse, and putting the bridle

---

6   Matthew 6:23.

7   "My father remain[ed] behind to help the poor Saints in getting away, as well as to assist the Prophet and his brethren in making their escape from prison. He being almost a stranger there could stay with less danger than Bro. Brigham, who was obliged to keep himself disguised, and he was seen but little with us in the daytime." Helen Mar Kimball Whitney, "Early Reminiscences," *Woman's Exponent* 9, no. 1 (June 1, 1880): 5.

over his arm laid down to sleep. Dr. Levi Richards, who was
traveling with us, and had also gone ahead of the wagons, soon
overtook him, and by hard shaking and a few well meaning
blows, which made him angry enough to fight, started the
blood to circulating and saved his life. We soon after arrived
at Bishop Vincent Knight's house, where his feet were found
to be badly frozen. We remained there until the next morning.
The Lord was with us, and although we never heard from my
father for nearly three months, yet we found friends as the
Lord told him that we should.[8]

Helen would never forget the Missouri nightmare, nor the
sufferings she and her people were forced to endure. Remarkably,
however, she conquered her feelings of bitterness and anger, choosing
instead to forgive the wrongs forced upon the families she loved, and
rejecting any inclination toward revenge. In 1880, she wrote:

// ... my heart aches for the suffering, even of our enemies. I pity
and feel to pray for them, for they know not what they do, but
the blood of the innocent is crying for vengeance. This nation
has a terrible debt to pay. . . . The Saints have borne all in patience
because they had faith in the Almighty who said, "Vengeance
is mine, I will repay."[9]

Helen's compassionate advocacy for forgiveness did not discount
or overlook the divine justice she knew would eventually come.
Instead of taking vengeance into her own hands, she utilized her pen
to remind Latter-day Saints to leave reparation in the hands of a God
whose promises are sure:

// ... Jesus said with the measure they meted to the Latter-day
Saints it shall be measured to them again or upon all those who
consented to it, *four-fold*, running over and pressed down, and
as the Lord God Almighty liveth I shall live to see it come to
pass." Missouri suffered all that at the time of the war between
the north and south, and one week ago that state and a portion

---

8   Ibid.
9   Helen Mar Kimball Whitney, "Early Reminiscences," *Woman's Exponent* 9, no. 2
(June 15, 1880): 10.

of Illinois was visited by a terrible cyclone which swept away whole towns and villages and men, women and children destroying everything before it. We scarcely take up a paper that has not some frightful account of deaths by cyclones, fires, railroad accidents, earthquakes, floods, the sea heaving beyond its bounds, famines, and also pestilence which is more terrible than all the rest and when I think of the good and the innocent who must suffer with the wicked, my heart pains me and these things we know have scarcely begun.[10]

Helen understood this life as a temporary shadow, merely one scene in a multi-act drama that, when concluded, would culminate in perfect justice, mercy, and restoration—for both victim and perpetrator. Helen continuously made the deliberate choice to cast her focus far into the future—to make decisions with the view of eternity as her guide. Her foresight gave her strength to forgive the horrific injustices she had witnessed and, in some cases, suffered personally—and it gave her the humility to entertain new doctrine and principles—some that the Lord entrusted to her from a very young age.

Settling a Mosquito-Infested Swamp

Helen's father eventually escaped from Missouri and made his way to Illinois where, at long last, the Kimball family was reunited under one roof. Unfortunately, the roof under which they found themselves domiciled turned out to be far from protective. Their first home in Illinois was a log shelter, poorly built and lacking even a floor. Helen recalled that "when it rained the water stood near ankle deep on the ground."[11] They had left the hostility of the Missouri mobs behind them, but their sufferings were far from over.

Soon thereafter, the Saints—weakened by their perilous winter exodus out of Missouri—were afflicted with widespread malaria from the mosquito-infested swamps surrounding their new 'home.' As the pestilence took its toll, "Nearly all were taken down, one after another. . . . Many had to see their dear ones die and not one of

10   Helen Mar Kimball Whitney, "Early Reminiscences," *Woman's Exponent* 8, no. 24 (May 15, 1880): 188; italicized in original.

11   Helen Mar Kimball Whitney, "Life Incidents," *Woman's Exponent* 9, no. 3 (July 1, 1880): 18.

the family able to follow [their remains] to their last resting place; hundreds were lying sick in tents and wagons."[12] Their determination and conviction to live the Gospel did not grant the Kimball family immunity against the suffering, and before long they all succumbed to the dreaded pestilence, until only Helen's little brother (Heber Parley, about four years old) was strong enough to bring water to the family:

> "... my little brother, upon whom we had depended to bring us water to drink as we lay sick with chills and fever, came in with his usual pail of water, and setting it upon the floor, laid down by it and said: "I b'eve I's goin' to have agu' too"; and sure enough the little fellow was shaking with it.
>
> ... None but those who have passed through similar sufferings can realize our condition, as the days and weeks dragged on, and most of the Saints were destitute of the commonest comforts, and were wanting for beds and even covering, having been robbed in the state of Missouri, and the nights were very cold. We know how the ague weakens and reduces a person's strength in two or three days, but there we had it for weeks and months at a time, and there was no alternative but to submit and make the best of it.
>
> Wrapped in our shawls or quilts we would sit cramped and shaking to the very marrow, hovering over the fire, which only increased the shivering, but would not leave it as long as we could sit up, and when the fever came on the pain and suffering were so intense that the patient generally became delirious.[13]

As the days and weeks passed by, the Saints huddled, exhausted and sick, on the banks of the Mississippi River in Illinois and across the river in Iowa. During this time, Helen witnessed incredible acts of Christlike sacrifice and compassion as she watched the Prophet Joseph, although oftimes sick himself, rise up and travel throughout

---

12 Ibid.

13 Helen Mar Kimball Whitney, "Scenes in Nauvoo," *Woman's Exponent* 10, no. 4 (July 15, 1881): 26.

the camps, nursing the sick.[14] In this she saw the fulfillment of Christ's teaching; she saw the greatest among them willingly stoop into the role of the servant. Helen remembered:

> The Prophet visited and administered words of consolation and often made tea and waited upon them himself and sent members of his own family who were able to go, to nurse and comfort the sick and sorrowful. He was often heard to say that the Saints who died in consequence of the persecutions, were as much martyrs as the ones who were killed in defence of the Saints or murdered at Haun's Mill.[15]

One extraordinary event occurred on July 22, when Joseph suddenly arose, full of the Spirit of God, and began administering blessings to the Saints. So many were healed, even some on the brink of death, that this day has been singled out and recorded in the annals of Church history as a remarkable "day of God's power." The miraculous healing began at the Prophet's own home, as he blessed the suffering Saints, beginning with those camped in his dooryard. Then, traveling from house to house and from tent to tent, he began healing those with the necessary faith. Wilford Woodruff recalled:

> While I was living in this cabin in the old barracks, we experienced a day of God's power with the Prophet Joseph. It was a very sickly time and Joseph had given up his home in Commerce to the sick, and had a tent pitched in his door-yard and was living in that himself. The large number of Saints who had been driven out of Missouri, were flocking into Commerce; but had no homes to go into, and were living in wagons, in tents, and on

---

14   Oliver B. Huntington recalled, "The prophet was our ... doctor, and he visited us nearly every day, in fact he was doctor for all the brethren and every day he went the circuit, to all, which took him pretty much all the time through the sickly season. He would lay on hands and apply simple proscriptions. He once ordered me a showering of cold water, and Carlos Smith layed hands on me and my chills turned to the real shaking ague, which was less dangerous." Elaine S. Marshall, "The Power of God to Heal: The Shared Gifts of Joseph and Hyrum," in *Joseph and Hyrum—Leading as One*, ed. Mark E. Mendenhall, Hal B. Gregersen, Jeffrey S. O'Driscoll, Heidi S. Swinton, and Breck England (Provo, UT: Religious Studies Center, Brigham Young University; Salt Lake City: Deseret Book, 2010).

15   Helen Mar Kimball Whitney, "Life Incidents," *Woman's Exponent* 9, no. 3 (July 1, 1880): 18.

the ground. Many, therefore, were sick through the exposure they were subjected to. Brother Joseph had waited on the sick, until he was worn out and nearly sick himself.

On the morning of the 22nd of July, 1839, he arose reflecting upon the situation of the Saints of God in their persecutions and afflictions, and he called upon the Lord in prayer, and the power of God rested upon him mightily, and as Jesus healed all the sick around Him in His day, so Joseph, the Prophet of God, healed all around on this occasion. He healed all in his house and door-yard, then, in company with Sidney Rigdon and several of the Twelve, he went through among the sick lying on the bank of the river, and he commanded them in a loud voice, in the name of Jesus Christ, to come up and be made whole, and they were all healed. When he healed all that were sick on the east side of the river, they crossed the Mississippi river in a ferry-boat to the west side, to Montrose, where we were. . . . As they were passing by my door, Brother Joseph said: "Brother Woodruff, follow me." These were the only words spoken by any of the company from the time they left Brother Brigham's house till we crossed the public square, and entered Brother Fordham's house. Brother Fordham had been dying for an hour, and we expected each minute would be his last.

I felt the power of God that was overwhelming His Prophet.

When we entered the house, Brother Joseph walked up to Brother Fordham, and took him by the right hand; in his left hand he held his hat.

He saw that Brother Fordham's eyes were glazed, and that he was speechless and unconscious.

After taking hold of his hand, he looked down into the dying man's face and said: "Brother Fordham, do you not know me?" At first he made no reply; but we could all see the effect of the Spirit of God resting upon him.

He again said: "Elijah, do you not know me?"

With a low whisper, Brother Fordham answered, "Yes!"

The Prophet then said, "Have you not faith to be healed?"

The answer, which was a little plainer than before, was: "I am afraid it is too late. If you had come sooner, I think it might have been."

He had the appearance of a man waking from sleep. It was the sleep of death.

Joseph then said: "Do you believe that Jesus is the Christ?"

"I do, Brother Joseph," was the response.

Then the Prophet of God spoke with a loud voice, as in the majesty of the Godhead: "Elijah, I command you, in the name of Jesus of Nazareth, to arise and be made whole!"

The words of the Prophet were not like the words of man, but like the voice of God. It seemed to me that the house shook from its foundation.

Elijah Fordham leaped from his bed like a man raised from the dead. A healthy color came to his face, and life was manifested in every act.

His feet were done up in Indian meal poultices. He kicked them off his feet, scattered the contents, and then called for his clothes and put them on. He asked for a bowl of bread and milk, and ate it; then put on his hat and followed us into the street, to visit others who were sick. . . .

It was the greatest day for the manifestation of the power of God through the gift of healing since the organization of the Church.[16]

Joseph spent the remaining week among the sick, giving counsel and endeavoring to bring relief through nursing and the administration of priesthood blessings,[17] leaving this period of time remembered as

---

16 Wilford Woodruff, *Leaves from My Journal* (Salt Lake City: Juvenile Instructor Office, 1882), 62-65; see also, July 22, 1839, Wilford Woodruff journal, 1838 January-1839 December, p. 109, Church History Library, https://catalog.churchofjesuschrist.org/assets/adc523d5-d74b-42ec-930a-557fdc7d05a2/0/108.

17 Joseph Smith's history records the following counsel given by the Prophet to the Saints a week later on Sunday, July 28, 1839: ". . . I spoke and admonished the church individually to set their houses in order, to make clean the inside of the platter, and to

Painting of Israel Barlow with Joseph Smith overlooking Commerce, Illinois the future site of Nauvoo, by Ken Corbett

one of the most memorable examples of faith and priesthood power as exercised by the Prophet.

Enduring the privations and persecutions in Missouri, suffering with debilitating sickness in Nauvoo, and feeling the sting of betrayal of those who once stood as friends was fulfillment to an acute degree the promise of the Lord who had said He would sit as a refiner and purifier of the Saints.[18] As the people began to heal, it would still require great faith, and patience to forgive and rise above. Would Helen and her family have the fortitude to go on? Would they pay the price that had been exacted?

---

meet on the next sabbath to partake of the Sacrament in order that by our obedience to the ordinances, we might be enabled to prevail with God against the destroyer, and that the sick may might be healed. All this week chiefly spent among the sick, who in general are gaining strength, and recovering health[.]" Joseph Smith, History, 1838–1856, volume C-1, p. 964, The Joseph Smith Papers.

18   Zechariah 13:9, "And I will bring the third part through the fire, and will refine them as silver is refined, and will try them as gold is tried: they shall call on my name, and I will hear them: I will say, It is my people: and they shall say, The Lord is my God."

The Lord was refining a chosen people, and in a revelation to Joseph Smith in 1842, He said, "Behold, the great day of the Lord is at hand; and who can abide the day of his coming, and who can stand when he appeareth? For he is like a refiner's fire, and like fuller's soap; and he shall sit as a refiner and purifier of silver, and he shall purify the sons of Levi, and purge them as gold and silver, that they may offer unto the Lord an offering in righteousness. Let us, therefore, as a church and a people, and as Latter-day Saints, offer unto the Lord an offering in righteousness; and let us present in his holy temple, when it is finished, a book containing the records of our dead, which shall be worthy of all acceptation." Doctrine and Covenants 128:24.

CHAPTER 5

Weighing the Cost & "Bitter Price"

~⌘~

T he Kimballs felt a united family commitment and dedication
to teaching the Gospel. Despite having only recently reunited
with his family, and with his wife and children bedridden, sick,
and taken with chills and fever, Heber C. Kimball accepted a call
to return to the mission field with Brigham Young in September
1839. The Lord needed him to return to Europe and gather out new
members—faithful souls who would strengthen and reinforce the
weakened Church after the horrors of Missouri.

Hurrah for Israel!

However, when the wagon arrived to take Heber and Brigham once
again to England, Heber had been sick throughout the night, and
lay prostrate from the effects of the ague (malaria). He could barely
rise from his bed. However, exerting almost inhuman determination
and strength, he staggered to his feet to bid his family goodbye.
We capture the poignancy of the moment in his own words as he
describes the pitiful scene:

// I went to the bed and shook hands with my wife, who was
shaking with the ague, having two children lying sick by her
side; I embraced her and my children, and bid them farewell; the
only child well was little Heber Parley, and it was with difficulty
he could carry a two-quart pail full of water from a spring at
the bottom of a small hill to assist in quenching their thirst.
It was with difficulty we got into the wagon and started down

the hill about ten rods; it appeared to me as though my very inmost parts would melt within me; leaving my family in such a condition, as it were, almost in the arms of death; it seemed to me as though I could not endure it.

I said to the teamster, "Hold up." Said I to Brother Brigham, "This is pretty tough, ain't it? Let's rise up and give them a cheer." We arose and swinging our hats three times over our heads, we cried, "Hurrah! Hurrah! Hurrah for Israel." Vilate hearing the noise arose from her bed and came to the door; she had a smile on her face and she and Mary Ann Young cried out to us, "Good-bye, God bless you." We returned the compliment and then told the driver to go ahead.

After this I felt a spirit of joy and gratitude at having the satisfaction of seeing my wife standing upon her feet, instead of leaving her in bed, knowing as I did that I should not see them again for two or more years.[1]

For 11-year-old Helen, the thought of bidding her ailing father farewell to an unknown fate brought out acute feelings of grief, buffered only by the greatness of the service to which they were called:

// ... we children wept bitterly when our father came to bid us farewell, not knowing that we would ever see him again in the flesh. Both he and Brother Young were going away so sick they were unable to get into the wagon without assistance. The scene is so vivid before me that my eyes are blinded with tears as I try to write; but words fail to describe it. Our grief for a time was very great, but the knowledge that they were messengers of the Almighty to carry glad tidings to those who were in darkness that they also might be partakers of the blessings of the gospel of salvation, sustained those who were left.[2]

The breaking of lost Israel's chains came with a heavy price for the Kimball family—but their willing offering unlocked the heavens and poured forth the blessings of eternity. The Lord had promised

---

1   Helen Mar Kimball Whitney, "Life Incidents," *Woman's Exponent* 9, no. 4 (July 15, 1880): 25.

2   Ibid.

that for those who followed the words of Joseph Smith, the gates of hell would not prevail, darkness would be dispersed, and the very heavens would shake for their good.[3] This assurance was fulfilled for the Kimballs and others in that day. The work of Heber and his fellow laborers blossomed in their mother country—Brigham Young recounted the miraculous progress the Lord opened before them:

❘❘ We landed in the spring of 1840, as strangers in a strange land and penniless, but through the mercy of God we have gained many friends, established churches in almost every noted town and city in the kingdom of Great Britain, baptized between seven and eight thousand, printed 5,000 Books of Mormon, 3,000 Hymn Books, 2,500 [copies] of the Millennial Star, and 50,000 tracts, and emigrated to Zion 1,000 souls, established a permanent shipping agency which will be a great blessing to the Saints, and have sown in the hearts of many thousands the seeds of eternal truth, which will bring forth fruit to the honor and glory of God, and yet we have lacked nothing to eat, drink or wear; in all these things I acknowledge the hand of God.[4]

Helen and her mother willingly shouldered the responsibilities that came with the sacrifice of losing their father and husband, their provider and protector. He was laboring far across the ocean in a foreign land, preaching the Gospel of life and salvation to a people whom the Lord was calling home, gathering them as an eternal family who had grown as numerous as the sands of the sea. Vilate understood that their family, as a whole, had been set apart to teach the restored Gospel—that they were part of a grand quest to redeem lost and scattered Israel.

---

3   Doctrine and Covenants 21:4-6.

"Wherefore, meaning the church, thou shalt give heed unto all his words and commandments which he shall give unto you as he receiveth them, walking in all holiness before me;

"For his word ye shall receive, as if from mine own mouth, in all patience and faith.

"For by doing these things the gates of hell shall not prevail against you; yea, and the Lord God will disperse the powers of darkness from before you, and cause the heavens to shake for your good, and his name's glory."

4   Brigham Young, *The Journal of Brigham*, comp. Leland R. Nelson (Provo: Council Press, 1980), 41.

Helen would later record the importance and timing of her father's first mission to Europe, including the powerful and rousing truth that the mission field had been prepared by one of the Three Nephite disciples.[5] This knowledge came from the Prophet Joseph Smith, who received:

> **❝** ... a visit from one of the Nephites, who told him he had been through England, Ireland and that the work of the Lord would be short and powerful in those places. He also told him many things about this land (America), many of which have been fulfilled. . . .[6]
>
> There are [no] doubt hundreds still living who heard the Prophet relate the circumstance mentioned in my mother's letter of one of the old Nephites visiting England, Ireland and Scotland, and they can bear their testimony to the fulfilment of Joseph's predictions on that day, as well as all the rest up to the present time.[7]

The astonishing conversion of the Saints who gathered from the isles of Great Britain was remarkable. For a five-year period during the early days of the Church, there were more Latter-day Saints in Great Britain than were in the United States.[8] During the 1970s, a survey of general Church membership revealed that an estimated 80% were of British extraction *alone*.[9] What was so fertile about the land of

---

5   In 3 Nephi 28, we learn that three of the original 12 Nephite disciples were blessed to "never taste of death" and remain on the earth, to continue teaching and ministering to "bring the souls of men unto [Jesus Christ]." Mormon revealed that these men would serve, without recognition, "among the Gentiles," "among the Jews," among "all the scattered tribes of Israel, and unto all nations, kindreds, tongues and people, and shall bring out of them unto Jesus many souls . . ." While Mormon folklore has sometimes imagined the 'Three Nephites' as wandering men changing flat tires and mysteriously offering random acts of service, the Book of Mormon clarifies that their work is to preach the gospel with "convincing power," to perform "great and marvelous" works to prepare the world for the final judgement.

6   Helen Mar Kimball Whitney, "Scenes and Incidents in Nauvoo," *Woman's Exponent* 10, no. 18 (February 15, 1882): 138.

7   Helen Mar Kimball Whitney, "Scenes and Incidents in Nauvoo," *Woman's Exponent* 10, no. 20 (March 15, 1882): 159.

8   "More Members Now outside U.S. Than in U.S.," *Ensign*, ed. Jay M. Todd, March 1996, 76-77.

9   "History of the Church in Great Britain," *Ensign*, September 1971, 25-29.

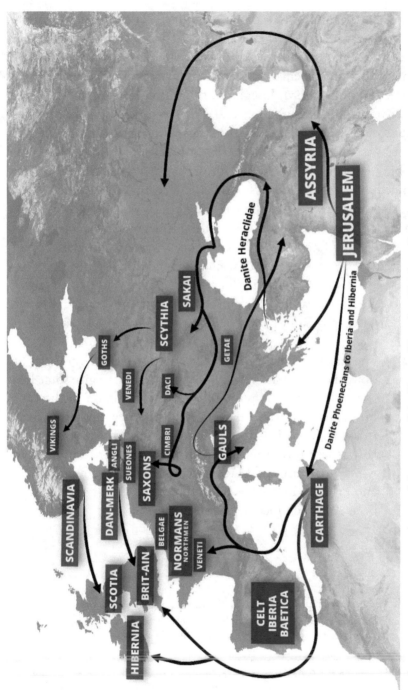

Ancient Migrations of the House of Israel in Northern Europe

England that allowed for the message of the Restoration to flourish? The answer is simple: They were Israel! They were the Lord's sheep, and when they heard the Shepherd's voice—delivered by humble, unsophisticated men—Israel ran to answer His call.[10] Under the direction of the Lord, Joseph Smith sent his choicest men—Heber C. Kimball, Brigham Young, and others as missionaries to Britain—not to convert every inhabitant of those isles, but instead, to find the elect—to find *Israel*. The lost tribes of Israel, truly a sleeping giant, a lion amid the beasts of the forest, had been scattered—lost and mixed among the Gentiles with only a remnant remaining.[11] This was no small event. The Kimballs and others were literally fulfilling latter-day prophecy—they were calling Israel to come *home*!

While her father served across the ocean in England, many grateful converts—men and women whom he taught—poured out their gratitude by sending gifts and toys to his family in Nauvoo. These gifts often came to Helen, who would then share liberally with other Latter-day Saint children:

// The majority of them were of the poor and meek of the earth, but none the less to show their love they desired to give some little token, if it was but a toy, and would insist upon the brethren taking them to the children. All who knew my father heard him speak of his little girl, and many and various were the things sent me, numerous handkerchiefs were among them, which generally had Queen Vic, as she was commonly called, and Prince Albert printed on them; her Majesty having lately been crowned Queen of Great Britain.

---

10   John 10:27.

11   The Son of God prophesied to the ancient Nephites regarding the work of Joseph Smith and the awakening of Israel in the latter days: "For in that day, for my sake shall the Father work a work, which shall be a great and a marvelous work among them; and there shall be among them those who will not believe it, although a man shall declare it unto them. . . . And my people who are a remnant of Jacob shall be among the Gentiles, yea, in the midst of them as a lion among the beasts of the forest, as a young lion among the flocks of sheep, who, if he go through both treadeth down and teareth in pieces, and none can deliver. Their hand shall be lifted up upon their adversaries, and all their enemies shall be cut off." 3 Nephi 21:9, 12-13.

I also received a variety of pretty little china dishes and a box of wooden ones as well as china dolls . . .[12]

Helen noted that as gifts poured in, some considered her too old (11-12 years) for amusing oneself with dolls.[13] Rather than keep them all for herself, she gave many away to others in need.

Helen's generous spirit defined her life—she was well known for her consistent sympathetic and charitable nature. After giving birth to another son in 1843, her mother Vilate's health sharply declined, and the mounting pressure and difficulties began to exact their toll on her weakened frame. Her mother's infirmity necessitated Helen stepping in to assist with the newborn. Joyfully, 14-year-old Helen shouldered the responsibility of caring for her infant brother:

// My mother being in a feeble state of health I had to take almost the whole care of him [her baby brother, Charles] during the first year or two. He was very delicate and had some severe spells of sickness, and my love and tender care increased with the days and months and I never wearied of my charge. When two years old he became strong, healthy and the pride of my heart . . . my affection for him surpassed any that I had ever felt for a baby.[14]

Helen's giving nature blessed her family greatly, but her reach would extend far beyond her intimate circle in the coming years.

Entrusted With Sensitive Knowledge

Heber C. Kimball returned to Nauvoo in 1841 and immediately set to work providing for the temporal necessities of his family while enjoying a closer working relationship with the Prophet Joseph Smith. These intimate settings allowed the Prophet to begin revealing the restoration of significant doctrines, ordinances, and principles with Heber and others whom he felt confident would not betray his trust.

12   Helen Mar Kimball Whitney, "Scenes in Nauvoo," *Woman's Exponent* 10, no. 5 (August 1, 1881): 34.

13   Helen would later advise parents not to cut childhood too short for their daughters, noting: "I sometimes think it a mistaken idea in American mothers to want their daughters to become sedate and womanly before they have fairly reached their teens. We can never be young but once in this life and I like children to enjoy themselves while they can for they will grow old soon enough." Ibid.

14   Helen Mar Kimball Whitney, "Scenes and Incidents in Nauvoo," *Woman's Exponent* 11, no. 4 (July 15, 1882): 26.

In 1843, Heber first introduced the order of marriage practiced by Abraham, Isaac, Jacob, Joseph, Moses, and many other Hebrew prophets, to his daughter, Helen, clarifying that this sacred principle was to be restored in the latter days. Helen was witnessing a literal fulfillment of the hymn she had sung in the Kirtland temple: "The Lord is extending the Saints' understanding, restoring their judges and *all as at first.*"[15] Helen heard and believed her father— but she also wondered, would she ever understand for herself?

Entrusting such a sensitive and potentially dangerous secret to a girl so young in years speaks to Helen's remarkable character and integrity. Throughout her life, Helen had been boldly independent. Her writings reveal her willingness to speak with raw authenticity—acknowledging doubts, analyzing questions, and facing struggles head on. As a spirited free thinker, she strove to establish her own opinions from a young age. Helen wrote that, at first, she felt "unwilling to sacrifice my earthly happiness for the promise of future reward." She wondered, could she not "content [herself] with a lesser glory"? Even as a young child bubbling with the curious imagination of a seven-year-old, Helen concluded she was just not cut out to be a "Saint"—she was too "fond of fun and amusement," but cleverly determined that if quickly alerted before she was to die, she would "sober down and prepare myself." Later in life, she would laugh at her past antics, commenting: "In that early day we were full of sectarian notions [about salvation and heaven] which took time to overcome."[16]

---

15   *Collection of Sacred Hymns for the Church of the Latter-day Saints* (Kirtland: F. G. Williams, 1835), 120, Church History Library, https://catalog.churchofjesuschrist.org/assets/ced69f72-4799-4b3d-9827-2006d64c5804/0/121.

16   "[My mother] enjoyed the love and respect of everyone, and she never wanted for anything if her circumstances were made known. She truly enjoyed her religion. I was her youngest child living; was hardly seven years old when my father went East on his first mission, but I remember how happy she used to seem. Often in the morning I would awaken and hear her praying, and then she would go about her daily duties singing so sweetly, it seemed to me as though heaven and the angels were not very far off. I used to think it impossible for me to ever become a Saint. I looked upon my parents as such, but thought that nothing short of perfection could take us to heaven, which I could never attain to, as I was so fond of fun and amusement that I could not possibly give them up, though I often had very serious reflections upon the subject, and used to think if I could only know just a little time before I was to die, I might be able to sober down and prepare myself. In that early day we were full of sectarian notions, and our ideas were rather contracted. We had many traditions which took time to overcome." Helen Mar Kimball Whitney, "Life Incidents," *Woman's Exponent* 9, no. 6 (August 15, 1880): 42.

As she grew and began contemplating life's greatest questions, Helen scrutinized every aspect of the Gospel and finally determined:

❙❙ ... I found that there was no real substance in any religious doctrine outside of "Mormonism," and I could not disbelieve one part (as many have professed to do) without rejecting it completely and considering Joseph Smith an impostor. I therefore listened to the counsel of my brethren until I became more firmly rooted in the true faith of the gospel.[17]

Helen's genuine honesty, coupled with her ability to balance autonomy and determination with humility and sacrifice, made her a woman who, by the age of 14, was worthy of being entrusted with the sacred principle of plural and Celestial marriage. She now wielded power to either protect or destroy the reputation, character, and position of both the Prophet Joseph Smith and her father. Helen would never betray that trust.

To truly comprehend the significance of the promises offered to Helen, one must look beyond the mortal moment in which these Restoration milestones occurred. In our 21st-century society, no one is entirely immune to the shadow cast by cultural evolution— influencing for good or ill our opinions and beliefs. We judge the past based on our present societal traditions and expectations, often failing to consider the spiritual stature of those noble and great ones whom God foreordained before this life. Many of the men and women who joined the early Church exhibited extraordinary character—like Moroni, Nephi, Samuel, and Noah, they could not be defined by their age. For the young Helen Mar, the choice of accepting the opportunity to be sealed to the Prophet Joseph Smith would set the stage for the rest of her life, being perfectly designed for a woman of superior standing in the eternities.

Helen soon received another, though not unpleasant, surprise when she discovered that she was now united with familial ties to her best friend, Sarah Ann Whitney. Helen's father "took the first opportunity to introduce Sarah Ann to me as Joseph's wife. This astonished me beyond measure; but I could then understand

---

17   Helen Mar Whitney, *Plural Marriage as Taught by the Prophet Joseph* (Salt Lake City: Juvenile Instructor Office, 1882), 37.

a few things which had previously been to me a puzzle."[18] With the knowledge that her beloved friend had also been sealed to the Prophet Joseph Smith, Helen discovered that she had a trusted confidante—a special gift for which she no doubt felt profoundly grateful, especially as persecution increased.

Helen's "Bitter Price"

At first, Helen had not considered that her sealing to the Prophet would cause any change in her daily life—certainly no inconvenience would result, she thought. Later in life, and with the panorama of many years' experience laid out before her, she articulated her feelings as a 14-year-old in poignant and poetic verse:

❯❯ ... through this life my time will be my own,

 the step I now am taking's for eternity alone.

 No one need be the wiser, through time I shall be free,

 And as the past hath been the future still will be.[19]

Time, however, taught her a lesson—a confession she made as she continued:

❯❯ Untutor'd heart in thy gen'rous sacrafise,

 Thou dids't not weigh the cost nor know the bitter price ...[20]

What was the "bitter price" Helen paid? First, as persecution mounted, so did Helen's distress over the danger and ostracization that constantly threatened those who practiced plural marriage. The sting came from the difficult circumstances faced by those who stood closest to the Prophet. Continuing in her poetic pen, she lamented that her "youthful friends grow shy and cold," and "poisonous darts

---

18 Helen Mar Kimball Whitney, "Scenes in Nauvoo after the Martyrdom of the Prophet and Patriarch," *Woman's Exponent* 11, no. 19 (March 1, 1883): 146.

19 Helen Mar Kimball Whitney Autobiography, March 30, 1881. Located within the "Helen M. Kimball Whitney papers, 1881-1882," p. 4, Church History Library, https://catalog.churchofjesuschrist.org/assets/2c0cb6bb-493b-417a-8bd5-dce48180827f/1/3.

20 Ibid.

from sland'rous tongues were hurled."[21] This was a time when she felt isolation and apparent slander directed toward herself and family— she felt *alone*:

❙❙ Thy happy dreems all o'er thou'rt doom'd alas to be

Bar'd out from social scenes by this thy destiny,

And o'er thy sad'nd mem'ries of sweet departed joys

Thy sicken'd heart will brood and imagine future woes,

And like a fetter'd bird with wild and longing heart,

Thou'lt dayly pine for freedom and murmor at thy lot . . .[22]

The rapid growth of the Saints' population in Nauvoo brought with it a number of apostates and antagonists toward the Prophet and the Church. The relentless infiltration of the enemy threatened those who were loyal to the faith, especially those endeavoring to live higher laws. With the increased danger came a necessary increase in the wariness exercised by all involved—including Helen, who keenly felt the effects of these safeguards and restrictions:

❙❙ During the winter of 1843, there were plenty of parties and balls, and many were held at the Mansion. The last one that I attended there that winter, was on Christmas Eve. Some of the young gentlemen got up a series of dancing parties, to be held at the Mansion once a week. My brother William put his name down before asking father's permission, and when questioned about it made him believe that he must pay the money for himself and lady, whether he went or not, and that he could not honorably withdraw from it. He carried the day, but I had to stay at home, as my father had been warned by the Prophet to keep his daughter away from there, because of the blacklegs and certain ones of questionable character who attended there. His wife Emma had become the ruling spirit, and money had become her God.

---

21   Ibid.

22   Ibid.

I did not betray William, but I felt quite sore over it, and thought it a very unkind act in father to allow him to go and enjoy the dance unrestrained with others of my companions, and fetter me down, for no girl loved dancing better than I did, and I really felt that it was too much to bear. It made the dull school still more dull, and like a wild bird I longed for the freedom that was denied me; and thought myself a much abused child, and that it was pardonable if I did murmur. I imagined that my happiness was all over, and brooded over the sad memories of sweet departed joys and all manner of future woes, which (by the by) were of short duration, my bump of hope being too large to admit of my remaining long under the clouds; besides my father was very kind and indulgen[t] in other ways, and always took me with him, when mother could not go, and it was not a very long time before I became satisfied that I was blessed in being under the control of so good and wise a parent, who had taken counsel and thus saved me from evils, which some others in their youth and inexperience, were exposed to, though they thought no evil.[23]

Another issue arose for Helen to sort out, regarding her social life. As a young woman who was married—sealed, albeit in secret, to Joseph Smith—she would necessarily find herself in conflict as other interested young men came calling. Understanding this challenge, her father conscientiously sought out alternative social opportunities for his cherished daughter. He wanted Helen to enjoy uplifting interactions and to participate in cultured recreation—to allow her to fully develop and express the many gifts and talents God had given her.

Helen joined a choir led by Stephen Goddard, and later remembered trudging toward the Mansion House in the midnight rain on New Year's Eve to serenade Joseph and Emma with a New Year's hymn. She recalled: "After singing one or two anthems he [Joseph] pronounced his blessing upon the orchestra and choir, which repaid the brethren and sisters for all their trouble."[24]

---

23   Helen Mar Kimball Whitney, "Scenes and Incidents in Nauvoo," *Woman's Exponent* 11, no. 12 (November 15, 1882): 90.

24   Ibid.

Helen also participated in a number of Nauvoo's theatricals, though initially with some trepidation due to her timidity. She received her first taste of performing as an actress in plays performed in the Nauvoo Masonic Hall. Helen played the Countess in *Thérèse, the Orphan of Geneva*,[25] and one of the virgins in *Pizarro*,[26] in addition to another role she did not identify. When the acting troupe presented *Pizarro* for the Nauvoo citizens, Helen recalled that no actor could excel Brigham Young, who played the part of the Incan high priest:

❝ ... no part in "Pizarro" was better played than was the Priest, by Brigham Young. There was some good acting done—some so life-like, that at times nearly the whole audience would be affected to tears. Joseph did not try to hide his feelings, but was seen to weep a number of times.[27]

Life was filled with blessings, as well as trouble. There were days when the sun shone brightly, and others that hung with foreboding clouds overhead—and Helen drew knowledge, wisdom, and experience from both. Over the years, she grew in appreciation for the guidance that her parents provided, and diligently wrote for the benefit of future Latter-day Saints:

❝ A moral may be drawn from this truthful story. "Children obey thy parents," etc. And also, "Have regard to thy name; for that shall continue with you above a thousand great treasures of gold." "A good life hath but few days; but a good name endureth forever."[28]

Helen felt a deep conviction that from an eternal perspective, the blessings and knowledge she would receive from life's temporary trials would ensure a future eternity of honor, peace, joy, and reward. She wrote:

---

25 *Thérèse, the Orphan of Geneva* was written by French novelist, Victor Ducange, who was an outspoken supporter of freedom principles in Europe. He was fined and imprisoned more than once for his stances.

26 Pizarro, a melodrama set during the Spanish conquest of Peru, was written by playwright Richard Sheridan in 1799.

27 Helen Mar Kimball Whitney, "Scenes and Incidents in Nauvoo," *Woman's Exponent* 11, no. 12 (November 15, 1882): 90.

28 Ibid.

// But could'st thou see the future & view that glorious crown,

Awaiting you in Heaven you would not weep nor mourn,

Pure and exalted was thy father's aim, he saw

A glory in obeying this high celestial law . . .[29]

In many ways, as with most girls, Helen might have had a general expectation for her future—but she soon learned by experience that the Lord has a singular way of altering one's projected mortal path with rather startling twists and turns—each calculated to provide a benefit for our good and greatest happiness. The struggles and toil that life brought provided a priceless understanding of the God she loved and chose to serve—also providing her wisdom for the poetry and prose that fell from her pen. She admitted to her children: "I am thankful that He has brought me through the furnace of affliction," as well as the promise she claimed from her Maker:

// For to thousands who've died without the light

I will bring eternal joy & make thy crown more bright.[30]

The "bitter price" Helen had paid thus far was but a harbinger of trials yet to come. Along with her fellow Saints, she would experience a world turned upside down during the summer of 1844, setting in motion a turbulent series of events—a turning point she would forever keep in her remembrance.

---

29   Helen Mar Kimball Whitney Autobiography, March 30, 1881. Located within the "Helen M. Kimball Whitney papers, 1881-1882," p. 4-5, Church History Library, https://catalog.churchofjesuschrist.org/assets/2c0cb6bb-493b-417a-8bd5-dce48180827f/1/3.

30   Helen Mar Kimball Whitney Autobiography, March 30, 1881. Located within the "Helen M. Kimball Whitney papers, 1881-1882," p. 5, Church History Library, https://catalog.churchofjesuschrist.org/assets/2c0cb6bb-493b-417a-8bd5-dce48180827f/1/4.

CHAPTER 6

A World Turned Upside Down

⌒

The night of June 24, 1844 was warm and humid under the light of a nearly full moon. Helen—just two months shy of her 16th birthday—and Emily Partridge[1] had been visiting friends before retiring to bed. The two were sleeping peacefully when they were suddenly awakened by an agitated clamor—anguished voices exclaiming the Prophet had been murdered! Life as young Helen knew it would never be the same.

The martyrdom of the Prophet Joseph Smith and his brother Hyrum, savagely enacted while they were incarcerated in Carthage Jail, threw the Kimball family into an anguished state of disarray. At the time, Heber was away from home on a mission to the Eastern states, while Helen and her mother had been eagerly preparing to join him. Without forewarning or anticipation, Helen felt "all the airy castles that I had been building [were] cruelly dashed to the ground."[2]

---

1   Emily Dow Partridge was sealed as a plural wife to the Prophet Joseph Smith on March 4, 1843, by Heber C. Kimball. Emily testified in firsthand accounts that her marriage was consummated with the Prophet Joseph Smith, and that her experience confirmed to her that he always conducted himself with the utmost respect and virtue. Many years later, in 1892, she was questioned by an RLDS attorney who asked her whether Joseph had ever initiated a physical relationship with her during their courtship, including laying his hand on her shoulder, putting his arm around her, or offering to take her hand. Emily was adamant that he did not, testifying that ". . . he never did for he was not that kind of a man, -he was a gentleman in every way and did not indulge in liberties like that. . . . not before we were married." Emily Partridge, deposition, Temple Lot transcript, United States testimony 1892, p. 357-358, Church History Library, https://catalog.churchofjesuschrist.org/assets/6ed3a142-524e-4471-852d-51e8ef422647/0/9.

2   Helen Mar Kimball Whitney, "Scenes and Incidents in Nauvoo," *Woman's Exponent* 11, no. 15 (January 1, 1883): 114.

Only days before the martyrdom, Helen stood with the Nauvoo Legion and "thousands" of fellow Saints—listening in rapt attention to what would later become known as Joseph's 'last address.' "I have had the honor of being your General," Joseph cried out before beginning to prophesy concerning the Saints' gathering to the Rocky Mountains—hinting of his own approaching departure:

" ... you will gather many people unto the fastness of the Rocky Mountains, as a center for the gathering of the people; and you will be faithful because of what you have been through: And many of those that come in under your ministry, because of their much learning, will seek for high positions, and they will be set up and raise themselves in eminence above you, but you will walk in low places unnoticed—and you will know of all that transpires in their midst, and those that are your friends will be my friends[.] this I will promise to you that when I come again to lead you forth[,] for I will to prepare a place for you, so that where I am you shall be with me.[3]

Joseph foresaw the fate that awaited him at Carthage, while the rest of the world paid little attention to the affairs rapidly unfolding in the little town a mere 25 miles from Nauvoo. Friends bid Joseph and Hyrum farewell as they rode away—but few, if any, could have known that the brothers' mortal sojourn was at its end—that neither would return alive to their beautiful 'City of Joseph.'

On that fateful Thursday—the day of the martyrdom—Helen stood by as a witness when Thomas Ford, governor of Illinois, visited Nauvoo to deliver what has been described as "one of the most infamous and insulting speeches that ever fell from the lips of an Executive."[4] Ford falsely accused the Saints of being violent criminals who should "atone" for their "misbehavior." Helen listened to Ford's hypocritical speech, but never suspected the "treachery nor the awful tragedy that was being enacted at Carthage. . . ."[5]

---

3   Joseph Smith, Discourse, 22 June 1844, as Reported by Unknown Scribe, p. 3, Joseph Smith Papers.

4   Historian's Office, Martyrdom Account, p. 67, The Joseph Smith Papers; Historian's Office, Martyrdom Account, Draft, p. 55, The Joseph Smith Papers.

5   Helen Mar Kimball Whitney, "Scenes and Incidents in Nauvoo," *Woman's Exponent* 11, no. 15 (January 1, 1883): 114.

Later, it would be discovered that Ford had been warned repeatedly of large-scale threats against the lives of Joseph and Hyrum, and though he had pledged his protection, he deliberately ignored the intelligence his sources were providing, when he had ample opportunity to take appropriate action. Instead of fulfilling his oath, Ford[6] left Carthage for Nauvoo on June 27, taking with him troops who were favorable to the Saints—and leaving behind a band of ruffians in Carthage composed of "known enemies of the Prophet, ostensibly to guard the jail."[7] Only a few hours later, the Prophet would draw his last breath, lying in his own blood against the well curb just outside the jail. He had been brutally shot amidst a hailstorm of bullets, and had fallen from the second-story jail window onto the stone pathway below.

Heber C. Kimball—prominent leader and a well-known, loyal friend of Joseph Smith—soon received word from a distraught Vilate, recounting the horrific scene and the volatile state of affairs in Nauvoo. Her words conveyed a heaviness that no doubt weighed on Heber's heart, and she expressed her distress and concern for his safety. Her anxiety is evident in the letter—but her faith shines through as well:

> Never before did I take up my pen to address you under so trying circumstances as we are now placed, but as Brother Adams, the bearer of this, can tell you more than I can write, I shall not attempt to describe the scene through which we have passed. I saw the lifeless bodies of our beloved brethren,

---

6   When Governor Thomas Ford wrote the *History of Illinois* some years later, he revealed when writing of the Latter-day Saints and the 1844 death of Joseph and Hyrum that he may not have been completely unaware of his own responsibility for the murders, "It is to be feared that in the course of a century, some gifted man like Paul, some splendid orator who will be able by his eloquence to attract crowds of thousands ... [will] make the name of the martyred Joseph ring as loud and stir the souls of men as much as the mighty name of Christ itself. Sharon, Palmyra, Manchester, Kirtland, Far West, Adam Ondi Ahman, Ramus, Nauvoo, and the Carthage Jail may become holy and venerable names ... like Jerusalem, the Garden of Gethsemane, the Mount of Olives, and Mount Calvary to the Christian.... And in that event the author of this history feels degraded by the reflection that [he]... stands a fair chance, like Pilate and Herod ... of being dragged down to posterity with an immortal name hitched on to the memory of a miserable imposter." Thomas Ford, *A History of Illinois*, vol. 2, (Chicago: The Lakeside Press, 1946), 221-223.

7   Historian's Office, Martyrdom Account, p. 67, The Joseph Smith Papers; Historian's Office, Martyrdom Account, Draft, p. 55, The Joseph Smith Papers.

when they were brought to their almost distracted families. Yea, I witnessed their tears and groans, which were enough to rend the heart of adamant.[8] Every brother and sister who witnessed the scene felt deeply to sympathize with them; yea, every heart is filled with sorrow, and the very streets of Nauvoo seem to mourn. Where it will end the Lord only knows. We are kept awake night after night by the alarm of mobs. These apostates say, "Their damnation is sealed, their die is cast, their doom is fixed," and that they are determined to do all in their power to have revenge. William Law says he wants nine more that were in his quorum, sometimes I am afraid he will get them; I have no doubt but you are one.

My constant prayer now is for the Lord to preserve us all to meet again. I have no doubt but your life will be sought, but may the Lord give you wisdom to escape their hands.[9]

A Church in Crisis

With the death of the Prophet Joseph Smith and his brother, Hyrum, the future of the Church appeared desolate and uncertain. The members of the Quorum of the Twelve Apostles scattered abroad hastily began making the trek back to Nauvoo. Once home, they found the Church in a state of confusion, with "Sidney Rigdon [former First Counselor in the First Presidency] busy among the Saints, trying to establish his claim to the presidency of the Church."[10] Six weeks to the day following the martyrdom, a special meeting was convened "to choose a guardian, or trustee for said church."[11]

The seeds of division and disputation were evident, and opinion sharply divided—especially between Sidney Rigdon and the Twelve,

---

8   Defined by Webster's 1828 Dictionary as "A very hard or impenetrable stone; a name given to the diamond and other substances of extreme hardness. The name has often been given to the load stone; but in modern mineralogy, it has no technical signification." Noah Webster, *An American Dictionary of the English Language* (New York: S. Converse, 1828), 110.

9   Helen Mar Kimball Whitney, "Scenes and Incidents in Nauvoo," *Woman's Exponent* 11, no. 15 (January 1, 1883): 114.

10   Jacob Hamblin and James A. Little, *A Narrative of His Personal Experience, as a Frontiersman, Missionary to the Indians and Explorer* (Salt Lake City: The Deseret News, 1909), 20.

11   "Special Meeting," *Times and Seasons* 5 (September 2, 1844): 637.

with Brigham Young at their head. With his customary poise and eloquence, Sidney arose and delivered a polished, articulate speech that lasted nearly an hour and a half.[12] Helen listened, unimpressed, as she stood alongside her lawyer friend, Mr. Hatch—a young man who suddenly began voicing his support for Rigdon, speaking repeatedly "in defense and praise." The more Mr. Hatch attempted to convince Helen that Rigdon "was the right man to lead the Church," the deeper Helen's annoyance grew. Opinionated herself, Helen found her temper rising—and before long, a spirited debate ensued:

> He very quickly learned my feelings, and how offensive he had made himself. My father was seated there with Brigham and the rest of the Apostles, and I became very indignant, and quite a war of words ensued, neither of us (of course) yielding the point. Not long after this he married one of Rigdon's daughters, which proved to be the only loadstone that attracted him in that direction.[13]

Finally, with Sidney Rigdon's lengthy oration concluded, the congregation took a well-needed break before reconvening. After a recommencement of the opening exercises, Brigham Young took the stand. Suddenly, the people arose "en-masse to their feet astonished, as it appeared that Joseph had returned and was speaking to the people."[14] As Brigham Young commenced speaking, hundreds in the audience heard and saw "in every possible degree it was Joseph's voice, and his person, in look, attitude, dress and appearance . . . Joseph himself, personified . . ."[15] This event—no small incident considering the uncertain times—would become known as the Transfiguration of Brigham Young. Helen was an eyewitness to the extraordinary miracle, later testifying:

---

12   Joseph Fielding Smith, *Essentials in Church History* (Deseret Book Company, 1972), 387.

13   Helen Mar Kimball Whitney, "Scenes in Nauvoo after the Martyrdom of the Prophet and Patriarch," *Woman's Exponent* 11, no. 17 (February 1, 1883): 130.

14   Lynne W. Jorgensen, "The Mantle of the Prophet Joseph Passes to Brother Brigham," *BYU Studies Quarterly* 36, no. 4 (1996-1997): 171.

15   ". . . I knew in a moment the spirit and mantle of Joseph was upon him then I remembered his saying to the Council of which Sidney Rigdon was never a member and I knew for myself who was now the leader of Israel." Ibid., 168.

❛❛ I can bear witness, with hundreds of others who stood that day under the sound of Brigham's voice, of the wonderful and startling effect that it had upon us. If Joseph had risen from the dead and stood before them, it could hardly have made a deeper or more lasting impression. It was the very voice of Joseph himself.[16]

Not every Latter-day Saint present at the Nauvoo meeting witnessed the spiritual manifestation of President Young's heaven-ordained calling. In one notable example, Orson Hyde was present with two of his wives, and later shared that while one was able to see the transfiguration, the other was not. The significance was not lost on him, as he compared and contrasted the difference between the women's respective experiences:

❛❛ I sat myself down in the midst of the congregation, with my two wives, whom Joseph had given and sealed to me. When President Young began to speak, one of them said: "It is the voice of Joseph! It is Joseph Smith!" The exclamation of the other was,—"I do not see him, where is he?" Well the thought

---

16   Helen Mar Kimball Whitney, "Scenes in Nauvoo after the Martyrdom of the Prophet and Patriarch," *Woman's Exponent* 11, no. 17 (February 1, 1883): 130.

Helen also included in her account the following story, illustrating that although Sidney Rigdon had endeavored to draw the Saints away after him, Brigham Young frankly forgave him:

"I will here mention a little circumstance to show that there was still a warm place in the heart of Prest. Brigham Young towards Elder Rigdon. It is now more than twenty years since his two eldest sons, Sidney and Wickliffe, came out west in search of gold, the latter hoping also to find health, which he lost while studying law, and had been for some time a sufferer from dyspepsia. Being old schoolmates, my husband invited them to share our hospitality while they stayed. They accompanied him to the office to see President B. Young, who gave them a kindly welcome, and the first opportunity that presented itself of speaking alone to my husband, he said: 'Horace, you give those boys a home with you, and you shall lose nothing by it.' Horace informed him that he had already done so. Everything that laid in our power was done to make them feel comfortable and at home. Wickliffe remained here through the summer, and Sidney stopped with us whenever he came in from the mines. Wickliffe was more religiously inclined than the other, and he expressed himself to Mother Whitney and to Sister E. R. Snow, that he would give all that he had if he could know of the truth of 'Mormonism.' He wrote after returning home and expressed his appreciation of the hospitality that they had met with, while wanderers in this far off land." Helen Mar Kimball Whitney, "Scenes in Nauvoo after the Martyrdom of the Prophet and Patriarch," *Woman's Exponent* 11, no. 17 (February 1, 1883): 130.

occurred to my mind respecting the Scripture which President Young has just quoted:—"My sheep know my voice and follow me." Where is the one that recognized the voice of Joseph in President Young? Where is she? She is in the line of her duty. But where is the other? Gone where I wish she were not. The sheep of the good shepherd will follow the voice they know; but they will not follow the voice of a stranger.

Now, this was a manifestation of the power of the Almighty—it was the power of God resting on an individual in the eyes of all the people; not only in feature and voice, but actually in *stature*. This is my testimony.[17]

Years later—and continuing in our present day—a growing number of skeptics began to view the accounts of the Transfiguration of Brigham Young as mere remnants of 'Mormon folklore.' In other words, some consider the phenomenon as merely an exaggerated legend from our pioneer past. However, an analysis of the historical data—including surviving firsthand accounts—contradicts the progressive dismissal of the miracle. Historical records reveal the Transfiguration to be one of the most documented events in Church History—testifying to the divinely sanctioned mantle passed to Brigham Young following the death of the Prophet Joseph Smith.[18]

Completing Joseph's Temple—A Sacred Trust

The transfiguration miracle settled the question of succession for the Latter-day Saint majority. As they began to pick up the shattered remains of life as they knew it following the martyrdom, these members demonstrated remarkable fortitude and commitment to the Prophet's legacy. Foremost in the minds of the faithful was the completion of the Nauvoo Temple—'Joseph's temple.' Responsibility for leading the advancement of the Restoration now shifted to the shoulders of Brigham Young, Heber C. Kimball,

---

17   Orson Hyde, "The Right to Lead the Church, Etc.," in *Journal of Discourses*, vol. 13 (Liverpool: Horace S. Eldredge, 1871), 181; italics in original. Discourse given on October 6, 1869.

18   Latter-day Answers, "Is there evidence for the transfiguration of Brigham Young?" LDSAnswers.org, February 2, 2017, https://ldsanswers.org/evidence-transfiguration-brigham-young/.

Wilford Woodruff, and other prominent families who had proven themselves before the Lord through deep personal sacrifice. The rise or fall of the latter-day work depended on the execution of this sacred trust.

As both a Kimball daughter and an intimate friend of Brigham Young, the magnitude and significance of Helen's own role in her family's mission began to settle on the young girl. This was *her* work, *her* Church, *her* mission, and *her* cause. Helen and Sarah Ann Whitney assisted in stitching the Nauvoo temple veil, and what joy must have been hers when she was blessed to receive her own endowment on January 1, 1846. Helen had already proven her commitment to sacrifice for the Kingdom, and she had demonstrated her willingness to speak boldly in defense of the keys passed to the Twelve—yet, an even greater work lay ahead for her.

Swirling like the menace of storm clouds about to break down in fury, the environment the Saints found themselves in was brimming with hostile threats from local mobs, the strain of poverty, and increasing persecution from both within and without the Church. Yet, in spite of it all, Brigham Young refused to let the spirit of discouragement prevent the Saints' completion of the sacred edifice. Despite the perseverance manifested by many of the men who worked without even shoes or shirts to shield them from the elements, temple funds soon ran out. Brigham Young, a master of resourcefulness, had innovated every possible solution, but was unable to obtain the needed money. He at last announced the heartbreaking news at a morning gathering in early July 1845—that without funds, "work on the temple would have to cease."[19]

Sitting among the congregation that day was Joseph Toronto, an Italian convert who had an unusual dream years before being introduced to the Gospel. In that dream, "a man stood before him, and told him to leave his money with 'Mormon Brigham' and he should be blessed."[20] Joseph had worked as a sailor and fisherman, and for years—unlike most of his companions—had carefully saved his earnings rather than squandering his treasure on "wine and

---

19   Samuel W. Taylor, *Nightfall at Nauvoo* (New York City: Avon Books, 1971), 356.

20   John R. Young, *Memoirs of John R. Young: Utah Pioneer, 1847* (Salt Lake City: Deseret News, 1920), 47.

women."[21] Joseph had no idea who "Mormon Brigham" was at the time, but he heeded the instruction of the dream by quietly laying aside the gold coins he accumulated, wrapping them in old rags and tin boxes as he waited for the Lord to reveal to him further light and knowledge. Little did he then know that his faithfully saved earnings would, years later, provide for the completion of a sacred, latter-day temple for the God of Israel to visit His people and pour down the blessings which heaven had long held in reserve for this time. Joseph Toronto's answer came to him in early July 1845. God provided deliverance for His people, this time in the form of an Italian convert who delivered his accumulated gold to President Young. In a world turned upside down, this tender mercy and many others assured Helen and her fellow Saints that the Lord was in control. Helen remembered:

// An Italian brother Joseph Toronto (now of this city), came [to Nauvoo] and gave up all he had, which was $2,600.[22]

... [this] Italian brother [made] an offering of all his money to the trustee in trust to carry on the work on the temple. Previous to this the work was almost completely at a stand still for want of means, and President Young had urged the brethren to have faith and go on and the Lord would provide means. On the day when Brother Toronto laid down his money the brethren were to meet in Council and consider the subject of means. President Young walked into the council with the gold in his pocket, when they were debating the question of giving up the work, and he said, "Brethren, will you go on with the work and trust in the Lord?" And they were doubtful. When President Young scattered the gold over the room the brethren were as much astonished as men could possibly be. Is not this a proof that the Lord provides means to carry on His work? Brother Toronto

---

21 Samuel W. Taylor, *Nightfall at Nauvoo* (New York City: Avon Books, 1971), 356.

22 Helen Mar Kimball Whitney, "Scenes in Nauvoo after the Martyrdom of the Prophet and Patriarch," *Woman's Exponent* 11, no. 22 (April 15, 1883): 170. William Clayton recorded Toronto's contribution as $2,599.75 in gold. William Clayton Diary, July 8, 1845; William Clayton, *An Intimate Chronicle: The Journals of William Clayton*, ed. George D. Smith (Salt Lake City: Signature Books, 1995), 173.

has since accumulated means and raised a family, been to Italy and Sicily, and in his native land, accomplished a good work.[23]

While critics of the Restoration—both past and present—have mocked, questioned, and slandered the character of Brigham Young, Helen remained ever firm in her eyewitness testimony of her lifelong friend's integrity and prophetic utterances—adding her own witness to those of many other Saints. She personally witnessed the Lord's seal of approval on President Young's words and work:

/ / We are able to testify that his [Brigham's] words have not failed—no one can deny their fulfillment. Our enemies were blinded and did not see that "the blood of the Prophet was the seed of the Church;"[24] nor that their predictions were so soon to be answered upon their own heads instead of upon those of the Saints, who that day recognized in Brigham Young the voice of the true shepherd.[25]

The house of the Lord was well on towards its completion, And they could truly say that this was one of the results of faith with works.[26]

Rekindling an Old Friendship—Horace Whitney

Shortly after the Prophet's death, an old friend returned to Nauvoo— an upstanding young man destined to become the Lord's chosen earthly companion for Helen. Horace Kimball Whitney was the older brother of Helen's dear friend, Sarah Ann.

Previous to the martyrdom, Helen had been astonished to discover that her dear friend, Sarah Ann Whitney, was also sealed to the Prophet Joseph Smith as a plural wife. However, in an effort to

---

23   Helen Mar Kimball Whitney, "Scenes in Nauvoo, and Incidents from H. C. Kimball's Journal," *Woman's Exponent* 11, no. 23 (May 1, 1883): 177.

24   Tertullian, an early Christian author from Carthage (155-220 AD), authored the phrase, "the blood of the martyrs is the seed of the church" in his defense of Christianity. Tertullian, Apologeticum, https://tertullian.org/works/apologeticum.htm.

25   Helen Mar Kimball Whitney, "Scenes in Nauvoo after the Martyrdom of the Prophet and Patriarch," *Woman's Exponent* 11, no. 17 (February 1, 1883): 130.

26   Helen Mar Kimball Whitney, "Scenes in Nauvoo after the Martyrdom of the Prophet and Patriarch," *Woman's Exponent* 11, no. 22 (April 15, 1883): 170.

conceal Joseph and Sarah's relationship due to mounting persecution, a front was arranged for Sarah Ann to marry Joseph C. Kingsbury on April 29, 1843. Only a few trusted members knew of the secret.[27]

Efforts to contain knowledge of plural marriage in Nauvoo—particularly among those who understood it in context and purity—largely failed. Rumors of polygamy began to fly throughout Nauvoo and surrounding settlements. Vile corruptions of the principle by some men caused threats against the Latter-day Saints to escalate, and only made the situation increasingly dangerous. Disaffected members, such as Francis and Chauncey Higbee, soon abandoned their faith altogether and became embittered toward Joseph Smith. Families became divided as loyalties were tested, and even the safety of human life was thrown on the line. Because Sarah's brother, Horace, had developed a friendship with the Higbee family prior to their change of sentiment, it was difficult to know whether or not he could be trusted with the knowledge of his own sister's sealing. Ignorant of the sealing between his sister and the Prophet Joseph, Horace left with his assumed brother-in-law, Joseph Kingsbury, to visit his grandparents and other relatives in Connecticut and Ohio in 1843.

With news of the martyrdom the following year, he hurried back to Nauvoo, where he was acquainted with the truth of his sister Sarah Ann's eternal relationship to Joseph Smith. Sarah patiently taught him the principles of Celestial marriage. Understandably surprised, Horace took it all in stride because of his close association with, and

---

27 Joseph Smith was sealed to Sarah Ann Whitney sometime around July 27, 1842. She was married to Joseph C. Kingsbury as a 'front husband' on April 29, 1843. Kingsbury later requested to be financially reimbursed for supporting Sarah during that time. Joseph Kingsbury recorded, "I according to President Joseph Smith Council & others agreed to stand by Sarah Ann Whitney as supposed to be her husband & had a pretended marriage for the purpose of bringing about the purposes of God in the last days as spoken by the mouth of the prophet Isiah Jeremiah Ezekiel and also Joseph Smith, & Sarah Ann should rec-d a great glory Honner & Eternal Lives and I Also Should Rec-d a Great Glory Honner & Eternal Lives to the full desire of my heart in having my companion Caroline in the first resurrection to hail her & no one to have power to take her from me & we Both shall be crowned & enthroned togeather in the Celestial Kingdom of God Enjoying Each others Society in all of the fullness of the Gospel of Jesus Christ & our little ones with us as is Recorded in this blessing that President Joseph Smith Sealed upon my head on the Twenty third day of March 1843 as follows—" Joseph C. Kingsbury, "History of Joseph C. Kingsbury," (photocopy of manuscript), in Ronald and Ilene Kingsbury Collection, MS 522 Box 3 Folder 2, Marriott Library, excerpt, transcript.

confidence in, the Prophet and his character. Helen described this relationship in her writings:

❙❙ Joseph had always treated him with the greatest kindness from the time that he came to live in his father's house in Kirtland, in fact they had attended the same school and studied Hebrew together, and had pitched quoits and played ball together many a time there and in Nauvoo, and he could hold nothing against him now he was dead. Joseph was noted for his child-like love and familiarity with children, and he never seemed to feel that he was losing any of his honor or dignity in doing so. And if he heard the cry of a child he would rush out of the house to see if it was harmed.[28]

Horace's experience with the Prophet Joseph Smith was not unique. The largesse of the Prophet among the mature members of society matched his cheerful—even jovial—care for the children of Zion, including his well-known willingness to break unnecessary and myopic conventions of the time. Not all agreed with Joseph's frolicking with the children, some judging such behavior as unbecoming for a 'prophet.' Undeterred, Joseph demonstrated by his actions—in similitude of the Lord Jesus Christ, whom he loved—that the greatest among the people was the servant in the Kingdom, and to "suffer little children, and forbid them not, to come unto me: for of such is the kingdom of heaven."[29] At a moment's notice, the Prophet would drop his ecclesiastical work for a chance to play ball with the boys or wipe the mud and tears from a child caught in a dirty, spring puddle. For many, these traits defined Joseph's character. For Horace, they apparently made such a deep impression that Helen remembered his sentimental response for decades following.

Shortly after Horace's return, Helen and her brother William joined Sarah and Horace for a somber visit to Carthage Jail, the scene of the martyrdom—a visit she described as generating "peculiar sensations" for the young women especially:

---

28   Helen Mar Kimball Whitney, "Scenes in Nauvoo after the Martyrdom of the Prophet and Patriarch," *Woman's Exponent* 11, no. 19 (March 1, 1883): 146.

29   Matthew 19:14.

// The wife of the jailor very kindly showed us up stairs. The walls of the room had been whitewashed and the floor had been scoured many times, but the stains of blood were still quite visible, and we saw a number of bullet holes in the door. We looked into the cell, into which Willard Richards had dragged Elder John Taylor after he was wounded and covered him up, hoping that he would be overlooked and his life spared to tell the tale; not expecting that he himself would ever escape alive.[30]

One can only imagine the emotions of the four friends—Helen, William, Horace, and Sarah—as they stood where bullet and blood split spirit and mortality until Resurrection morn. Even more so must we contemplate the poignant feelings felt by Sarah and Helen, who stood gazing at the bloodstains of the man to whom they had been eternally sealed as plural wives. What lamentable scenes played out in their minds as they stood below, at the well outside the jail?:

// As we stood by the well-curb where Joseph fell, Horace picked up a small chip covered with blood, and which he still has in his possession, though the blood is hardly discernible— nearly thirty-nine years having elapsed since that awful tragedy was enacted . . .[31]

Perhaps it was with the wisdom of hindsight that Helen and her parents understood *why* it had been necessary to facilitate the sealing of Helen to the Prophet Joseph Smith, despite her young age. Conventional logic and prudence might have delayed the conversation with Helen until she was older—for, like the disciples of old who were stunned by the crucifixion and death of the Son of God, Joseph's friends never suspected that he would be taken from them only one year later. However, the Lord knew time was short, and had apparently seen fit to hasten events and timelines.

Eventually, Helen received unshaken confirmation through personal revelation regarding the validity of her sealing to the Prophet, allowing her to embrace her identity as one of his wives. Throughout her life, Helen witnessed and testified of the Prophet

---

30   Helen Mar Kimball Whitney, "Scenes in Nauvoo after the Martyrdom of the Prophet and Patriarch," *Woman's Exponent* 11, no. 20 (March 15, 1883): 153.

31   Ibid., 154.

Joseph Smith—a testimony she carried until the day she died. Her obituary noted that:

> **❝** During her childhood she was almost constantly associated with Joseph Smith the Prophet and his successor Brigham Young, and her recollections of these two great men, prophets, seers and revelators, were always interesting to those with whom she conversed. It was a pleasure and satisfaction to her to bear testimony of the divine mission of those two great leaders.[32]

Years later in Utah, a frequent stream of visitors approached Helen with curiosity to learn of her firsthand interactions with the Prophet Joseph, plural marriage in Nauvoo, and her testimony of the Gospel. Such visits were welcomed, and they brought her personal relief—lifting her spirits as she struggled with discouragement from debilitating chronic disease. Bearing testimony gave her life purpose; she considered it a central part of her identity. Throughout her life, Helen found joy in reviewing treasured keepsakes—documents that contained the Prophet's handwriting—and she celebrated his birthday each year on December 23. She believed Joseph Smith was the foretold Latter-day Moses who would "lead this people out of bondage."[33] She even recorded with joy several dreams wherein Joseph came to visit her, and she looked forward to his future return with a sense of hope and anticipation.[34]

---

32   "Helen Mar Whitney: Her Death—A Sketch of Her Personal History," *Deseret Evening News*, November 16, 1896, 2.

33   October 10, 1887. Charles M. Hatch and Todd M. Compton, *A Widow's Tale: 1884-1896 Diary of Helen Mar Kimball Whitney* (Logan: Utah State University Press, 2003), 262.

34   Joseph Smith promised the Latter-day Saints that he would one day return as a resurrected being to finish his mission and to "lead" his people again. Brigham Young, Heber C. Kimball, and other early leaders prophesied that the Prophet's work as dispensation head was not finished, and that, in the future, he would fulfill *every promise* made to him in his priesthood blessings. For quotes and historical sources, see the documentary The Prophet Joseph: More than we know (DVD), as well as the Latter-day Answers article, "What can we learn from Joseph Smith's patriarchal blessings?" June 27, 2018, https://ldsanswers.org/what-can-we-learn-from-joseph-smiths-patriarchal-blessings.

CHAPTER 7

Horace & Helen

RECONNECTING LOVE &
ETERNAL BLOODLINES

After the death of the Prophet and his brother in June 1844, the Saints gathered the pieces from their overturned world and began to make sense of how to continue the work and legacy Joseph had left them. It was during this time that a beautiful attachment developed between Horace and Helen. Horace's sister, Sarah Ann—one of Helen's best friends, and now an anticipated sister-in-law[1]—was delighted by the budding union. The two were married on February 3, 1846. Horace was 22, and Helen was 17. Helen fondly remembered:

" At early twilight on the 3rd of February a messenger was sent by my father, informing H. K. Whitney and myself that this day finished their work in the Temple, and that we were to present ourselves there that evening. The weather being fine we preferred to walk; and as we passed through the little graveyard at the foot of the hill a solemn covenant we entered into—to cling to each other through time and, if permitted, throughout all eternity, and this vow was solemnized at the holy altar. Though gay and highminded in many other things we reverenced the principles taught us by our parents and held them sacred, also the covenants which we had previously

---

1 Sarah Ann Whitney was already sealed to the Prophet Joseph Smith, technically making her a sort of sister-in-law to Helen before Helen's marriage to her brother Horace, but that fact would not become public knowledge until some time later. Sarah would later choose to be sealed to Heber C. Kimball, Helen's father, for time—while she retained her sealing to Joseph for eternity.

made in that house, so much so that we would as soon have thought of committing suicide as to betray them; for in doing either we would have forfeited every right or claim to our eternal salvation.[2]

Helen was married to Horace for time, and at the same time, resealed to the Prophet Joseph Smith for eternity. The next day, Helen stood in as proxy for Elizabeth Sikes, a deceased member of the Church who was sealed eternally to Horace.[3] Not much is known about Elizabeth, or why Horace chose to have her sealed to him, but Helen clearly gave her consent. The notable events of these two days bring to light certain aspects about the eternal nature of marriage and relationships that extend beyond the veil. Under her own hand, Helen expressed an exceptional love for Horace in her letters, yet also affirmed the eternal nature of the relationship she had with Joseph—of which Horace was well aware and presumably in support. Furthermore, Helen demonstrated her love toward the eternal nature of Horace's immediate family by standing in for another sister who was sealed to him eternally.

Horace and Helen's unique marital circumstances, however, do not infer that the young couple did not share a marriage of deep love and affection. In fact, Helen's letters, journals, and memorabilia reveal quite the opposite. In a touching letter written by Horace to Helen in 1849, we can observe the affectionate bond between them. After assuring Helen that her image is "sacredly enshrined within the inmost recesses of my heart," Horace continues:

---

2   Helen Mar Kimball Whitney, "The Last Chapter of Scenes in Nauvoo," *Woman's Exponent* 12, no. 11 (November 1, 1883): 81.

3   On February 4, 1846, Horace Whitney was sealed to Elizabeth Ford Sikes, the deceased wife of Wilson Law. Wilson and his brother William had turned against the Prophet Joseph Smith and conspired to kill him. Wilson was excommunicated on April 18, 1844, and afterward assisted his brother in publishing the inflammatory *Nauvoo Expositor*, a newspaper designed to incite the public and provoke violent persecution against Joseph Smith. Elizabeth's husband had broken his covenants and become an aggressive apostate. All sealings were done under the direction of Brigham Young, the key holder at that time. Accordingly, Horace "married Elizabeth Ford Sikes (deceased at the time, but Horace had evidently known her before her death) for eternity on February 4, 1846, in the Nauvoo Temple, with Helen standing proxy ..." Charles M. Hatch and Todd M. Compton, *A Widow's Tale: 1884-1896 Diary of Helen Mar Kimball Whitney* (Logan: Utah State University Press, 2003), 37.

". . . the love that I bear towards you is founded upon a deep respect & knowledge of your worth, & has something more substantial for its basis than the mere fleeting evanescent and romantic passion . . . When oppressed with sorrow, or weighed down by affliction, <u>you will always be the one and the only one to whom I shall resort to pour out my griefs, and from whom I shall expect that consolation which man sometimes stands in need of, and which can only be administered with effect by a dutifuly and affectionate companion, which you have always proved yourself to be.</u>[4]

Helen began to understand, on a new level, the depth of covenantal relationships and the sealing of families for eternity as restored by the Prophet Joseph Smith. For the early Latter-day Saints, the bonds of friendship, brotherhood, and sisterhood far transcended mortality,[5]

---

4 Horace Whitney to Helen Mar Kimball Whitney, April 17, 1849, Helen Mar Whitney Collection, Merrill Library, Box 1, fd 12, as quoted in Todd Compton, *In Sacred Loneliness* (Salt Lake City: Signature Books, 1997), 512; underline in original. It is interesting to note that the context of Horace's letter included assurances of his love and devotion toward Helen as he, with Helen's support, was preparing to marry a second wife, Lucy Bloxham. Helen later wrote appreciatively of Horace, "He studied my feelings and took one whom he had cause to believe loved me and my children, and would cause me the least trouble." Helen Mar Kimball Whitney, *Why We Practice Plural Marriage* (Salt Lake City: Juvenile Instructor Office, 1884), 11.

5 Orson F. Whitney made an observation on what he called "spirit memories" in *The Improvement Era* in 1919:

"Spirit Memories

"Writing one day upon the subject of spirit memories, I was led to indulge in these reflections: Why are we drawn toward certain persons, and they to us, as if we had always known each other? Is it a fact that we always have? Is there something, after all, in that much abused term 'affinity,' and is this the basis of its claim? At all events, it is just as logical to look back upon fond associations, as it is to look forward to them. We believe that ties formed in this life will be continued in the life to come; then why not believe that we had similar ties before we came into this world, and that some of them, at least, have been resumed in this state of existence?

"After meeting someone whom I had never met before on earth, I have wondered why that person's face seemed so familiar. More than once, upon hearing a noble sentiment expressed, though unable to recall that I had ever heard it until then, I have found myself in sympathy with it, was thrilled by it, and felt as if I had always known it. The same is true of some strains of music; they are like echoes of eternity. I do not assert pre-acquaintance in all such cases, but as one thought suggests another these queries arise in the mind.

"When it comes to the Gospel, I feel more positive. Why did the Savior say: 'My sheep know my voice?' Did a sheep ever know the voice of its shepherd if it had never heard that voice before? They who love the Truth, and to whom it most strongly appeals—were they not acquainted with it in a previous life? I think so.

as the Prophet had taught that "that same sociality which exists among us here will exist among us there, only it will be coupled with eternal glory, which glory we do not now enjoy."[6]

Many of the early Saints believed the teachings of Joseph Smith about the eternities without reservation—that covenantal relationships had been forged in premortality, and would exist ever after.[7] Although Helen was sealed to the Prophet Joseph Smith for eternity, Horace—presumably a dear friend from before this life—

I believe we knew the Gospel before we came here, and that is what gives to it a familiar sound." Orson F. Whitney, "Spirit Memories," *The Improvement Era*, vol. 23, no. 2, December 1919, 100.

6   Doctrine and Covenants 130:2.

7   Orson F. Whitney, son of Helen Mar Kimball, recorded a dream he was given in 1887 revealing familial ties that extended into the premortal world: "Last night, in a dream, a beautiful woman, angelic in appearance was shown to me as in a vision. She told me she was my wife, that she lived in heaven and that I left her in charge of my home there when I came down upon the earth. Her face was entirely new to me, so far as recollection went, and she was very beautiful. This dream illustrates a doctrine I have believed for several years." Orson F. Whitney Journal, November 15, 1887, p. 54, USU Digital History Collections, https://digital.lib.usu.edu/digital/collection/p16944coll11/id/235/rec/9.

Other plural wives of the Prophet spoke of the role the premortal life played in their sealing to Joseph. Mary Elizabeth Rollins Lightner commented that she and Joseph had a relationship "before the foundation of the earth was laid." "Mary Elizabeth Rollins," copy of holograph in Susa Young Gates Papers, USHS, box 14, fd 4.

"Joseph said I was his before I came here and he said all the Devils in Hell should never get me from him." Mary Elizabeth Rollins Lightner, "Statement," signed February 8, 1902, Vesta Crawford Papers, MS 125, box 1, fd 11. Original owned by Mrs. Nell Osborne, SLC (courtesy Juanita Brooks). See also, Juanita Brooks Papers, USHS, MSB103, box 16, fd 13; BYU special collections, MS 1132.

Joseph Lee Robinson heard the Prophet Joseph Smith:

"... say that God had revealed unto him that any man who ever committed adultery in either of his probations that that man could never be raised to the highest exaltation in the Celestial Glory and that he felt anxious with regard to himself and he inquired of the Lord and the Lord told him that he, Joseph, had never committed adultery. This saying of the Prophet astonished me very much. It opened up to me a very wide field of reflection. The idea that we had passed through probation prior to this and that we must have been married and given in marriage in those probations or there would be no propriety in making such an assertion and that there were several exaltations in the Celestial Kingdom of our God, the highest we supposed to be the Godhead and we conclude that there are several grades of exaltations in servants to the Gods. Be this as it may, this is what he said. We will know the truth of the matter some day." Joseph Lee Robinson, Autobiography and journals, 1883-1893, p. 12, Church History Library, https://catalog.churchofjesuschrist.org/assets/b61a941d-fe2b-4f61-bec0-a1557fd14fe6/0/0.

had accepted the opportunity to love and care for Helen in mortality.[8] Their mutual respect, trust, love, and familial bond was a union they did not take lightly—prized as an association that would never end, regardless of the cessation of their marital union after death. Horace and Helen had known one another long before, and they would know and work with one another far into future eternities.

The Whitney and Kimball families, already united in an eternal cause, became inseparably close—even constructing their cabins side by side in Winter Quarters. Helen's father, Heber, and Horace's father, Newel, developed a friendship deeper than that of most brothers. While sheltering in Winter Quarters before heading west, Heber commented that "We [he and Brother Whitney] always had the same feelings in common, and our views always met, and our thoughts always flow in the same channel—I don't know why it is so." Heber considered Helen's father-in-law a "worthy, good and exemplary man," and said "there was 'no person living in the world' in whom he placed more confidence than he did in Brother Whitney . . ."[9] Not surprisingly, Newel K. Whitney was sealed as a son to Heber C. Kimball through the Law of Adoption.[10] The

---

8   A scriptural parallel can be seen in the life of Mary, mother of the Son of God, who was married to Joseph for time. Joseph understood Mary's true identity after it was revealed to him by an angel of the Lord (Matthew 1:20-25), giving him the courage to proactively fulfill his life's mission in caring for her.

9   Helen Mar Kimball Whitney, "Scenes and Incidents at Winter Quarters," *Woman's Exponent* 14, no. 7 (September 1, 1885): 54.

10   The Law of Adoption involved sealings that were performed in the early days of the Church where men were sealed in an eternal father-son relationship to other men who were not their biological fathers. These were actual ordinances that involved revelation and solemnization through authorized priesthood authority. Brigham Young recorded a vision or dream he had of the Prophet Joseph Smith after the martyrdom, where the Prophet explained that in the premortal world, "Our Father in Heaven organized the human family [before they came into the world], but they are all disorganized and in great confusion." Joseph Smith counseled that if the Saints focused on cultivating humility, faithfully keeping the commandments, and maintaining the Spirit, the Lord would restore families into their proper order.

"Joseph stepped toward me [Brigham Young], and looking very earnestly, yet pleasantly said 'Tell the people to be humble and faithful, and be sure to keep the spirit of the Lord and it will lead them right. Be careful and not turn away the small still voice; it will teach them what to do and where to go; it will yield the fruits of the kingdom. Tell the brethren to keep their hearts open to conviction, so that when the Holy Ghost comes to them, their hearts will be ready to receive it. They can tell the spirit of the Lord from all other spirits; it will whisper peace and joy to their souls; it will take malice, hatred, strife and all evil from their hearts; and their whole desire will be to do good, bring forth righteousness and build up the kingdom of God.

mutual respect shared between the Whitney and Kimball families gave Horace and Helen the blessing of in-laws who were entirely committed to the Gospel, and who adored and revered one another with loyalty rarely seen in the world today.

In the sense that Horace was not on equal standing with the Prophet Joseph Smith, he may have also not been Helen's equal in an eternal sense—but he certainly complemented her mortal strengths and weaknesses. As a 22-year-old, Horace was honest, well-educated, intellectually brilliant, musically talented, and a competent mathematician. Although he served as a major in the Utah Territorial Nauvoo Legion,[11] Horace was not a leader, nor

---

"'Tell the brethren if they will follow the spirit of the Lord, they will go right. Be sure to tell the people to keep the spirit of the Lord; and if they will, they will find themselves just as they were organized by our Father in Heaven before they came into the world. Our father in Heaven organized the human family, but they are all disorganized and in great confusion.'

"Joseph then shewed me the pattern, how they were in the beginning. This I cannot describe, but I saw it, and saw where the Priesthood had been taken from the earth and how it must be joined together, so that there would be a perfect chain from Father Adam to his latest posterity. Joseph again said 'Tell the people to be sure to keep the spirit of the Lord and follow it, and it will lead them just right.'" Journal History of the Church, February 23, 1847, pg. 181-182, Church History Library, https://catalog.churchofjesuschrist.org/assets/75cc4e9f-bfcb-4ac2-8309-19d1a3e82e8e/0/180.

While some apostate teachers have attempted to hijack this teaching and use it for their own abusive purposes, Brigham Young clarified that the Law of Adoption is an ordinance that can only be performed in the proper order, and by proper authority. "We will administer in the Temple which we have now begun and that is one point gained and we will seal men to men by the keys of the Holy Priesthood. This is the highest ordinance. It is the last ordinance of the kingdom of God on the earth and above all the endowments that can be given you. It is a final sealing an Eternal Principle and when once made cannot be broken by the Devil." Brigham Young, *The Complete Discourses of Brigham Young*, vol. 1, ed. Richard S. Van Wagoner (Salt Lake City: The Smith-Pettit Foundation, 2009), 1033-1034.

Brigham Young also taught that we only have a "smattering" of revelation given to us on this subject, and that more will be revealed in the future, dependent upon the righteousness and obedience of the people. Brigham Young, *The Complete Discourses of Brigham Young*, vol. 1, ed. Richard S. Van Wagoner (Salt Lake City: The Smith-Pettit Foundation, 2009), 184-187.

11   The original Nauvoo Legion was organized in December 1840, and by 1844, had grown to include over 5,000 men. After the death of the Prophet in 1844, the Legion was disbanded when the State of Illinois repealed the Nauvoo Charter. The Saints carried the original Nauvoo Legion flag and other accouterments with them to the new Utah territory, and in March of 1849, the legislative council of the State of Deseret organized the Nauvoo Legion as a militia in the State of Deseret. Ralph Hansen, "Administrative History of the Nauvoo Legion in Utah" MA diss., Brigham Young University, Provo, 1954.

was he ambitious; but he could be *trusted*—a fact demonstrated in one instance by the confidence placed in him to copy the only manuscript of the revelation on marriage (later to be included in the Doctrine and Covenants as Section 132). Horace was among the first to enter the Salt Lake Valley, and he later served as a loyal secretary to President Brigham Young. He was industrious, and worked well with his hands, although he struggled throughout his life to provide for two large families. When Horace passed away in 1884, 12 years before Helen's own death, the loss of her beloved companion was a source of deep grief and sadness.

Both Horace and Helen were of choice lineage. The Prophet Joseph Smith had prophetically declared that the Whitney and Kimball families "were descendants from one and the same branch of the priesthood."[12] Heber C. Kimball believed the Lord revealed to him that he was a descendant of the Davidic royal house.[13] Moreover, the text of Sarah Ann Whitney's sealing ordinance to Joseph Smith specifies that their marriage was essential in restoring the royal house and throne of David,[14] affirming the Whitney family's descendancy

---

12   Helen noted, "Grandfather Whitney was in Nauvoo at the time. He had come from Kirtland to receive the holy ordinances in the Temple, and his last words to me were, "I shall try and secure the old homestead, in Kirtland, for you and Horace; I want you to come and live there by us." His wife was in Kirtland, and he was taken sick on his way back and died in a day or two after; and she survived him but a short time. Her maiden name was Kimball, and her son, Bishop Whitney, thought so much of her that he adopted it as a middle name to his four eldest sons. After he and my father became acquainted in Kirtland they traced relationship. Both were natives of Vermont, and the Prophet Joseph afterwards told them that they were descendants from one and the same branch of the priesthood." Helen Mar Kimball Whitney, " The Last Chapter of Scenes in Nauvoo," *Woman's Exponent* 12, no. 11 (November 1, 1883): 82.

13   The early leaders of the Church taught repeatedly that Jesus Christ was married, fathered children, and that His descendants had been hidden among "the poor and humble." Heber C. Kimball, George Q. Cannon, Joseph Smith and others were specifically identified as His descendants. Evidence found in Jewish culture, ancient writings, and even scripture, all lend credibility and support that these early brethren taught the truth. For extensive documentation on these sources, please see the documentary Hidden Bloodlines: The Grail & the Lost Tribes in the Lands of the North (DVD).

14   "Revelation received at Nauvoo, Illinois, on 27 July 1842 for Newel K. Whitney concerning Sarah Ann Whitney to be a wife of Joseph Smith ... If you both agree to covenant and do this then I give you S. A. [Sarah Ann] Whitney my Daughter to Joseph Smith to be his wife to observe all the rights betwe[e]n you both that belong to that condition I do it in my own name and in the name of my wife your mother and in the name of my Holy Progenitors by the right of birth which is of Priest Hood vested in me by revelation and commandment and promise of the liveing God obtained by

from Judah, as well as Joseph. Newel K. Whitney's patriarchal blessing, given in Kirtland, reveals significant insights into his family's sacred bloodline. The bestower of the blessing, Joseph Smith Sr., stated that Newel was a descendant of Melchizedek, and that one of his descendants would grow to become like the same great High Priest:

/ / Inasmuch as thou knowest thy progenitors, and art assured concerning the lineage through which thou hast descended, I bless thee with a father's blessing, for thee and thy children after thee, for their inheritances, to the end. And as thou art a descendant of Melchizedek, one of thy posterity shall be like unto him before the Lord; for his heart shall be filled with the same spirit from his youth up, and he shall be a benefit to thy posterity.[15]

Newel's wife, Elizabeth, who also received her patriarchal blessing under the hand of Joseph Smith Sr., was told that she was of the same lineage and descent as her husband, and that her lineage had been concealed from the world, for she had a significant mission to perform:

/ / ... the Lord has so ordained that those of the same family and descent might be one to fulfil his purposes; for thou art of the same lineage of thy husband, thy life has been hid also,[16] and thou mayest rejoice, for thy posterity shall be blessed. Thou hast

---

the Holy Milchisdick Gethrow and other of the Holy Fathers commanding in the name of the Lord all those Powers to concentrate in you and through [you] to your po[s]terity for ever

"all these things I do in the name of the Lord Jesus Christ that through this order he may be glor[i]fied and [that] through the power of anointing Davied [David] may reign King over Iseral [Israel] which shall hereafter be revealed let immortality and eternal life henc[e]forth be sealed upon your heads forever and ever." Revelation for Newell K. Whitney, July 27, 1842, as quoted in Michael Marquardt, *The Joseph Smith Revelations: Text and Commentary* (Salt Lake City: Signature Books, 1999), 315-316.

15   Blessing was given September 14, 1835. H. Michael Marquardt, *Early Patriarchal Blessings of The Church of Jesus Christ of Latter-day Saints* (Salt Lake City: The Smith-Pettit Foundation, 2007), 46-47.

16   Doctrine and Covenants 86:9.

a gift to sing the songs of Zion, and if thou wilt be humble before the Lord and keep all his commandments, it shall be increased.[17]

For Horace and Helen, the uniting of the Whitney and Kimball families stood as a testament to building an everlasting temporal *and* spiritual 'kingdom'[18]—an eternal estate based on covenantal family relationships. Their vow to preserve the association "through time and throughout all eternity" is reflective of this kingdom-building perspective. Whether one shares the beliefs of the early Latter-day Saints, or sees this worldview as stemming from imaginative or strange teachings—understanding Horace and Helen's perception of doctrine is critical to comprehending the life decisions they made. From their perspective, we can begin to appreciate that Helen's choices had far more to do with her understanding of *who* she was and who she was destined to *become*, than simply an adoption of plural marriage. Her identity fueled her mission and informed her familial decisions.

"the Lord has so ordained that those of the same family and descent might be one to fulfill his purposes"

For the Kimball and Whitney families, the Prophet Joseph Smith opened the heavens and enlightened the Saints' understanding of both premortal, mortal, and postmortal worlds. To many early Saints, Helen's association with Joseph Smith did not begin in this mortality—but existed long before. She was considered a noble woman of high standing.

---

17   Blessing was given September 14, 1835. H. Michael Marquardt, *Early Patriarchal Blessings of the Church of Jesus Christ of Latter-day Saints* (Salt Lake City: The Smith-Pettit Foundation, 2007), 47.

18   The Prophet Joseph Smith taught: "... Jesus said their was many mansions in his fathers house & he would go & prepare a place for them. House here named should have been translated -[kingdom]- & any person who is exhalted to the highest mansion has to abide a celestial law & the whole law to[o] ..." Joseph Smith, Discourse, 21 January 1844, as Reported by Wilford Woodruff, p. 183, The Joseph Smith Papers.

"14th ch. of John. 'In my Father's house are many mansions.' It should be, 'in my Father's Kingdom are many Kingdoms', in order that ye may be heirs of God and joint heirs with me." May 12, 1844. Joseph Smith, History, 1838–1856, volume F-1, p. 19, The Joseph Smith Papers.

Love & Labor, by Lynde Mott

Equipped with the perspective of Joseph Smith's teachings, Helen welded a link with Joseph's kingdom that would bless Horace and his posterity for eternity. Horace's sacrifices were believed to render him blessings he could only begin to comprehend. Although Horace and Helen were sealed for time only, the early doctrine of the Restoration taught them that their association would never end, continuing throughout the eternities; the deep friendship they enjoyed on earth would stay with them forever, independent of the severance of their earthly marital union.

Following her marriage to Horace, Helen's family hosted a joyful wedding reception. Though it lacked the glamor typical of most contemporary events, Helen's description of the dancing, music, and guests paints a beautiful picture of their marriage—a humble celebration consecrated to God:

> President B. Young, and Bp. N. K. Whitney were invited with members of their families and a few of our most intimate friends to attend an infare given at my father's house in honor of our marriage—reception is the more modern name, and perhaps

the most proper as things are carried out in these days. . . . We had no glittering surroundings, nor had we any use for rich and costly gifts, but we had what is better, warm and loving hearts, that were knitted together by past scenes of sorrow and suffering. It was the pure and genuine friendship that could neither be bought nor sold. The lively airs played on the violin and flute and the bass viol drove dull care away, and all joined in the merry dance till the clock struck twelve, when the music ceased and the blessings of God were invoked upon us and all of His people, of whatever nation they might be.[19]

The Kimball and Whitney families shared far more than a close kinship and familial bond—they shared a common vision and mission based on their faith and testimony. Like the Kimballs, Newel and his wife, Elizabeth Ann, had prayed long and diligently for the truth prior to their introduction to the Gospel. Elizabeth Ann shared how their perseverance was rewarded while praying one night in 1829:

// It was midnight—my husband and I were in our house at Kirtland, praying to the Father to be shown the way when the Spirit rested upon us and a cloud overshadowed the house. . . . A solemn awe pervaded us. We saw the cloud and felt the Spirit of the Lord. Then we heard a voice out of the cloud saying, "Prepare to receive the word of the Lord, for it is coming." At this we marveled greatly. [B]ut from that moment we knew that the word of the Lord was coming to Kirtland.[20]

Following this vision, the Whitneys were introduced to the Restoration and subsequently, joined with the Saints in November 1830. The Whitney family sheltered the Prophet Joseph Smith in their upper floor, and were richly repaid for their hospitality. Revelations came (including the Word of Wisdom, the 89th section of Doctrine and Covenants), the Prophet organized and conducted the School of the Prophets, and a significant portion of the Joseph

---

19   Helen Mar Kimball Whitney, "The Last Chapter of Scenes in Nauvoo," *Woman's Exponent* 12, no. 11 (November 1, 1883): 81-82.

20   Andrew Jenson, *Latter-day Saint Biographical Encyclopedia*, vol. 1 (Salt Lake City: Andrew Jenson History Company, 1901), 223.

Smith Translation of the Bible was completed—all within the walls of the Whitney family establishment.

When Helen married Horace, she found herself immersed into a family rich in prophetic gifts. For example, her mother-in-law, Sister Elizabeth Whitney, possessed the gifts of healing and speaking in tongues, often through beautiful music.[21] Joseph Smith titled her the "Sweet Songstress of Zion," and William Clayton[22] recorded a Nauvoo gathering where Elizabeth suddenly began singing in the Adamic tongue. This melodic prophecy foretold the pioneer immigration to Utah, and the glorious gathering of Israel:

---

21   Helen Mar Kimball Whitney, "Scenes in Nauvoo after the Martyrdom of the Prophet and Patriarch," *Woman's Exponent* 11, no. 21 (April 1, 1883): 162.

Later in life, as Helen reviewed her father's papers and journals, she was reminded of other miraculous healings. One in particular occurred in 1845:

> "I find many things mentioned in my father's journal which I remember as I read them, and they bring to my mind other incidents which had it not been for his record, would probably have been buried in oblivion.... 'I and others of the Twelve were sent for by Sister Jennetta Richards, (Brother Willard's wife,) to meet there and pray for her, as she felt that she could not live long. We also prayed for my wife, who is very sick—and offered up prayer for Bishop Whitney, who has gone to St. Louis—that he may be prospered....['] 'Returned home and found Sister Whitney. She anointed my wife and sang in tongues; I also sang and the Lord blessed us.' 'June the 20th, I again met with my brethren to read history—were in that part which describes the persecutions in Jackson Co. Missouri.' 'We stopped reading at two o'clock in the afternoon. I found my wife worse—sent for Sister Whitney. We clothed ourselves according to the order of the holy priesthood and anointed and prayed for her. The Lord heard us, for she was better and had a good night's rest. The Lord shall have the glory.' 'All is quiet in our city.'" Helen Mar Kimball Whitney, "Scenes in Nauvoo after the Martyrdom of the Prophet and Patriarch," *Woman's Exponent* 11, no. 21 (April 1, 1883): 162.

22   William H. Clayton was a trusted clerk and scribe to the Prophet Joseph Smith. He was the author of "Come, Come, Ye Saints," "When First the Glorious Light of Truth," and other hymns. William Clayton was a member of the Council of Fifty as organized by the Prophet, as well as one of the first to receive his endowments. Joseph Smith trusted William Clayton and shared intimate knowledge with him concerning Celestial plural marriage, as well as many other doctrines and principles. In 1842, William Clayton wrote to William Hardman: "My faith ... in the prophet and officers is firm, unshaken, and unmoved; nay, rather, it is strengthened and settled firmer than ever.... For me to write any thing concerning the character of president Joseph Smith would be superfluous. All evil reports concerning him I treat with utter contempt.... I will add that, the more I am with him, the more I love him; the more I know of him, and the more confidence I have in him; and I am sorry that people should give heed to evil reports concerning him, when we all know the great service he has rendered the church." William Clayton to William Hardman, March 30, 1842, as quoted in "Correspondence," *The Latter-day Saints Millennial Star*, vol. 3, no. 4, August, 1842, 75-76.

❞ The labors of the day having been brought to a close at so early an hour (half past eight) it was thought proper to have a little season of recreation; accordingly, Brother Hans Hanson was invited to produce his violin. He did so, and played several lively airs; several excellent songs were sung, in which several of the brethren and sisters joined. The 'Upper California' was sung by Erastus Snow; after which Sister Whitney, being invited by President Young, stood up, and invoking the gift of tongues, sang one of the most beautiful songs in tongues that was ever heard. The interpretation was given by her husband, Bishop Whitney. It related to our efforts to build this house, and to the privilege we now have of meeting together in it—of our departure shortly to the country of the Lamanites, and their rejoicing when they hear the Gospel, and of the ingathering of Israel. Altogether it was one of the most touching and beautiful exhibitions of the power of the spirit in the gift of tongues, which was ever witnessed, (so it appeared to the writer of this, William Clayton). After a little conversation of a general nature the exercises of the evening were closed by prayer by President B. Young.[23]

As further evidence of the Whitneys' spiritual legacy, Samuel Whitney, Helen's new grandfather-in-law and father of Newel K. Whitney, carried the distinctive title of a "natural prophet."[24] Helen

---

23   Helen Mar Kimball Whitney, "Scenes in Nauvoo, and Incidents from H. C. Kimball's Journal," *Woman's Exponent* 12, no. 7 (September 1, 1883): 50.

24   Helen Mar Kimball Whitney, "The Last Chapter of Scenes in Nauvoo," *Woman's Exponent* 12, no. 11 (November 1, 1883): 82.

Note that the Prophet Joseph Smith defined a "prophet" as "every man who has the testimony of Jesus. 'For the testimony of Jesus is the Spirit of prophecy.'" Joseph Smith, May 8, 1838, in History, 1838–1856, volume B-1, p. 794, The Joseph Smith Papers.

Moses taught, "Would God that all the Lord's people were prophets, and that the Lord would put his spirit upon them!" Numbers 11:26-29. Joseph Smith echoed Moses' sentiments, explaining that, "Salvation cannot come without revelation; it is in vain for any one to minister without it. No man is a minister of Jesus christ without being a prophet. No man can be the minister of Jesus Christ except he has the testimony of Jesus, and this is the spirit of prophecy. Whenever salvation has been administered it has been by testimony." Joseph Smith, Discourse, between circa 26 June and circa 4 August 1839–A, as Reported by William Clayton, p. 18, The Joseph Smith Papers.

Wilford Woodruff taught: "[Brigham Young] is a prophet, I am a prophet, you are, and anybody is a prophet who has the testimony of Jesus Christ, for that is the spirit of

recorded the fulfillment of one of his prophecies given in Nauvoo as the Saints were preparing to migrate west:

/ / Bishop Whitney said that his father was a natural prophet, and he put a great deal of confidence in his words. He said to Mother Whitney before leaving Nauvoo for Kirtland: "I can only see N. K. till he gets to the mountains, but you, Ann, will live a great many years."

This was a very hard thing for them to believe as she had always been a delicate woman and was subject to habitual spells of sick headache, when Bishop Whitney would nurse her, and he always treated her with the tenderest care, and had never placed any hardships or responsibilities upon her. But when on the 23rd of September, 1850, a little over three years after the arrival of the pioneers Bishop Whitney took sick and died, leaving his delicate wife to survive him for many years, the beginning of the prophecies' fulfillment was made manifest.[25]

With the death of her eternal husband, Joseph Smith, and a transition from her father's household into her new role as a wife of Horace Whitney, Helen closed one chapter and prepared to initiate another as they packed their belongings and bade a melancholy farewell to their beloved City of Joseph and the beautiful temple in Nauvoo.

---

prophecy." Wilford Woodruff, "The Holy Ghost—Laboring in Faith—The Kingdom of God—Patriarchal Marriage," in *Journal of Discourses*, vol. 13 (Liverpool: Horace S. Eldredge, 1871), 165. Discourse given on December 12, 1869.

While some have confused the title of "prophet" as referring only to the President of the Church, both scripture as well as the teachings of the Presidents of the Church are clear that the two terms are not synonymous. While a President of the Church may be a prophet, seer, revelator and translator, the title 'President of the Church' refers to the "President of the High Priesthood of the Church," (see Doctrine and Covenants 107:65) the man authorized with priesthood keys to preside over ordinances within the Church, while the title of 'prophet' is a man with the "spirit of prophecy" as defined by the Prophet Joseph and others.

25   Helen Mar Kimball Whitney, "The Last Chapter of Scenes in Nauvoo," *Woman's Exponent* 12, no. 11 (November 1, 1883): 82.

CHAPTER 8

Walking the Valley
of the Shadow

❧

In the midst of an exceptionally cold winter, in February 1846, with the landscape hidden under a blanket of snow,[1] a steady stream of wagons and teams began congregating on Parley Street in Nauvoo. Counted among the dedicated families assembling there—bundled in whatever clothing they could layer on to protect their shivering bodies from the freezing temperatures—was that of Heber and Vilate Kimball. Like others throughout the city, they loaded their belongings into the wagons and hitched up their teams as the Saints bade farewell to the temple and slowly departed from their beloved city. Due to the immediacy of their departure, wagons were in short supply, so Helen and others "carried our change of apparel in bags" to lighten the load.[2]

Many of the Saints suffered from illness—including Helen's mother, who, in addition to her own sickness:

> ❞ . . . had three little boys with the whooping cough—the babe was thirteen months old, who, as soon as he commenced coughing,

---

1   The coldest month in Nauvoo is January, with an average low of about 21°F, rarely dropping to 2°F. However, the exceptional cold of the winter of 1845-1846 brought the temperature down to -2°F (with some reports listing -17°F) in February 1846. *History of the Church*, vol. 7 (Salt Lake City: Deseret Book Company, 1950), 598. However, the extreme cold had the fortuitous effect of creating an ice bridge about a mile wide across the Mississippi, allowing the Saints to drive their teams across the river. *History of the Church*, vol. 7 (Salt Lake City: Deseret Book Company, 1950), 603.

2   Helen Mar Kimball Whitney, "The Last Chapter of Scenes in Nauvoo," *Woman's Exponent* 12, no. 11 (November 1, 1883): 82.

would lose his breath, and we would have to toss him out into the cold air, which seemed the only thing to bring him to.[3]

Helen—now a member of the Whitney family, but still organized under her father's company—remembered later that her husband's family and many others found themselves in dire straits, far worse than the Kimballs. And yet when the call came to leave Nauvoo, "they left their comfortable homes and the graves of their loved ones and followed the voice of the one whom they knew the Lord had chosen to lead His people."[4] The cost of discipleship was steep, and many wondered—*Was remaining true to the Restoration really worth the price?*

With wisdom gained from living through many harsh midwestern winters, the Saints had originally planned to leave in the spring of 1847. They faced an impossible choice: to stay would mean "death by 'fire and sword,'" but to leave unprepared would be 'death by starvation.'"[5] With heartless abandon, the mobs continued to harass the Saints. On the one hand, they bullied the city's inhabitants with legal action, including a repeal of the Nauvoo city charter—and on the other hand, they threatened bodily harm, including attempted kidnappings and other darkened deeds. Finally, the governor of Illinois responded, but did so in a manner revelatory of his cowardice and/or collusion. He informed the leaders of the Church that if they did not leave, the government could not—or would not—step in to prevent the inevitable massacre. Abandoned by the rule of law and by their own government, the Saints were forced to capitulate—it was better to starve or die from exposure than to give their lives into the hands of the "mobocrats." With breaking hearts, they chose to hand over their homes, their beautiful, prosperous city that they had built up with their own hands out of a swamp, and to leave even their own country to make their way through sleet, blizzard, and mud to an uncertain destination. Cold, destitute,

---

3   Ibid.

4   Ibid.

5   Helen Mar Kimball Whitney, "Our Travels Beyond the Mississippi," *Woman's Exponent* 12, no. 13 (December 1, 1883): 102; "Chapters from the Life of Prest. Brigham Young," *The Latter-day Saints Millennial Star*, vol. 39, no. 5, January 29, 1877, 66.

and unprepared, they were obliged to face an unknown journey of faith and fortitude that would take them through the valley of the shadow of death itself.

Helen covered the first day's distance by traveling on her pony, but soon found that the freezing temperatures left her too chilled to continue without walking to keep her blood circulating. A few days later, on February 17, the Kimball party arrived at the Sugar Creek camp, where they were compelled to spend the night on the frozen ground. Upon waking, they discovered "The snow was deep so that paths had to be made with spades between the wagons and tents."[6] Brigham Young's company had arrived a few days prior, and on their first night[7] nine babies were born.[8]

In addition to the already arduous journey, Helen and other members of her family made needed trips back to Nauvoo to procure oxen teams and resolve unfinished business. Helen returned to Sugar Creek by the end of February, and the following month, her father's company broke camp, resuming the journey westward. Helen's 1883-1884 articles in the *Woman's Exponent* provide many details of their "travels beyond the Mississippi." Hardship was a constant companion—food supplies were low,[9] and the Saints did not have the animals or wagons to make the journey—but they persevered nonetheless.

In spite of the intense adversity that followed them like a shadow, those Saints who finished the trek would prove themselves loyal and faithful to the cause of Zion—it was, for them, a refiner's fire. Those lacking the spiritual strength or testimony sufficient to withstand such hardship either remained behind in Nauvoo or abandoned the trek midway, leaving only those souls fashioned from the purest gold to emigrate to Utah:

---

6   Helen Mar Kimball Whitney, "The Last Chapter of Scenes in Nauvoo," *Woman's Exponent* 12, no. 11 (November 1, 1883): 82.

7   It is interesting that the February Moon, also called the Snow Moon, was at full phase on February 11, 1846, just six days before the Kimball party arrived at the Sugar Creek camp.

8   Joseph Fielding Smith, *Essentials in Church History* (Deseret Book Company, 1972), 332, footnote B.

9   Ibid., 333.

⫻ Much of the dross had been left behind, and the "fair weather friends," as they were called by Col. Thomas L. Kane, had forsaken the tents of Israel and had sought the tents of ease. In this manner the camps were purged of those who were not faithful enough to face the perils and deprivations of the eventful journey. Although there were difficulties and differences to be settled from time to time, President Young was led to declare that he doubted if there had ever been a body of people, since the days of Enoch, who had done so little grumbling under such unpleasant and trying circumstances.[10]

Helen was about to find herself being tested once again, and her soul would be stretched beyond its former limits. *How* loyal was she to the Gospel of Jesus Christ? Was her desire sincere enough for her to be counted as a part of His Kingdom? Helen's experiences transformed her from a faithful girl struggling to comprehend the world around her, wrestling with uncertainty, to a passionate woman with a calling—a wife, mother, and Saint who *knew*.[11]

Winter Quarters: "Saddest Chapters in My History"

The Saints established various camps across the Mississippi River in Iowa, including Garden Grove, Mount Pisgah, and Council Bluffs—finally establishing a permanent camp in Winter Quarters—now Omaha, Nebraska—266 miles from Nauvoo. Families prepared for the 1846-47 winter cold by constructing homes, with nearly 4,000 Saints moving to Winter Quarters by December.

The bleak winter of 1846-47 proved both a 'valley of the shadow,' as well as a stage for many sacred experiences among the refugee Saints. Death loomed as a constant companion; weakened bodies and poor nutrition took a heavy toll. More than 600 died in Winter Quarters during the winters of 1846-47 and 1847-48. Many succumbed to the black scurvy, caused by a lack of vegetables in the pioneer diet. Helen described the painful, distressing experiences she witnessed along the way as an eighteen-year-old young woman:

---

10   Ibid., 334-335.

11   Alma 56:45-48.

"A Monument in the Mormon Pioneer Cemetery at Winter Quarters, Florence, Nebraska," by Avard Fairbanks under CC BY-SA 2.0

"Some 2,000 Latter-day Saints died [in Winter Quarters] and across the river between June 1846 and October 1848." A sculpture stands today in Omaha, Nebraska, in remembrance of their sacrifice. "That the struggles, the sacrifices, and the sufferings of the faithful pioneers and the cause they represented shall never be forgotten, this monument is gratefully erected and dedicated." —Heber J. Grant, J. Reuben Clark Jr., and David O. McKay, 1936, inscription on the Winter Quarters Cemetery Monument

❝ ... many cases had proved fatal. It would commence with dark streaks and pains in the ends of the fingers or toes, which increased and spread till the limbs were inflamed and became almost black, causing such intense agony that death would be welcomed as a release from their suffering. It was caused by the want of vegetable food and living so long on salt meat without it.

It was now a year or more since the majority had left their homes and civilization behind, and our trail was marked by the lonely mounds of the dead, who had made a happy escape from the sufferings and want to which we were so many years subjected, through the wickedness and injustice of man.[12]

Few today can truly comprehend the misery, suffering, death, and disease through which these poor souls passed—but Helen acquired painful firsthand experience that remained forever etched in her memory. Decades later, she could not recall those trying days "without weeping":[13]

---

12   Helen Mar Kimball Whitney, "Scenes and Incidents at Winter Quarters," *Woman's Exponent* 14, no. 4 (July 15, 1885): 31.

13   Pioneer autobiographies, journals, and letters describe the suffering and want during that first winter in Winter Quarters, as exemplified by accounts from Lucy Meserve Smith and Margaret Phelps:

"We moved down to winter quarters when my babe was two weeks old, there we lived in an osnaburg cloth tent til December, then we moved into a log cabin ten feet square with a sod chimney, only the soft wet ground for a floor, and poor worn out cattle beef and corn cracked on a hand-mill for our food, here I took the scurvy not having any vegatables to eat. I got so low I must wean my babe and he must be fed on that coarse cracked corn bread, when he was only five months old. . . .

"My dear child used to cry till it seemed as though I would jump off my bed when it came night I would get so nervous, but I could not even speak to him. I was as helpless as an infant for I could not move myself in bed or speak a loud word. . . .

"When I began to get better I had not a morsel in the house that I could eat as my mouth was so very sore I could not eat the corn bread I have cried hours for a morsel to put into my mouth, then my companion would take a plate and go around among the neighbours and find some one cooking may be a calfs pluck. He would beg a bit to keep me from starving. I would taste it, then I would say Oh, do feed my baby, my apetite would leave me when I would think of my dear child. my stomach was harding for want of food.

"The next July my darling boy took sick and on the 22nd, the same day that his Father and br. O. Pratt came into the valley of the Great Salt lake my only child died. I felt so overcome in my feelings I was afraid I would lose my mind as I had not recovered from my sickness the previous winter." Lucy Meserve Smith, Family history and autobiography, 1889 June, p. 34-36, Church History Library, https://catalog.churchofjesuschrist.org/assets/1ec56bac-d51d-48ee-9b1c-6e98d8d7a290/0/33.

Margaret Phelps remembered, ". . . winter [1846-1847] found me bed-ridden, destitute, in a wretched hovel which was built upon a hillside; the season was one of constant rain; the situation of the hovel and its openness, gave free access to piercing winds and water flowed over the dirt floor, converting it into mud two or three inches deep; no wood but what my little ones picked up around the fences, so green it filled the room with smoke; the rain dropping and wetting the bed which I was powerless to leave." Daniel Tyler, *A Concise History of the Mormon Battalion in the Mexican War* (1881), 130.

// ... death was sweeping away its victims, and want and suffering seemed to be staring us in the face, which required courage, and a mighty effort to obtain the requisite amount, to be able to bear up under it. That was among the saddest chapters in my history; and it made so vivid an impression that though years have elapsed, and erased many a scene of later date they have not been able to obliterate it from my memory, nor can I ever dwell upon it without weeping.[14]

In the midst of the suffering, however, Helen would not allow herself to succumb to despair—recognizing instead the bright hope of a Divine Deliverer, even during the darkest of times:

// ... the Lord was very merciful ... we were brought into tight places, and many even to the point of death, [but] there came deliverance when most needed. There was always a bright star of hope glimmering between the heavy clouds as they bore down upon us, till at last it seemed as though the very heavens were being opened to pour down a healing balm upon the wounded and disconsolate—proving that "Earth has no sorrows that heaven cannot heal."[15]

Some may question why God would inflict a life of adversity, pain, and sorrow on His choicest children. Helen, a wife of the presiding priesthood leader over the entire dispensation—truly a queen of the Restoration—along with the Prophet's friends and allies, had already passed through numerous fiery trials as they built up Zion. Did they win an unlucky lottery draw for a tormented mortal life, or was there a far *deeper* pattern being repeated once again? Do these principles continue today? As we consider the lives of the early Saints, their struggle and perseverance can help us answer the question: What is the life of a committed disciple like—*What is the true cost of discipleship?*

The Saints could have stayed in Nauvoo or relocated to another desirable city—if they would have simply renounced the controversial aspects of Joseph's ministry and assimilated into the crowd. Many

---

14   Helen Mar Kimball Whitney, "Scenes and Incidents at Winter Quarters," *Woman's Exponent* 14, no. 8 (September 15, 1885): 58.

15   Ibid.

who died might have lived, and most would have prospered—the pleasures of life could have been theirs. When opposition arose to crush the work of Joseph Smith, many wavering souls *did* recoil from the fight. Others gave their all and faced the advancing fire head on. While mobs may not drive contemporary Latter-day Saints from their homes today, two enduring questions remain for us to answer: What is the price required to keep the Restoration alive? And who is willing to pay that price—whatever it may be?

Helen's First Child—Helen Rosabelle

In April 1847, Horace Whitney nervously left his young bride behind, traveling with the first company to establish a gathering place in the Rocky Mountains. It was a formidable journey with the purpose of paving the way for others to follow.[16] Helen was expecting their first child, and the difficult circumstances and treacherous, unknown path ahead weighed heavily on her,—especially with there being no guarantee that she would ever hear from her husband again:

> How far they were going, or how long would be our separation, no one could tell. They were going beyond the trackless wastes of the Great American Desert . . . . Nor were they to turn back till they found some suitable spot where they could form a colony, and make homes that they thought would not be coveted nor encroached upon by their white brethren, who had so mercilessly driven them from their midst. The out look was indeed a gloomy one, and needed all the faith and hope that could be mustered to sustain us under the circumstances. . .[17]

Adding to the complexity of the situation, many of the men were asked by Brigham Young to demonstrate their loyalty to the Constitution by serving the US Army in the 1846-48 Mexican-American War. This was a sacrifice that would also provide critical

---

16   Helen included entries from her husband's diary in her 1885 article in the *Woman's Exponent*. One entry of note records that the men joining that first company to enter Utah were encouraged to "not go hunting or fishing" on Sunday, "for if they did so, they should not be prospered, as this was a day set apart for the service of the Lord, not for trivial amusements." Helen Mar Kimball Whitney, "Scenes and Incidents at Winter Quarters," *Woman's Exponent* 14, no. 8 (September 15, 1885): 58.

17   Helen Mar Kimball Whitney, "Scenes and Incidents at Winter Quarters," *Woman's Exponent* 14, no. 8 (September 15, 1885): 58.

funds to aid the Saints' westward migration.[18] Recognizing that prolonging their stay at Winter Quarters would only lead to increased death and disease, Brigham Young prioritized the trek west in 1847, leading a company of the strongest brethren to the Rocky Mountains. The goal was to secure a settlement and plant crops as soon as possible, and then return to assist the women and children left behind; it was the only practical solution. Those remaining in Winter Quarters endeavored to survive as best they could, although they faced the very real possibility of starvation. "When one meal was eaten, how the next was to be obtained was something of a puzzle."[19]

Helen had another concern weighing anxiously on her mind—at 18 years old, she was about to give birth for the first time. In the morning hours of May 6, 1847, Helen went into labor and delivered a beautiful baby girl, but alas, the anticipation of celebrating new life and new hope was dashed to pieces. Patty Sessions, also a plural wife of the Prophet Joseph Smith and a renowned midwife, recorded in her journal that the baby was stillborn.[20]

---

18   A few months after the first pioneer companies had been forced to abandon Nauvoo, Captain James Allen of the U.S. Army arrived in their destitute camp, asking for volunteers to help the United States fight the Mexican-American War. While the Saints felt betrayed by this request from a government who had refused to protect their rights as its citizens, President Young realized the service would supply funding for the trek west and reinforce the Latter-day Saints' commitment to the Constitution of the United States, in spite of corruption in local and federal governments. Sergeant William Hyde reported that the men were charged "to remember their prayers, to see that the name of the Deity was revered, and that virtue and cleanliness were strictly observed. [The troops were instructed] to treat all men with kindness . . . and never take life when it could be avoided." Daniel Tyler, *A Concise History of the Mormon Battalion in the Mexican War* (1881), 129.

President Young promised that if they made this sacrifice, their "lives should be spared and [their] expedition result in great good, and [their] names be handed down in honorable remembrance to all generations." He also made the promise "that they would have no fighting to do." William Hyde, *The Private Journal of William Hyde* (privately published, 1962?), 19; spelling standardized. These promises were all fulfilled. The Mormon Battalion consisted of 541 men, 32 women, and 50 children. The battalion made other significant contributions in creating many wagon roads and settling areas in California, gaining the respect and gratitude of all they came in contact with.

19   Helen Mar Kimball Whitney, "Scenes and Incidents at Winter Quarters," *Woman's Exponent* 14, no. 10 (October 15, 1885): 78.

20   May 6, 1847. "May Thursday 6 put Helen Kimbal to bed the child still born." Patty Sessions Diary, Volume 1, 1846 February-1849 February, p. 134, Church History Library, https://catalog.churchofjesuschrist.org/assets/46802f09-24c4-4aa8-9ddc-7f4da4bef67a/0/133.

The struggle and travail of birth and death shattered the young mother's world. Helen's heart broke nearly in two: "The only bright star, to which my doting heart had clung, was snatched away...." A devastated Helen struggled to understand the higher purpose of it all:

❝ ... though it seemed a needless bereavement, and most cruel in the eyes of all who beheld it, their sympathies were such that, by their united faith and prayers, they seemed to buoy me up to that degree that death was shorn of its sting, till I could say, 'Thy will, not mine, be done.'[21]

Helen struggled to rally her wits about her and find strength as a young mother deprived of both her husband, albeit temporarily, as well as her first child for the remainder of mortality. Helen named the babe, with whom she spent so little time, 'Helen Rosabelle.' Then, with resolute determination, she interred her little body in a cold earthen grave. One can imagine the bereaved mother sitting alone at the final resting place of her little one, pondering her past, her present, and her future. Was this price to keep the Restoration alive really worth it?

Refusing to succumb to the darkening spirit of despair, she intentionally walked through the "dark hours" knowing that "the Lord was there."[22] In June 1847, Helen broke the news of her firstborn's passing in a tender letter to Horace:

❝ I have passed through serious trying scenes since you left. I have been called to part with my little babe, which has been harder to bear than all my bodily suffering, (although that has been very great) for I had doted much on its society in your absence, but the Lord has certainly been with me to comfort me through all my trials and I have <u>more</u> than realized the blessings, which were pronounced upon my head before you left, they have caused me to meditate more upon eternal things than I ever did before in my life. I feel now as though we had a treasure laid up in

---

21   Helen Mar Kimball Whitney, "Scenes and Incidents at Winter Quarters," *Woman's Exponent* 14, no. 10 (October 15, 1885): 78.

22   Augusta Joyce Crocheron, *Representative Women of Deseret* (Salt Lake City, J. C. Graham & Co.), 110.

heaven, to draw our hearts there, instead of settling them upon anything on earth[23]

Seeking to console her husband as she herself sought to be consoled, Helen eagerly encouraged Horace by sharing the prophetic utterances with which she had been blessed from Eliza R. Snow Smith, also a plural wife of Joseph Smith. She told him of Eliza speaking in tongues, with the immediate interpretation provided by "Sister Sessions"[24]:

// Saturday 6th My dear Horace I am quite happy today, for I have had such bles[s]ings poured out upon my head, by sister Eliza Snow in the gift of tongues, (and interpreted by sister Sessions) that my heart is so full to overflowing. She prophesied things concerning you and myself, she nor sister sessions could have thought of (not knowing the desires of our hearts) had not the spirit of the Lord dictated them what to say, she told me I should see you again, and Great many other things which I will tell you when you come home. Oh that you could have heard them for it would have rejoiced your heart as much as it did mine.[25]

In her own diary, Eliza also recorded her experience as ". . . a time of blessing at sis. K[imball]'s . . . sis[ter] Sess[ions] & myself blest Helen. I spoke and she interpreted. I then blest the girls in a song, singing to each in rotation."[26]

Mournful loss weighed heavily on Helen—yet she again demonstrated her refusal to abandon hope by reaching out to her Lord in faith, determined to trust that He would fulfill every heaven-sent promise made to her. With a heart that ached with loneliness, she roused her courage by remembering that one day she would be

---

23 Letter from Helen to Horace, June 4, 1847. Utah State University, Merrill Library, MSS 179, box 1, fd 1; underline in original.

24 Patty Bartlett Sessions was sealed as a plural wife to the Prophet Joseph Smith on March 9, 1842. She was a celebrated midwife among the Latter-day Saints and kept detailed diaries during the early pioneer migration to the Salt Lake Valley.

25 Letter from Helen to Horace, June 4, 1847. Utah State University, Merrill Library, MSS 179, box 1, fd 1; underline in original.

26 Journal entry of Eliza R. Snow, dated June 6, 1847. Diary of Eliza R. Snow, vol. 2, p. 3, Church History Library, https://catalog.churchofjesuschrist.org/assets/ca0aca76-26a7-4560-821c-e7902b7a393a/0/2. Limited digital access (approval required).

reunited with her child again—she would nurture and raise the dear little soul in a day of peace, without sorrow or tears.[27] To her dear Horace she wrote:

// I have had many lonely feelings since you left as well as many joyful ones, when I have been meditating upon the future when we shall receive our little infant back to our arms when sorrow and affliction shall be done away. I am happy for the blessing is surely ours, it has been promised by your father, and many others and it causes my heart to rejoice.[28]

No great man or woman has lived a life free of affliction. God's work is accomplished by seemingly ordinary men and women— often without wealth, significant talent, resources, or prestige—but men and women possessing purity. Through the broken hearts and tested mettle of humble families, stripped from worldly accolades and esteem, the Lord was forging the Restoration, a kingdom, and a message that would eventually revolutionize the entire world.

Overcoming the loss of her first child was not Helen's only challenge; the effects of labor and childbirth, coupled with her naturally delicate health, left her in a seriously compromised condition. Mental distress and day-to-day hardship added to the crippling effect on her physical strength:

---

27   The Prophet Joseph Smith taught, "They rest from their labors for a long time, and yet their work is held in reserve for them, that they are permitted to do the same works after they receive a resurrection for their bodies." Joseph Smith, Instruction on Priesthood, circa October 5, 1840, p. 7-8, The Joseph Smith Papers.

"'… we have again the warning voice sounded in our midst which shows the uncertainty of human life. And in my leasure moments I have meditated upon the subject, & asked the question Why is it that, infant innocent children are taken away from us, esspecially those that seem to be most intelligent beings' Answer 'This world is a vary wicked world & it is a proverb that the world grow weaker & wiser, but if it is the case the world grows more wicke[d] & corrupt. In the early ages of the world A richeoos [righteous] man & a man of God & intell[i]gence had a better chance to do good to be received & believed than at the present day, but in this these days such a man is much opposed & persecuted by most of the inhabitants of the earth & he has much sorrow to pass through, hence the Lord takes many away even in infancy that they may escape the envy of man, the sorrows & evils of this present world & they were two pure & to[o] lov[e]ly to live on Earth, Therefore if rightly considerd we have, instead of mo[u]rning we have reason to rejoice, as they are deliverd from evil & we shall soon have them again …'" Joseph Smith, Discourse, March 20, 1842, as Reported by Wilford Woodruff, p. 134, The Joseph Smith Papers.

28   Letter from Helen to Horace, June 4, 1847. Utah State University, Merrill Library, MSS 179, box 1, fd 1; underline in original.

❝ Three weeks of suffering followed, when I was dressed one day, but I took cold and was again prostrated, and lay in a critical state for another three weeks, a part of that time in a cold clammy sweat, until everything on me was as wet as though it had been drenched in cold water, and death seemed determined to claim me, but I was saved for a purpose. Before I was able to sit up, the scurvy laid hold of me, commencing at the tips of the fingers of my left hand with black streaks running up the nails, with inflammation and the most intense pain, and which increased till it had reached my shoulder. Poultices of scraped potato, the best thing, it was considered, to subdue the inflammation; it would turn black as soon as applied, and for all they were changed every few minutes for fresh ones, it was all to no effect. By this time I had lost all faith, and patience, too, and, with a feeling of desperation, I arose, and, taking the wrap and everything with it, I threw it with such force that it went into the fireplace on the opposite side of the room, saying, "There you can stay, for I will never do another thing for it!" and to my great surprise I had no occasion to, as the pain and disease had left me, and from that moment I felt no more of it. Still there were other obstacles in the way of my full recovery; though I was free from pain, I remained in a feeble state for some time, so that I had to lie down a goodly portion of the time.[29]

Helen's father and mother-in-law, Newel and Elizabeth Ann Whitney, visited Helen often, taking on the responsibility of her care as if she were their own child.[30] Helen's beloved "Aunt Fanny"[31] stood in as another angel of mercy during her bitter trial. In a letter to Helen's uncle dated July 5, 1847, Fanny described the anguish of Helen's suffering—but also noted her triumph over the hardship:

---

29   Helen Mar Kimball Whitney, "Scenes and Incidents at Winter Quarters," *Woman's Exponent* 14, no. 10 (October 15, 1885): 78.

30   Letter from Helen to Horace, June 4, 1847. Utah State University, Merrill Library, MSS 179, box 1, fd 1; underline in original.

31   Fanny Young was sealed as a plural wife of the Prophet Joseph Smith on November 2, 1843. Fanny had been the widow of Vilate Kimball's father, Roswell Murry, until his passing in 1839. Helen would often refer to her endearingly as "Aunt Fanny."

Painting of Winter Quarters, by C. C. A. Christensen

❦❦ When her time of trouble came, she was very sick, but very patient. It seemed as though the Lord was teaching her a great lesson. She at length gave birth to a beautiful little daughter, but mother and child could not both live, and she was destined to yield up to death the dear little object on which she had doted with her whole heart. You know how natural it is for our hearts to cleave to earthly objects, and how easy it is with the Lord to blast every ray of comfort, that we may seek our all in Him. Helen's affection is indeed a savor of life unto her. She sunk into the will of God with all her heart, and her soul was so filled with the joy of heaven that she enjoys rather than suffers her bereavement. How I should love you to see her and all the family.[32]

In all of the trials and difficult circumstances Helen faced, she was not alone. A path had been forged before her—a step-by-step journey guarded by a loving Father in Heaven who led Helen along as she walked by faith. By degrees, He had been drawing her closer to Him, preparing her to receive her own witness.

---

32 Helen Mar Kimball Whitney, "Scenes and Incidents at Winter Quarters," *Woman's Exponent* 14, no. 11 (November 1, 1885): 82.

CHAPTER 9

Unity Among Sisters

VISIONS, THE GIFT OF TONGUES, & PROPHECY

Newness of life within the soul is often born when treading the deepest waters—surrendering to God's will at your lowest point amidst the greatest depths of struggle and pain. For Helen and her pioneer sisters, the suffering in Winter Quarters was soon eclipsed by powerful spiritual experiences poured out by the Lord in response to their steady faithfulness. This oft-repeated pattern appears throughout the lives of faithful and valiant women in the history of the Church—both past and present.

In May 1847, with the bitter cold of winter finally behind them, Helen began meeting two to three times a week with other sisters, including Eliza R. Snow and Zina D. Young—both fellow wives of the Prophet Joseph Smith. "Some had visions, and by the gift of tongues there were things foretold, some of which we have seen the fulfillment of . . ."[1] Helen became a witness to the active power of fasting and prayer that is manifest when sisters come together to unite their faith in purpose:

❝ We had but few men, mostly aged and disabled, but to see the union of the sisters; the fasting and prayers for the preservation of our battalion and the pioneers; and for the destroyer to be stayed; the great and marvelous manifestations, even the power of the resurrection, experienced there—proved that they

---

1   Helen Mar Kimball Whitney, "Scenes and Incidents at Winter Quarters," *Woman's Exponent* 14, no. 13 (December 1, 1885): 98.

Winter Quarters, by Jon McNaughton

were encircled by a mighty power, and that "the prayers of the righteous availeth much."[2]

With the Restoration of the Gospel came the unlocking of a lost, ancient understanding of womanhood in God's Kingdom. Eliza R. Snow would later teach that women "acting in a united capacity and their prayers being one, they should have power with God, for Father hears the prayers of his daughters as well as his sons, when they are *united*."[3] The women assembled in Winter Quarters—reaching within the depths of their souls to call upon the Lord with all the energy of their hearts. The Father answered in tender, yet powerful, approbation—pouring down revelations in such abundance as to define this period as one of the most remarkable experiences of Latter-day Saint women in our history. Morning light was beginning to pierce the darkened nights of despair.

2   Augusta Joyce Crocheron, *Representative Women of Deseret* (Salt Lake City, J. C. Graham & Co.), 110.

3   Eliza R. Snow, Seventeenth Ward Relief Society minutes and records (1856-1973), March 12, 1868, p. 69, Church History Library, https://catalog.churchofjesuschrist. org/assets/364b9038-7a3d-484f-849b-2726c7c58356/0/15; emphasis added.

Experiencing the Gift of Tongues, Visions, & Prophecy

Three of the sisters who gathered in the spring of 1847—Presendia Kimball,[4] Frances Kimball[5], and Emmeline Whitney[6]—shared the appellation of being "gifted in the interpretation of tongues." Helen recorded the details of one experience:

❧ The two former, with a few others, met at the house occupied by Sister Presendia and Laura P. Kimball, and while conversing upon some of the spiritual manifestations the same power rested down upon them, and an open vision appeared to Frances. I have not heard it related for years, but as nearly as my memory serves me, they that were there said she arose, and her countenance beamed with a brightness like unto one transfigured; her voice and language was heavenly, and grace was in every movement, as she stood there and related over scenes in the experience of

---

4   Presendia Lathrop Huntington was sealed to the Prophet Joseph Smith on December 11, 1841. Following the martyrdom, she married Heber C. Kimball for time. Presendia was the older sister of Zina D. Huntington, who was also a plural wife of the Prophet. Presendia was present at the dedication of the Kirtland Temple, and witnessed a choir of angels singing overhead. She faithfully endured the persecution in Missouri and Nauvoo and, with her children, labored to settle the barren desert of Utah. During a famine in 1856, Presendia recorded: "Some lived on nothing but roots and greens for weeks together. Verily it was a time of trial that pierced men's souls; to hear one's children crying for bread without a morsel to give is something that even strong men shrink from, and the tender hearts of mothers in times like these are torn with anguish." Presendia's response to the crisis is a testament to her selfless faith and love: ". . . I asked the Lord in prayer to take away my appetite and give me strength to keep up without it, so that I might give my rations to the poor children who had nothing. Strange as it may seem the Lord heard and answered my prayers. I was enabled to keep up my usual strength with scarce any food at all, and the desire of my heart was granted me that I might impart my share to those who had none." Presendia Lathrop Huntington, "A Venerable Woman," *Woman's Exponent* 12, no. 13 (December 1, 1883): 98.

Such was the character of many of the women sealed to the Prophet, who assisted in laying the foundation of the Church.

5   Frances Swan Kimball was a plural wife of Heber C. Kimball. Sadly, shortly after arriving in Utah, the toil and sacrifice proved too much for her, and she abandoned the Kimball family and moved to California where she married George L. Clark.

6   Emmeline B. Wells was one of the plural wives of Helen's father-in-law, Newel K. Whitney. She served as the fifth Relief Society General President from 1910-1921, and edited the *Woman's Exponent* for 37 years. She served as president of the Utah Woman's Suffrage Association, and also represented Utah in the National and American Women's Suffrage conventions for nearly 30 years.

some of those sisters, which were some of the most acute trials that had been their lot to pass through during their earth-lives, or while being driven from place to place in Missouri, Illinois, and at various times since they took upon themselves the name of Latter-day Saint. She seemed to be addressing one or more personages, who recorded each one's story as they were told them, only one entering their presence at a time, Frances being voice for them, as well as for the personage, who, in return, addressed them with a look of approval, and with a countenance beaming with joy and satisfaction, they were welcomed, and a bright crown of glory was placed on each one's head, attended with words suitable to their station and the occasion. Sister Frances had known little or nothing of their previous experience, and had never heard the incidents related, but she described them as accurately as if told by themselves.[7]

Throughout that spring, the Lord continued to open the heavens and answer the sisters' fervent prayers. During this time, "many consoling things were spoken by the spirit concerning our brethren, the Pioneers and Battalion, to the truth of which they testified when they returned."[8] Prophecies foretelling future events were given— many eventually occurring within their lifetimes, while others awaited fulfillment in times to come.[9] The sisters were told that a Zion society would be established in the mountains, with the word

---

7   Helen Mar Kimball Whitney, "Scenes and Incidents at Winter Quarters," *Woman's Exponent* 14, no. 13 (December 1, 1885): 98.

8   Ibid.

9   Presendia Young's biography in the *Woman's Exponent* records, "The Sisters had greater need to draw near to the Lord, and the manifestation of his goodness and power were indeed marvelous, especially in healing the sick. The gift of tongues and interpretation, and the gift of prophecy were given them for their comfort and consolation in this trying time. . . . a meeting was held, at which Sister Eliza R. Snow, Zina D. Young and Elizabeth Ann Whitney were present, also Sisters Vilate and Presendia Kimball and some others. Brother Leonard spoke in tongues in an Indian language, and prophesied of the destruction of this nation before the coming of the Savior. The power that rested upon him was so great as to produce such intense sympathy with those in the room, that they were all wonderfully affected. Sister Eliza Snow walked the floor to keep her breath. All felt the distress and agony that awaited the nation, more particularly the priests and harlots being destroyed in their wickedness. Sister Eliza Snow spoke afterwards in the pure language of Adam, with great power, and the interpretation was given." "A Venerable Woman," *Woman's Exponent* 12, no. 1 (June 1, 1883): 2.

Emmeline B. Whitney Wells resided with
Heber C. Kimball Company in Winter Quarters

of God serving as the legal foundation.[10] Peace and righteousness would be found among the people—but not until many future Latter-day Saints had shed their lifeblood. The sisters were shown that there would be many missionaries who would yet be martyred for the faith:

// Many were the things revealed by the spirit concerning the judgments that would be poured out upon the nations after they rejected the Gospel, and smote and slew others of God's messengers who should be sent out to proclaim the Gospel of

---

10   Helen wrote, "There were many great and glorious manifestations—some had visions, and by the gift of tongues there were things foretold, some of which we have seen the fulfillment of, and others that are coming swiftly upon those who have turned away and are uniting their voices and influence against that Zion which we were told should be established in these mountains, where the laws of God were to rule, and the honorable of the earth would come to dwell within its borders, because the wicked were allowed to rule elsewhere, and peace was taken from the earth, except it were in Zion, a place where righteousness would reign, and naught should molest or make afraid in all the holy mount." Helen Mar Kimball Whitney, "Scenes and Incidents at Winter Quarters," *Woman's Exponent* 14, no. 13 (December 1, 1885): 98.

salvation to an erring world, and the righteous would barely escape, and many of them would be called upon to lay down their lives in their struggle for the truth; also of the wars that were right at our doors, famine, pestilence, etc., and the anguish that would rend the hearts of the suffering and bereaved; that the time would be when hunger would overcome every tender feeling, and even mothers would eat their own babes.[11]

Helen remembered that the portrayal of some of the future events shown to them were so violently graphic that they prayed for "the Lord to close the vision of our minds."[12]

Spiritual Warfare: Light & Darkness

The sisters would typically gather in the morning at the home of Vilate Kimball, or another relative.[13] Those who came would fast and rejoice, spending "the day singing, praying and prophesying." Men were not excluded—whenever they could break away from their work they "united with us and received great blessings in connection with the sisters." Whenever the Saints were willing to follow God's laws with exactness and lay down their lives for the standard of truth, miracles always followed. Helen wrote of the incredible, ongoing experiences they shared:

Presendia Lathrop Huntington

---

11   Helen Mar Kimball Whitney, "Scenes and Incidents at Winter Quarters," *Woman's Exponent* 14, no. 13 (December 1, 1885): 98.

12   Ibid.

13   "Frequently, without eating or drinking, we would meet in the morning, either at my mother's, or some other of father's houses, and spend the day singing, praying and prophecying; occasionally some of the brethren who could leave their work united with us and received great blessings in connection with the sisters." Ibid.

❙❙ The spirit that began to be poured out while they were with us, continued to burn in the bosoms of those who met often one with another, and the love of God flowed from heart to heart, till the wicked one seemed powerless in his efforts to get between us and the Lord, and his cruel darts, in some instances, were shorn of their sting.[14]

According to Helen, their joy did not go unnoticed by the adversary, and it was not long before the "wicked one" began to manifest his annoyance. Helen remembered that since they were "so frequently ... enjoying the outpourings of the Holy Spirit," it became necessary for them to "meet and contend with the opposite." The women could not truly appreciate the sweet without tasting the bitter. Firsthand accounts described cunning darts aimed at the target that would cause these sisters the most acute pain—toward that which was dearer to them than their own lives—their children. Helen wrote, "The love and union that prevailed seemed to enrage the evil one, and, not being able to cause a division among us, he vented his wrath upon the little ones."[15] The sisters felt that united prayer was the surest way to combat the enemy—but this did not prevent the manifestation of evil influences from time to time. The worldviews of Helen and her companions were forever altered by their experiences:

❙❙ At one of the meetings which I attended at Sister Presendia's, there was a powerful manifestation of the Holy Spirit, and many comforting words were uttered, and prophecies of blessings which it was our privilege to obtain, if we would unite in fasting and prayer.

... [My mother's] house was the place appointed by the voice of the Spirit to hold the fast meeting, and the great blessing to be gained thereby was the administration of an angel or angels. I had a promise that day that I should be healed by the power of God. Up to this time I had remained feeble and unable to sit up but little, or to walk to a neighbor's without having to lie down,

---

14 Ibid.

15 Helen Mar Kimball Whitney, "Scenes and Incidents at Winter Quarters," *Woman's Exponent* 14, no. 14 (December 15, 1885): 105.

and this I desired more than anything else of a temporal nature. In obedience to that spirit Mother Whitney, her daughter, Sarah Ann, Sisters Louisa Pitkin, Presendia Buel, Sarah Lawrence, Frances Swan, Harriet Sanders, Persis Young and two or three others who were there, all being my father's wives but Sister Persis and Mother Whitney, met the next morning without eating or drinking. But no sooner had we begun to offer up our united prayers than the devil commenced his operations on the three little ones that were there, mother's Brigham and her little babe, and Sarah Ann's son, who was born on the journey from Nauvoo. It would be one and then the other. The eldest was playing in the room adjoining, and without any known cause, he commenced screaming; floundering and going into the most frightful contortions, which obliged us to stop and administer to him and rebuke that spirit in the name of Jesus, when the child quieted down and went to sleep. We had no sooner begun again to seek in prayer for the promised blessing, than we were again interrupted by my mother's babe screaming, and it had lain sleeping peacefully till then. He was operated upon in a similar manner to the other, so we were under the necessity of again stopping to administer to him, when he was immediately relieved, and went to sleep. But just as soon as we commenced again to struggle for the blessing that had been promised, the third one was seized, and this continued through the day, and every time the evil spirits were rebuked by the power of the priesthood, which had been conferred upon us in the house of God in connection with our husbands.[16] This only stimulated us to persevere . . . We broke our fast [that night], and [Bishop Whitney] came about dusk and spent the best portion of the night in answering questions and explaining doctrines and things which the sisters had never before understood. . . . He said it was only through similar struggles that any great manifestations from on high were ever obtained. There were things that he uttered that night that he did not know of himself, but by the Spirit some choice truths were revealed through him, and they were of a most consoling nature to women, particularly to those who were making a willing sacrifice in helping their

---

16   See Chapter 14, "Rolling Waters & Power from Heaven" for a discussion on women and the priesthood in the early days of the Church.

husbands to accomplish the great and mighty purposes which the Lord had commanded them to do, and they were promised that eventually all that were true and faithful would enjoy all that their hearts desired, or could conceive of; their trials and sufferings here would be swallowed up in the glory they had attained to through obedience, and they would be enthroned and reign as queens in the presence of God, eternities without end.[17]

... [I] am able to testify to the enjoyment of many happy seasons after the mighty struggle with the destroyer was over, and we were again in the enjoyment of health, a blessing that none could appreciate more fully than myself.[18]

While the other sisters were eagerly discussing the traumatic events of the day with Bishop Whitney, Helen retired to lay down and rest. She was still in the process of recovering her health, and the ordeal had thoroughly exhausted her. Helen was also left feeling somewhat disappointed, for "not having been healed as I had been told I should be, my faith was considerably shaken."[19] As she retired for the night, however, the prophetic promises made by her father-in-law earlier that evening left her "comforted," and she "forgot [her] disappointment in the hope of that happiness which I believed would be mine, in connection with those I loved, in a day to come."[20]

Helen is Healed

Like Mary of old, the mother of Jesus, Helen laid hold on the promises of God—promises she knew would be fulfilled.[21] She felt that her strenuous exertions of faith, hope, and long-suffering were richly rewarded in an unanticipated blessing the next morning, when, during the early hours, Sister Persis Young stopped by to visit, "saying that she had been impressed by the Spirit to come and

---

17 Helen Mar Kimball Whitney, "Scenes and Incidents at Winter Quarters," *Woman's Exponent* 14, no. 14 (December 15, 1885): 105-106.

18 Helen Mar Kimball Whitney, "Scenes and Incidents at Winter Quarters," *Woman's Exponent* 14, no. 18 (February 15, 1886): 138.

19 Helen Mar Kimball Whitney, "Scenes and Incidents at Winter Quarters," *Woman's Exponent* 14, no. 14 (December 15, 1885): 106.

20 Ibid.

21 Luke 1:45.

administer to me, and I would be healed."[22] Sister Young disclosed that she had been unable to sleep from the urgency of the prompting, and so "had come there in obedience to that Spirit." The Lord had not forgotten Helen, and her fervent prayers of long-suffering would be answered in a most profound way:

// She had been so long under its influence that she shook as though palsied when she laid her hands upon my head with my mother. She rebuked my weakness, and every disease that had been, or was then afflicting me, and commanded me to be made whole, pronouncing health and many other blessings upon me, nearly all of which have been literally fulfilled. From that morning I went about to work as though nothing had been the matter. Thus did the Lord remember one of His unworthy handmaidens and fulfill the promise that had been given by the gift and power of the Holy Ghost.[23]

Helen was learning through personal experience to wait patiently on the Lord without doubt. Humiliation opened the door to exaltation. As she pressed forward in faith and obedience, her confidence grew as the Lord continued to bless her by pouring out revelation, healing, and strength:

// The experience had at Winter Quarters taught me that it was only through obedience and great humiliation, more especially through fasting and prayer, that we could obtain any great manifestations from on high, or the power to enable us to overcome the adversary.

Could we as a people, lay aside the world, and bring our own evil natures into subjection to that spirit, which would make us of one heart and one mind, and valiant to do all that is required of the Saints of God. I know that we would not be long as we are now, bending under the yoke of oppression, but would soon become that people whom we have been told from

---

22   See Chapter 14, "Rolling Waters & Power from Heaven" for a discussion on women and the priesthood in the early days of the Church.

23   Helen Mar Kimball Whitney, "Scenes and Incidents at Winter Quarters," *Woman's Exponent* 14, no. 14 (December 15, 1885): 106.

Vilate Murray Kimball

the beginning, should be honored, not only by the noble, but by the Great Lawgiver of the whole earth.[24]

Power comes from purity. Helen learned by experience that there was no power in a religion that did not require significant sacrifice.[25] Many could *believe* in God, and many could *profess* a great love for

---

24 Helen Mar Kimball Whitney, "Scenes and Incidents at Winter Quarters," *Woman's Exponent* 14, no. 15 (January 1, 1886): 118.

25 "Let us here observe, that a religion that does not require the sacrifice of all things, never has power sufficient to produce the faith necessary unto life and salvation..." Lectures on Faith, Lecture Sixth, found in the 1835 Doctrine and Covenants, p. 60, The Joseph Smith Papers.

the Savior—but powerful spiritual experiences, revelation, visions, healings, the gift of tongues, and so forth, came only after paying the commensurate price. The Kirtland Lectures on Faith, directed and approved by the Prophet Joseph Smith, expounded on this timeless principle:

// Let us here observe, that a religion that does not require the sacrifice of all things never has power sufficient to produce the faith necessary unto life and salvation; for, from the first existence of man, the faith necessary unto the enjoyment of life and salvation never could be obtained without the sacrifice of all earthly things. It was through this sacrifice, and this only, that God has ordained that men should enjoy eternal life; and it is through the medium of the sacrifice of all earthly things that men do actually know that they are doing the things that are well pleasing in the sight of God. When a man has offered in sacrifice all that he has for the truth's sake, not even withholding his life, and believing before God that he has been called to make this sacrifice because he seeks to do [H]is will, he does know, most assuredly, that God does and will accept [H]is sacrifice and offering, and that he has not, nor will not seek his face in vain. Under these circumstances, then, he can obtain the faith necessary for him to lay hold on eternal life.[26]

Helen and her sisters in the Gospel experienced great miracles because of how they *lived*. Helen longed for each member to experience the joy that comes through "lay[ing] aside the world." The opportunity is open to all—past and present—but how many brave souls are eager to take this 'road less traveled'? For those willing to live a higher standard in entertainment and media, diet, recreation, fashion, education, and so forth—for those prepared to consecrate their time, embracing the tumultuous life of a genuine disciple of Christ, for those ready to pay any price to further the Restoration, miracles and signs did follow—and still do *today*. Helen answered 'yes' to the call, and testified throughout her life that the reward was indeed worth the cost.

---

26   Lectures on Faith, Lecture Sixth, found in the 1835 Doctrine and Covenants, p. 60-61, The Joseph Smith Papers.

CHAPTER 10

A Witness in the Fiery Furnace

With the passing of summer, a change in the air heralded October's fall colors and a joyous reunion between Helen and Horace—the latter having recently returned to Winter Quarters with Brigham Young after six months of trying separation. With the location out west secured, the men returned to gather their families and migrate to their new home in the Rocky Mountains. The following spring, Horace and Helen left Winter Quarters, closing this bittersweet chapter as they traveled in Heber C. Kimball's pioneer company.

Helen was expecting again as they made their way across the plains of the midwest, and she came to term while crossing through Wyoming. To the delight of the young parents, Helen's labor produced a beautiful baby boy. But again, sadly, their joy would be short lived, and in yet another bitter test, she would lose her son just five days later—on her 20th birthday, August 22, 1848. The Lord giveth and the Lord taketh. Helen had given birth to two children, and the Lord had required them both. The grief-stricken couple would bury their precious son, leaving his little body beside the trail that crossed the lonely, windswept Wyoming territory. This tiny resting place would join those of many other Saints whose graves stood as sentinels of sacrifice along the way.

Descending the Depths of Despair

This second tragedy soon proved too much for Helen to bear: her health plummeted, and darkness gathered around her. She had already submitted patiently to her daughter's death, had suffered hunger, illness, and fatigue in Winter Quarters, and had laid her home, her ambitions, and her longings all on the altar for the sake of the Gospel. But still, she felt her heart continually being torn asunder—again and again came the trials, and she "mourned incessantly, and that with my intense bodily sufferings soon brought me to death's door."[1] While en route to the Salt Lake Valley, Helen's health, spirits, and even mental stability, continued to decline until she had sunk into a dark valley of depression.

Helen could never share the full details—the true depth of her suffering during the fall and early winter of 1848:

❝ No one but God and the angels to whom I owe my life and all I have, could know the tenth part of what I suffered. I never told anybody and I never could. A keener taste of misery and woe, no mortal, I think, could endure.[2]

From a personal letter to a woman named Mary Bond, and from the details Helen shared in her short biographical history in *Representative Women of Deseret*, the understanding of an intense conflict begins to form—a struggle not unlike Alma the Younger's experience recorded in the Book of Mormon. Progressive historians have interpreted the accounts as indicative of a period of psychological disorder fueled by a psychotic, superstitious—some even suggest a religiously abusive— 'early Mormon worldview.' Conversely, Helen saw her experience as a profound spiritual rebirth where she encountered the forces of good and evil, each contending for her allegiance. Regardless of varying interpretations, the following history is related according to Helen's firsthand accounts and personal perspective:

❝ It is true that my body was prostrated by sickness, but my spirit & my understanding was quickened & I was shown the workings of the Devil & his Agents or his Angels. I was overwhelmed by the power of darkness & really believed for a time that Satan had possession of me[.] I suffered what I am confident

---

1   Augusta Joyce Crocheron, *Representative Women of Deseret* (Salt Lake City: J. C. Graham & Co., 1884), 111.

2   Ibid., 112.

that those will suffer who have once received the light of this Gospel & then rejected it. I saw what I had lost & that I by my own misdeeds my disobedience & murmurings against the Providence principles, of this gospel with the more per . . . the principle of Celestial . . . marriage.[3]

Alma the Younger, nearly two millennia before, described a similar experience of being "racked with eternal torment," and "tormented with the pains of hell," including "inexpressible horror" as his soul was "harrowed up to the greatest degree and racked with all [his] sins." Alma had been raised by a faithful father and leader of the Nephite Church in Zarahemla. Yet, he rebelled against the Gospel and actively engaged in persecuting the members of the Church. Alma's deliverance came when he called on the Son of God for deliverance: "O Jesus, thou Son of God, have mercy on me . . ."[4] Helen believed she was walking through a similar experience, though for different reasons:

// I knew that it was from God. & I felt the power of the Priesthood when my father was near me the evil spirits departed, but when duties called him and he left me they returned ten fold & none but the Lord & his Angels knew this . . . that I was enduring for I never made any outward demonstrations, [line obscured by fold] Every . . . life passed before me like a panorama. The scriptures which I knew very little about previous to this I was made familiar with in [t]he anguish of my soul I longed to be annihilated or if my soul must be cast into Hell & remain there till I had paid the debt I desired to go that I might the sooner be redeemed. The [evil] Spirit made me to believe that I was doomed to remain there two thousand years. They missed just enough truth to make me believe their lies. I was told that God & his Angels were too far off from me to be heard & it was [useless] for me to pray, for a long time I believe it to be true. I was very sick & for a time became to all outward appearance as dead, & I was dead

3   Brian Hales' Mormon Polygamy Documents, 71.040-71.045, https://mormonpolygamydocuments.org/jsp-document-book-71/.

4   Alma 36:18.

to every thing in this world. They my family afterwards told me that the only way they could found out that life was in my body was to put the ear to my mouth . . .[5]

Death seemed only too sweet a respite, and Helen's losses far too great to bear. "I was very weak & gave way to my sorrow until my bodily suffering rendered me powerless to think," she wrote. Having surrendered the strength to resist any longer, she had given up her very will to live:

▐▐ one evening after all had retired but one who was to watch me, all my family were worn out, all at once my pain left me my limbs were cold & my pulse had almost stopped beating & I felt as though my body did not touch the bed & I was perfectly happy thinking that I was go[i]ng to my little one my mind was remarkably clear I felt as if my breath was leaving me without a struggle I desired to see my father & mother and Horace.[6]

One by one, Helen's family members came to bid her farewell. First, her father arrived, "weeping & talking as though for the last in this world." Then her dear mother came, followed by Horace, and finally her father and mother-in-law. Completely overcome with sorrow, Vilate collapsed—her daughter's impending death being too much to bear:

▐▐ My poor mother was shocked as so overcome . . . that she sunk to the floor of the carriage speechless & looked as though she might be dying. I begged her not to weep telling her she would soon follow me . . .[7]

---

5   Brian Hales' Mormon Polygamy Documents, 71.040-71.045, p. 45-46, https://mormonpolygamydocuments.org/jsp-document-book-71/.

6   Brian Hales' Mormon Polygamy Documents, 71.040-71.045, p. 46, https://mormonpolygamydocuments.org/jsp-document-book-71/.

Representative Women of Deseret records Helen's account of this time as follows: "I was cold, but oh, how peaceful, as I lay there painless and my breath passing so gently away; I felt as though I was wafting on the air and happy in the thought of meeting so soon with my babes where no more pain or sorrow could come." Augusta Joyce Crocheron, *Representative Women of Deseret* (Salt Lake City, J. C. Graham & Co., 1884), 111-112.

7   Brian Hales' Mormon Polygamy Documents, 71.040-71.045, p. 46, https://mormonpolygamydocuments.org/jsp-document-book-71/.

Helen's words "went like lightning to [her] father's heart . . ."[8]
It was in this moment of crisis—with his beloved daughter's life
ebbing away, his wife weeping disconsolately, and Helen's husband
and family in grave distress—that Heber suddenly stood erect,
filled with the spirit of prophecy. He knew this was not to be, and
called on the Lord to heal his daughter:

// My words struck father like a sudden thunderbolt, and he spoke
with a mighty voice and said—"Vilate, Helen *is not dying!*" but
my breath which by this time had nearly gone, stopped that
very instant, and I felt his faith and knew that he was holding
me; and I begged him to let me go as I thought it very cruel
to keep me, and believed it impossible for me to live and ever
recover. The destroyer was then stirred up in anger at being
cheated out of his victim and he seemed determined to wreak
his vengeance upon us all.[9]

So great was the faith of Helen's father that it seemed to defy death
itself—the ever-present trials of sickness and despair *demanded*
such unyielding faith. "It felt that i was being held by faith," Helen
would write to Mary Bond. "I did not want to live & begged of
him to let me die."[10] A later account of this incident added that,
"her mother was also very sick at the same time, and it seemed that
only Brother Kimball's mighty faith kept them alive."[11] It was not
only the potential loss of a daughter, but also the loss of his loyal
wife that stared Heber in the face. It was moments like this—when
nearly *all* seemed lost—that the love of God shone through and, in
this case, endowed the family patriarch with prophetic knowledge
from on high. Orson Whitney, Helen's son, would later write:

---

8   Brian Hales' Mormon Polygamy Documents, 71.040-71.045, p. 46, https://
mormonpolygamydocuments.org/jsp-document-book-71/.

9   Augusta Joyce Crocheron, *Representative Women of Deseret* (Salt Lake City, J. C.
Graham & Co., 1884), 112.

10   Brian Hales' Mormon Polygamy Documents, 71.040-71.045, p. 46, https://
mormonpolygamydocuments.org/jsp-document-book-71/.

11   "Helen Mar Whitney: Her Death—A Sketch of Her Personal History," *Deseret
Evening News*, November 16, 1896, 2.

❝❝ Vilate herself was prostrated by her daughter's deep distress, and it was only by dint of Heber's mighty faith and powerful will, that either of them were kept alive. Again and again he administered to the sufferers, praying that God would spare their lives, and declaring in prophetic words to them and the whole camp that they "should not die." Thus it was, throughout the entire journey to the mountains. That season of dire trouble Heber and his family ever after looked back upon as one of the extraordinary trials of his life.[12]

Helen begged her father to summon the doctor to prove she was dying: "He gratified my wishes & the Dr. said the same as he did that I was not dying. They all were united in faith for me to live & I felt . . . that they were very cruel . . ."[13] Helen stood at a crossroad like never before—resurrect hope and continue to struggle for new life, or succumb to the oppressive intimidation of the adversary. She felt herself enveloped in a tremendous conflict being waged between God and "the destroyer"—manifested to her as an intense, fiery trial.

Helen wanted to die—she had lost her strength and her will to live. However, she would later testify that this furnace of affliction would ultimately offer a spiritual rebirth, as well as the opportunity to gain a testimony and witness greater than any she had ever before experienced. To her family and friends, her illness appeared to render her "like one dead," but she felt that though her body was immobile, her mind had entered another realm:

❝❝ In a short time reason forsook me. I could not tell all that I felt & realized during those days I suffered in spirit more than all that my body has ever felt & that has been a great deal. The worst thing I endured in body was thirst. I lost all power of speech & did not make a sound. The[y] afterwards told me like any word, but I thought I spoke correctly & that I was made to suffer it as a just punishment for my sins. They could not prevail on me to eat for I was made by the evil one,

---

12   Orson F. Whitney, *Life of Heber C. Kimball* (Salt Lake City: Kimball Family, 1888), 398.

13   Brian Hales' Mormon Polygamy Documents, 71.040-71.045, p. 46, https://mormonpolygamydocuments.org/jsp-document-book-71/.

to believe that every thing they fed me would cause me to rot alive. My jaws were closed as tight as though they were locked & no one could open them. Father would come & try to get me to take a little nourishment. I layed . . . senseless at the time, except when they [r]oused me for a moment. I can remember so well of father laying down the spoon after trying in vain to get me to swallow & closing his eyes to pray. I felt my jaws unlocking & I knew that I must take it & I could not help it. I was perfectly sensible of [t]he power of the priesthood being superior to that of the devil, but I though[t] that [?] would only add & prolong my separation [?]. I was in purgatory whether sleeping or waking & realized the loss that I had sustained, & that I was unworthy to live & associate with them. The devil predicted hundreds of terrible things which were to befall me & would set the time, but all of them passed unfulfilled by degrees. I lost confidence, & in time I ventured to look to higher power. My body . . . became very weak. I could b[e] buffeted & was made to believe that it was of no use for me to pray & then for two or three days I would again be sunk in despair, but all that they told me would come to pass failed & I gained in strength of mind until at last I determined to be buffeted by the evil one no more.[14]

The pioneer company pressed on toward their destination, arriving in the Salt Lake Valley on September 24, 1848. Helen continued her battle of life and death and describing her experience in the book *Representative Women of Deseret*, Helen emphasized this as her 'born of God' turning point, not unlike Alma the Younger in the Book of Mormon:

// For three months I lay a portion of the time like one dead, they told me; but that did not last long. I was alive to my spiritual condition and dead to the world. I tasted of the punishment which is prepared for those who reject any of the principles of this Gospel. Then I learned that plural marriage was a celestial principle, and saw the difference between the power of God's priesthood and that of Satan's and the necessity of obedience

---

14   Brian Hales' Mormon Polygamy Documents, 71.040-71.045, p. 46-47, https://mormonpolygamydocuments.org/jsp-document-book-71/.

to those who hold the priesthood, and the danger of rebelling against or speaking lightly of the Lord's annointed.

I had, in hours of temptation, when seeing the trials of my mother, felt to rebel. I hated polygamy in my heart, I had loved my baby more than my God, and mourned for it unreasonably. All my sins and shortcomings were magnified before my eyes till I believed I had sinned beyond redemption. Some may call it the fruits of a diseased brain. There is nothing without a cause, be that as it may, it was a keen reality to me. During that season I lost my speech, forgot the names of everybody and everything, and was living in another sphere, learning lessons that would serve me in future times to keep me in the narrow way.[15]

Helen slowly began to recover her health and regain her reason, but despite her father's faith and repeated priesthood blessings, she continued to battle through bouts of evil spiritual artillery, confessing that at times she felt so weak that it left her "discouraged in trying to pray, as the evil spirits caused me to feel that it was no use."[16]

A Christmas Fast & New Year's Feast

With time marching inexorably on, soon Christmas was upon them, and still Helen struggled. In the midst of this spiritual forge, we see the true grit and heart of this young woman as she was being shaped and fashioned into a tool for the Lord's work—refined metal that would one day come forth as a bright sword of truth. The day following Christmas—December 26, 1848, Helen arrived at a point of decision:

" I commenced to fast & continued it that whole week. I increased in faith every day & the last day of the year I had gained the victory. I was perfectly happy & realized the presence of holy Angels around my bed just as sensibly as I had felt the opposite Power. I only had to raise my heart in prayer & my desires were

---

15   Augusta Joyce Crocheron, *Representative Women of Deseret* (Salt Lake City: J. C. Graham & Co., 1884), 112-113.

16   Ibid., 113.

granted. The vision of my mind was open to see & understand the will & design of the Allmighty. I had a view of the order of plural marriage. The beauty & the glory which I saw in it was enough to make up for the trials in this life. I have passed through the trials which have been as keen to me as to anyone, but I have kept my eyes upon [. . . the joy?] of them who have entered into that principle ["who hold" or possibly "not at"] it with my eyes single to the glory of God it will make their damnation sure.[17]

Helen would later express her deep gratitude for the Lord's mercy in walking with her through the midst of her own Gethsemane. In the past, to a great degree, she had relied on the testimony of her parents; their word had been enough to lean on, and she had come to depend on their strength. Now this crutch was taken away, and she knew she must rise up and stand in her own place—carry her own witness of truth and error, light and darkness:

// I never disbelieved this doctrine nor fought against it, but I at times felt to murmur at what I now understood to be the providences of a wise creator, when young I could not see the necessity of enduring so many . . . Temptations. I had not learned that God intended to try us & that we had to [come] up through much tribulation before we could inherit His promises. His son Jesus is our pattern & He had to suffer more than any of us, that we might be redeemed. . . . I felt after I was delivered similar to Jesus. & I am just as positive of the truth of my testimony as I am that He is Christ our savior. I thanked the Lord that He had spared my life for the needful lessons which I had been taught though I had suffered so much I prayed that I might never forget them, & I also prayed that I'd never have to endure them again, & that I might live long enough & be able to prove myself worthy of a place in the Celestial Kingdom.[18]

---

17   Brian Hales' Mormon Polygamy Documents, 71.040-71.045, p. 47, https://mormonpolygamydocuments.org/jsp-document-book-71/; brackets in original.

18   Brian Hales' Mormon Polygamy Documents, 71.040-71.045, p. 47, https://mormonpolygamydocuments.org/jsp-document-book-71/.

Every event—every step marked by the milestones in Helen's life—led her to this point. She had consistently exercised childlike faith in God, submitting her own will through heart-rending sacrifices. She had stepped forward to assist her family in accepting their new position and responsibility following the martyrdom of the Prophet. She had witnessed the higher planes of spiritual warfare waged by her sisters in Winter Quarters. But then the enemy turned its attention to her person directly, and as both light and darkness had striven for mastery, she had faced Apollyon[19] herself. Finally, Helen emerged from the spiritual chrysalis of her fiery furnace victorious—a girl reborn as a resilient woman with a mission:

> ... had I been differently situated like many were without a father and a mother to love and counsel me, probably my dependence, like theirs, would have been on the Lord, but I leaned not upon His arm. My father was my teacher and revelator, and I saw no necessity then for further testimony; but in after years the Lord, in His far-seeing and infinite mercy, suffered me to pass through the rough waves of experience, and in sorrow and affliction, I learned this most important lesson, that in Him alone must I trust, and not in weak and sinful man; and that it was absolutely necessary for each one to obtain a living witness and testimony for him or herself, and not for another, to the truth of this latter-day work, to be able to stand, and that like Saul, we "must suffer for His name's sake." Then I learned that "The fear of the Lord is the beginning of knowledge;" and that "He is nigh unto all those that call upon Him in truth, and healeth the broken in heart and bindeth up their wounds."[20]

With each passing day, Helen grew stronger, gaining faith and confidence to a degree she had never before thought possible. The end of the year brought such remarkable change that when New Year's Eve arrived, Helen experienced indescribable joy. It would be

---

19   Greek word meaning "destroyer." In ancient and apocryphal texts, this title is used to refer to Lucifer. In John Bunyon's classic, *The Pilgrim's Progress*, the faithful pilgrim Christian battles with the monster Apollyon and is only preserved by the armor of God as a metaphorical description of spiritual conflict between the adversary and true Christians.

20   Helen Mar Kimball Whitney, "Scenes and Incidents in Nauvoo," *Woman's Exponent* 11, no. 5 (August 1, 1882): 39.

a day she would remember as being "one of the happiest days of my life." After walking through her own valley of the shadow of death, she immediately began to look outward, endeavoring to strengthen, lift, and build those around her:

❝ I was moved upon to talk to my mother. I knew her heart was weighed down in sorrow and I was full of the holy Ghost. I talked as I never did before, I was too weak to talk with such a voice (of my own strength), beside, I never before spoke with such eloquence, and she knew that it was not myself. She was so affected that she sobbed till I ceased. I assured her that father loved her, but he had a work to do, she must rise above her feelings and seek for the Holy Comforter, and though it rent her heart she must uphold him, for he in taking other wives had done it only in obedience to a holy principle. Much more I said, and when I ceased, she wiped her eyes and told me to rest. I had not felt tired till she said this, but commenced then to feel myself sinking away. I silently prayed to be renewed, when my strength returned that instant.[21]

The next day, her father's family held a New Year's fast culminating with a feast of thanksgiving. Helen had experienced a mighty change of heart—she had been spiritually reborn—but still she yearned for a conviction that her God would accept her—would love her and recognize her as one of His daughters:

❝ New Year's day father had set apart to fast and pray, and they prepared a feast at evening. I had prayed that I might gain a sure testimony that day that I was acceptable to God, and my father, when he arose to speak, was so filled with His power, that he looked almost transfigured! He turned to me and spoke of my sufferings and the blessings I should receive because of the same. He prophesied of the great work that I should do, that I should live long and raise honorable sons and daughters that would rise up and call me blessed, and should be a comfort to my mother in her declining years, and many more things which I have fulfilled. Many who knew me then have looked at me

---

21   Augusta Joyce Crocheron, *Representative Women of Deseret* (Salt Lake City: J. C. Graham & Co., 1884), 113.

and seen me working with my children around me, with perfect amazement and as one who had been dead and resurrected.[22]

Helen's response was one of humble gratitude, elation, and joy: "I was perfectly overcome & wept for joy, I had received more than I had asked for." Helen would later share with Mary Bond her father's instrumental role, and her own testimony forged in fire:

// He [My father] said that the destroyer would have been pleased to have taken me & was perfectly willing that I should die easy & happily, but he was mad at him & took the next step to cause him all the trouble that he possibly could but he should not accomplish his end. . . . Though the whole I knew that my father's faith was the cause of my not dying & I know too that the Lord gave it him & this is my testimony to you Mary whether you accept it or not. If your eyes could see & your heart understand all the glorious truths contained in this the Gospel of Christ your faith would become much smoother. Jesus said, "He that taketh not his cross & followeth after me is not worthy of me. He that findeth [h]is life shall lose it. He that loseth his life for my sake shall find it."[23]

Counseling with Eliza R. Snow

During this period of refinement and growth, Helen drew strength from the wise counsel of her dear friend, Eliza R. Snow. As a small child,

---

22   Helen's letter to Mary Bond records: "I . . . was in bed but I fasted as I had been do[i]ng the whole week I had not desired food. I felt as full as though I'd eaten. I had but one desire & t[h]at was that I might receive a testimony that day that would satisfy me that my sins were all forgiven & that I could enter into the celestial Kingdom I did no[t] express my desires to any but the Lord. & my prayer was fully answered when my father rose up & spoke I prayed that He would speak through him to me & almost as soon as he had commenced he turned to me and began to talk of my sufferings & how hard the destroyer had tired[tried] to cut short my glory because he knew that I would do a good work & prove true to the principles that God had established in the earth & he prophesied many things upon my head among them was that I should live & should bear sons & daughters who would be a great blessing & an honor to me & others also, & to the Kingdom of God. I was perfectly overcome & wept for joy, I had received more than I asked for. He said that the destroyer would have been pleased to have taken me & was perfectly willing that I should die easy & happily, but he was mad at him & took the next step to cause him all the trouble that he possibly could but he should not accomplish his end." Brian Hales' Mormon Polygamy, p. 47-48, Documents, 71.040-71.045, https://mormonpolygamydocuments.org/jsp-document-book-71/.

23   Ibid., p. 48.

Eliza R. Snow Smith

Helen had been a student in Sister Snow's Kirtland school—and then years later, had watched as this beloved sister moved about in Winter Quarters, wandering from hut to destitute hut as she administered hope to her afflicted sisters. Now Helen and Eliza were living in Utah, and both were suffering from debilitating health challenges. Although they lived only half a block from one another, their illnesses prevented them from enjoying the felicity of in-person visits. Consequently, they turned to writing—communicating through a stream of letters. Helen received the elder sister's counsel with joy, and Eliza's missives gave Helen the strength to persevere through her moments of shadow, when a ray of light was most welcome:

// Many a time have her words dropped like refreshing dews from the heavens, like manna they have come when most needed, reviving and giving new hope to the weary and hungry soul. Our intimacy began the first winter after we came to this valley; we were both invalids and though we lived within half a block's distance of each other, we were unable to walk it; but we could communicate our thoughts and feelings by letter which we often did, though paper like every other commodity at that time was very scarce; we never left any blank space. Her notes contained many things which were to me as precious treasures, which I have preserved among other choice relics of the past.[24]

---

24   Helen Mar Kimball Whitney, "Life Incidents," *Woman's Exponent* 9, no. 22 (April 15, 1881): 170.

These experiences of ultimate triumph over pain, tremendous loss, exquisite heartache, and even her own impending death left Helen strengthened and assured. This was her moment of conversion—the instance when her faith became *certain knowledge* and testimony.

Helen's remarkable journey had taken her from a young teenage girl, struggling with doubts and inner conflict, to a young bride driven from her home into the untamed wilderness, to a young mother grieving the loss of her first two children, and then had culminated at last into a rebirth and spiritual endowment of power that few women, regardless of their age, ever have the opportunity to experience. She later acknowledged in her writings:

// I truly rejoice that I have had the privilege of being numbered with those who have come up through much tribulation and gained a knowledge for myself that this is the work of God which neither wealth nor worldly honors could tempt me to part with. This is a world of sorrow and disappointment. Life and every thing here is uncertain, but beyond is eternal life and exaltation.[25]

Helen endured suffering—tremendous suffering—but through it all, she *overcame*. She listened to her father's prophetic utterances, which, no doubt, gave her peace—but it was gaining a victory in her own fiery struggle, and triumphing over her internal spiritual battle, that endowed her with great joy and a personal witness of eternal principles—a firm foundation where she learned to trust solely in God. She found herself basking in newfound strength and confidence with the ushering in of the new year, even a new chapter of her life. Helen had a great work to do, a legacy that would leave its mark on her family and the Church she so loved. Her voice would live on to change the lives of generations of Latter-day Saint women— including, for us, those in the past, present, and future. But long before this triumph was possible, Helen would have to accept a new sacrifice—the vulnerability of laying bare her trials and experiences to the public eye. Would she be willing to set aside personal comfort to speak up and testify?

---

25   Helen Mar Kimball Whitney, "Early Reminiscences," *Woman's Exponent* 8, no. 24 (May 15, 1880): 188.

CHAPTER 11

A Quiet Voice Urges Helen to Speak

⸺

Helen's newfound witness and spiritual rebirth initiated a fresh, new chapter in her life. Helen would utilize her wisdom and experience to bless those she came in contact with—both in person and through the medium of pen, paper, and ink. Trials and afflictions were far from over, but she now embraced her calling with an enduring anchor—a firm foundation established on the Rock of Jesus Christ. Her crucible planted the seeds that would direct her life's mission, defining her legacy.

True testimony always bears fruits of action, for it is not enough to merely know—all must stand as witnesses. Helen could not, and *would not*, keep her cherished testimony to herself. Speaking to Latter-day Saint women in her day, as well as those in the distant future, she pled:

" Until my faith was established and I knew for myself that this work was true, and that my future happiness or misery depended upon the course I took here whether I received or rejected the principles contained in the everlasting gospel, I was like a ship without an anchor liable to be tossed to and fro by the various trials and temptations that beset me. . . .

To my young friends who may have experienced similar trials I will say *"seek first the kingdom of God and its righteousness and all other things shall be added thereto;"* for this is the only legitimate way for us to obtain happiness; *I know this to be true* and would that it were possible for me to impress it upon the minds of the youth that they might not have to suffer sorrow and perhaps despair and everlasting woe.[1]

Settling into the Salt Lake Valley, Horace and Helen "made their home on the bank of City Creek, just east of where the [Salt Lake] Temple stands . . ."[2] To provide for his family, Horace taught school, wrote as a journalist, and later served as a clerk in the Tithing Office.

In September 1849, Helen would give birth to her third child—yet another infant who would tragically pass into eternity, joining his brother and sister. Helen's longing for children weighed heavily on her, and it would be another four long years before she would be blessed at long last with a daughter, born in June 1853 and named Vilate Murray—a beautiful and fitting tribute to Helen's own dear mother. At last, she would revel in the delighted squeals and pitter-patter of tiny feet that bring so much joy to a mother's heart. Two years later, the Whitney household would grow again when a son, Orson Ferguson, was born. Orson would later become a bishop at the tender age of 23, and be called as a member of the Quorum of the Twelve Apostles just before his 51st birthday, in 1906. Other Whitney children would follow—namely, Elizabeth Ann (Lillie), Genevieve (Gen or Genny), Helen Kimball (Henty), Charles Spaulding (Charley), Florence Marian (Flod) and Phebe Isabel.

"Publish to the world . . . a true history"

Horace and Helen began living the principle of Celestial plural marriage together when Horace married Lucy Amelia Bloxham in October 1850. Helen struggled at first to transition plural marriage from a theoretical doctrine into practical daily life, but this perplexity came to an abrupt halt when Lucy passed away less than a year later during childbirth. Helen cared for Lucy's newborn infant, but sadly, he too passed away, leaving yet another hole in the Whitney household. Later, Horace would be sealed to Mary Cravath, with whom Helen had a good relationship overall.

Helen often reflected on the near-indescribable and profound experiences she'd lived through, and as time passed, she felt the

---

1   Helen Mar Kimball Whitney, "Retrospection," *Woman's Exponent* 10, no. 3 (July 1, 1881): 18; italics in original.

2   "Helen Mar Whitney: Her Death—A Sketch of Her Personal History," *Deseret Evening News*, November 16, 1896, 2; italicized in original.

gentle nudge of a sacred, quiet voice stirring within, compelling her to document the history of her people and to share the testimony that now burned brightly within her. "Publish to the world not only the principles of your faith, but a true history of facts," the voice urged—a *true history*:

❝ . . . concerning the injustice done to an innocent people, and the trials and sufferings which they have endured from the world, because they would not deny their faith in revelation. Publish them upon the housetops, that they may reach the ears of the just and the honest in heart in all nations.[3]

Helen did not consider herself the only woman called to this responsibility; she felt that all faithful women of the Church were commissioned with a sacred trust. Helen believed that women play an indispensable role in the marvelous work and wonder of the latter days. She and her sister Saints had stood side by side with the elders in laying the very foundation of the Church. The sisters of Zion had toiled with their fathers, brothers, and sons in laying upon the sacrificial altar every earthly possession—every carnal and selfish inclination—that they might herald the Prophet Joseph Smith's revelations. But then, after a life so lived, "Should we not write [our history]," Helen reasoned, "to be handed down to our children and all future generations, that they may know the true history of those who endured all things which their enemies saw fit to place upon them, for the sake of establishing this work upon the earth"?[4] Her voice would echo the sentiments of the patriarchs and prophets of this dispensation—she knew she had a sacred duty to defend the Restoration.

Helen's testimony was sorely needed. During the mid-to-late 1800s, fresh, deadly venom was flowing rapidly from the pens of bitter enemies of the Church. Men and women who had once called themselves 'Mormons'—who had been regarded as cherished brothers and sisters in the Gospel, who had borne testimony of the Restoration and received incredible heavenly manifestations, and who had even made sacred covenants and been ordained with the

3 Helen Mar Kimball Whitney, "Scenes and Incidents in Nauvoo," *Woman's Exponent* 10, no. 15 (January 1, 1882): 114.

4 Ibid.

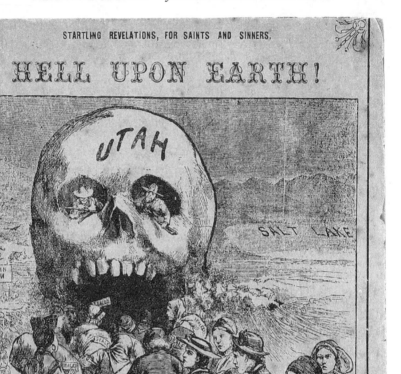

*"Startling Revelations for Saints and Sinners. Hell Upon Earth!
How Women and Girls are Ensnared"*

1882 Illustration by former member of the Church, W. Jarman.

holy priesthood—now exhausted their energy in spreading distorted slander and inciting anger against the Latter-day Saints.

No family was immune to these attacks—least of all the President of the Church, Brigham Young, who was divorced by one of his wives, Ann Eliza, in 1875. The year following, Ann Eliza published her sensational 'exposé of Mormonism,' evoking unmerited sympathy across the United States through her wild, emotionally-charged tales of supposed abuse and exploitation.[5] Among her many accusations, Ann Eliza claimed Brigham Young had threatened to excommunicate her parents and destroy her brother financially if she did not marry him. Alleging coercion into plural marriage through this ultimatum, Ann Eliza wrote dramatic portrayals of President Young as an adulterous husband who abused his wives and exercised manipulative control over his household. She also publicly mocked and exploited the temple endowment and many other sacred rites and ordinances. Ann Eliza went on to join an active crusade against the Church, arguing that she desired to:

// . . . impress upon the world what Mormonism really is; to show the pitiable condition of its women, held in a system of bondage that is more cruel than African slavery ever was, since it claims to hold body and soul alike . . .[6]

However, Ann Eliza's facade would not hold up forever, and as her true colors began to show, she became increasingly estranged from those closest to her—her two sons and their families. Her grandson later remarked: "I hope to hell I never see her again."[7] Carried away by the sensationalism she had created, Ann Eliza lived the life of a celebrity pro tempore—but truth always emerges over time, and soon, her life began to unravel. Ann Eliza had already been divorced once before her marriage to Brigham Young. After leaving the Church, she entered a third marriage, which also ended in divorce. Ann Eliza charged her third husband with adultery, and then disappeared from the public scene in a flurry of financial problems.

---

5   Ann Eliza Young, *Wife No. 19* (Chicago: Dustin, Gilman & Co., 1876).

6   Ibid., 32.

7   Irving Wallace, *The Twenty-seventh Wife* (New York: Simon & Schuster, 1961), 427.

Although the names and character of those who promoted such gross slander against the Church have largely been forgotten in the dusty annals of history, the lies and scandals they perpetuated never seemed to end. A series of lurid novels published in the 1850s spread like wildfire throughout the United States—depicting Mormon women as naive and overly sheltered victims trapped in harems—tortured, abused, and exploited.[8]

As Latter-day Saint women read with disgust the outrageous lies printed in newspapers across the country, their blood began to boil with righteous indignation. Among those incensed with the blatant misrepresentation of her people, Helen Mar herself wrote the editor of the *Woman's Exponent* in October 1880:

"The Judge," with the caption, "An Unsightly Object—Who Will Take an Axe and Hew It Down?" (1882)

---

8   Examples are seen in works such as *Boadicea: the Mormon Wife* (1855, Alfreda Eva Bell), *The Prophets: Or, Mormonism Unveiled* (1855, Orvilla S. Belisle), *Mormon Wives; A Narrative of Facts Stranger Than Fiction* (1856, Metta Victoria Fuller Victor) and *Female Life Among the Mormons: A Narrative of Many Years' Personal Experience by the Wife of a Mormon Elder, Recently from Utah* (1855, Maria Ward, a pseudonym).

"*The Mormon Octopus Enslaving the Women of Utah*" (1882)

"*The Mormon Question,*" *Daily Graphic* (1883)

❙❙ When reading in last evening's [*Deseret*] *News* the proceedings of our would-be tyrants, I confess that for a moment I felt warmed up and really indignant. It seems that we "poor, down-trodden women," whose sorrows and sufferings called forth so much PITY until it was disgusting to every true hearted "Mormon" woman have disappointed our very "liberal" and sympathetic friends! We really love our husbands and prefer to be governed by our brethren instead of by our acknowledged enemies.[9]

Helen Reevaluates Her Priorities

Heber C. Kimball had communicated to his daughter Helen his desire for her to write her own autobiography nearly a decade before, but she had put off acting on his counsel. Where was the time for such a commitment? Eight years following her father's death, however, a re-evaluation of Helen's priorities commenced after a refreshing visit with Eliza R. Snow and Margaret Thompson Smoot in 1876. With wisdom and foresight, Eliza and Margaret encouraged Helen to make the necessary sacrifices to become an author and defender of the Restoration:

❙❙ My Father when on his last mission East wrote me a letter and in it requested me to write my history in one of his large Books & when his own was written said that mine should go in with it but I never felt inclined to until the year 1876, in the 47th year of my age Being very feeble, so much so that I was confined to my room through <the> winter . . .

The Dr could not cure <u>me</u> so <u>I'd</u> <u>no</u> <u>other</u> source to look to but my Father in Heaven so concluded to send for Sister Snow who came soon bringing sister Smoot. They washed & anointed me & I was greatly comforted. We talked about many things & among the rest I told some of my experience. Sister Smoot told me she thought I would be a great benefit to the young sisters to hear my history & she considered it my duty to tell them. She had told me the same when I was at her house in Provo, and that night I made up my mind to commence my biography as it

---

9   Helen Mar Kimball Whitney, "Our 'Liberal' Clique!," *Woman's Exponent* 9, no. 9 (October 1, 1880): 70; italics in original.

Helen Mar Kimball Whitney

would serve two purposes, my mind would be occupied & this last reason stimulated me more than any other to undertake it.[10]

Eliza and Margaret's counsel seemed to unleash Helen's pen, as she began documenting history and current events for the benefit of her fellow sisters, and for future generations—a valuable perspective

---

10   Helen M. Whitney reminiscences and diary, 1876, p. 3-4, 22-23, Church History Library, https://catalog.churchofjesuschrist.org/assets/3d699b7f-4abd-43d1-b3fc-f05f20b64368/0/3; underline in original.

from a female eyewitness. As she engaged in this new endeavor, Helen felt the Lord endow her with strength and comfort while writing:

❝❝ I was up stairs in a peaceful pleasant room where I had nothing to disturb my thoughts & after I commenced writing I gained in strength. —I became so absorbed in the past that I lost sight of the present, & almost fancied that I was young and living my life over again. Some portions of which brought sweetest joy, & others never failed to bring tears to my eyes, I realy felt that I was blessed in doing this & never again was I lonesome while occupied in that way.[11]

Helen took comfort in reliving her personal history through her writing, but also in following her father's counsel. As she did so, she felt him prompting her in the furtherance of her work:

❝❝ ... last night [I] Dreamed that father came to me & told me to get that article ready for publication—meening one that I'd partly written some time ago, & had thought a day or two past, that this was the propper time for it to come out, and in my prayer—asked to know, and to be guided by the true spirit, what I should do. Whether this was the answer I am not able to say. but think, may be[12]

Helen loved the Gospel of Jesus Christ with all her heart. Her primary themes as an author centered on defending plural marriage and promoting an accurate history of the Church. However, she occasionally branched out into other topics of interest.[13] Ultimately, Helen's greatest desire was to defend truth and preach the Gospel by sharing her personal experiences and understanding as an early member of the Church of Jesus Christ of Latter-day Saints.

---

11   Helen M. Whitney reminiscences and diary, 1876, p. 23, Church History Library, https://catalog.churchofjesuschrist.org/assets/3d699b7f-4abd-43d1-b3fc-f05f20b64368/0/22.

12   October 1, 1885. Charles M. Hatch and Todd M. Compton, *A Widow's Tale: 1884-1896 Diary of Helen Mar Kimball Whitney* (Logan: Utah State University Press, 2003), 106.

13   "Finished my article for publication—The subject being the signs of the Times and the necessity of every soul obtaining a knowledge for themselves that this Latter day work is true to be able to endure to the end—quoted from early teachings of the Prophet Joseph." August 29, 1888. Ibid., 318.

CHAPTER 12

A Voice Unleashed

HELEN DEFENDS JOSEPH

Since her early childhood, Helen had felt an inner calling to "plead the cause of suffering innocence—to go on the side of the oppressed at all times."[1] Being gifted with the ability to express herself in writing, she would use this consecrated talent as a latter-day Esther to step forward and defend her own oppressed people. She published her first periodical in the *Woman's Exponent* in 1880, coincidentally also the 50-year jubilee celebrating the organization of the Church in 1830. This date was significant to her, she felt, as she opened her writing with the following observation:

> // This has been proclaimed as a year of jubilee to the Latter-day Saints and I truly rejoice that I have had the privilege of being numbered with those who have come up through much tribulation and gained a knowledge for myself that this is the work of God which neither wealth nor worldly honors could tempt me to part with. This is a world of sorrow and disappointment. Life and every thing here is uncertain, but beyond is eternal life and exaltation. The experience of the Latter-day Saints during the past fifty years has disciplined and prepared them in a measure for the great and wonderful changes which are coming, while those who know not God are groping as it were in midnight darkness.[2]

---

1 Helen Mar Kimball Whitney, "Life Incidents," *Woman's Exponent* 9, no. 5 (August 1, 1880): 38.

2 Helen Mar Kimball Whitney, "Early Reminiscences," *Woman's Exponent* 8, no. 24 (May 15, 1880): 188.

Helen's first periodical was published on May 15, with successive writings published on June 1 and June 15, 1880. This was a fortuitous year for her, as she also celebrated the birth of her first grandchild a few months later in October. Helen was a mother, a grandmother, a wife, and a local Latter-day Saint, endeavoring to juggle her responsibilities and daily demands. She had no career as an author, there was no funding for her work, and no leader had set her apart with this calling—in essence, Helen was a busy woman with a chaotic life who sacrificed to carve out the time needed. She did not wait to be commanded in all things—she saw a need and took it upon herself to fill the void. Joseph Smith and the doctrine of the Gospel needed to be sustained—she would sustain them.

It seems that throughout history, the greatest work for the Lord has almost always been accomplished by seemingly unqualified men and women lacking the funding or position to build the Kingdom— whether a shepherd boy from ancient Israel, a 14-year-old farm boy from upstate New York, or a simple potter, like Helen's father. All of these stalwart servants, and many more, carried the unseen credentials of foreordination from before the foundations of the Earth were laid. Lacking worldly means, these men and women utilized the powers of faith, inspiration, discipline, and obedience to forge through conflict and accomplish incredible deeds in spite of the competing demands around them. They saw a need, and they volunteered to fill that deficiency, saying: 'Lord, here am I; send me.'[3] Likewise, today, each one of us has an ember of opportunity within us—a calling to actively build up the Kingdom of God, and the fire of our own foreordination that we must *remember* notwithstanding our personal limitations and our busy, distracted lives.

Helen Challenges the Reorganized Church

Helen continued writing through 1881—but in 1882, she undertook a new challenge by publicly confronting the son of her 'sister wife,' Emma Smith (now Bidamon), who had taken a decidedly antagonistic stance toward the Church centered in the Salt Lake Valley. Helen would publish this challenge in 1882 under the title, *Plural Marriage as Taught by the Prophet Joseph: A reply to Joseph Smith [III], Editor of the Lamoni (Iowa) "Herald."*

---

3   See, for example, Isaiah 6:8.

Joseph Smith III[4] was the first biological child of Joseph and Emma to survive to adulthood, and became the first "Prophet-President" of the Reorganized Church.[5] He asserted a claim to authority as a birthright from his father, and he expressed extreme hostility toward Brigham Young and the Church in Utah. Joseph III also denied that his father ever practiced plural marriage. He organized an effort to send missionaries to Utah to "reclaim" the people from Brigham Young's 'tyranny.'[6] For Helen, however, this was not just a theological

---

4   Joseph Smith III was born November 6, 1832 to Joseph Smith, the Prophet, and Emma Hale. His cousin, Joseph F. Smith, was born six years later on November 13, 1838, to Hyrum Smith and Mary Fielding. The two cousins would become leaders of their respective churches, with Joseph F. Smith leaving a powerful legacy of defending the Prophet Joseph's character and doctrine.

5   The Church of Jesus Christ of Latter-day Saints claimed Brigham Young and the Quorum of the Twelve Apostles jointly held that role, but others disagreed. Founded originally with the support of Joseph Smith III and Emma Smith Bidamon, The Reorganized Church of Jesus Christ of Latter Day Saints (RLDS), known today as the Community of Christ, upheld Joseph's son, Joseph Smith III, as the true successor. Emma's other sons, Frederick, Alexander, and David, became zealous defenders of the Reorganized Church, expressing extreme antagonism toward the "Brighamites" who had emigrated to Utah after being exiled from Nauvoo.

6   When Joseph Smith III first spoke as leader of the Reorganized Church of Jesus Christ of Latter-Day Saints at Amboy, Illinois, on April 6, 1860, he expressed his unqualified aversion to the Mormon doctrine of plural marriage: "There is but one principle by the leaders of any faction of this people that I hold in utter abhorrence; that is a principle taught by Brigham Young and those believing in him." Then in April 1863, the Reorganized Church approved of sending missionaries to Utah in order to 'reclaim' the Mormons from the authoritative leadership of Brigham Young, and to vocally condemn the practice of plural marriage. The Reorganized Church also never adopted or taught the doctrines and ordinances restored by the Prophet Joseph Smith related to baptism for the dead, temple endowments, or eternal marriages, including monogamous sealings. Roger D. Launius, "Methods and Motives: Joseph Smith III's Opposition to Polygamy, 1860-90," *Dialogue: A Journal of Mormon Thought* 20 (Winter 1987): 105-120.

"Their method of proselyting was of the unusual nature, a tirade of abuse and false accusation hurled at the authorities of the Church. Encouraged by the anti-'Mormon' help, they became extremely vindictive in their references to Brigham Young and the present Church authorities. Their sermons were so bitter and malignant—which has been the character of most of their work from the beginning, in Utah—that they raised considerable protest from many respectable citizens. Even non-'Mormons' declared that in no other community would such vicious attacks be tolerated. It appeared at times that these missionaries were attempting to provoke the 'Mormon' people to some act of violence, that it might be seized upon and published to the world through the anti-'Mormon' press that they had been mobbed, and thus capital for their cause be made of it. Fortunately they were not molested to the credit of the people so constantly abused. One of these meetings was attended by a prominent gentleman from the East who was somewhat acquainted with Utah and her people, he said, in conversation with the writer a few days later, that never in his experience has he witnessed such a thing before. 'If that fellow'—referring to a Reorganite who

debate, but familial friction, and—because she was the sister wife of Joseph III's mother, Emma—she recognized his accusations as a slanderous indictment of adultery and deceit against both herself and the other women who faithfully practiced the doctrine, who suffered character assassination and societal humiliation for their testimonies. Helen strongly defended the doctrine in a letter to Mary Bond, writing:

> *//* . . . the Josephites are not the true church. Emma [S]mith died with a wicked falsehood upon her lips if that printed testimony was hers, for my mother & Mother Whitney as well as many others, who are yet living were knowing to the fact of Emma's accepting the principle & she gave three young . . . women who lived with her to Joseph Smith her husband & I testify that I was intimately acquainted with them as well as others who were sealed to him and my father taught it me, the first time that I ever heard of it, as a saving pure and holy principle. I afterwards [sat?] in my father's house with him & my mother listened to the Prophet teach it. I believed that it was right . . .[7]

A heated debate ensued when Joseph III responded directly to Helen Mar after she published an article in the *Woman's Exponent* on June 1, 1882. In her article, she described her parents' conversion to Celestial plural marriage, as well as Joseph Smith's struggle to introduce it in Nauvoo. She also recalled a time when Joseph had attempted to raise the subject during a Sabbath meeting, but was met with such a general uproar among his listeners that he found himself being forced to retreat from the subject and reserve it only for those whose hearts were more aptly prepared:

> *//* Although the Lord had revealed the principle of Celestial Marriage to Joseph Smith in an early day, the astounding revelation and command to proclaim it was not given until

---

has since been promoted in his church—'should come to our town and abuse the ministers of our church, calling them murderers, thieves, and liars, as he did Brigham Young and your churchmen, we would kick him off the streets.'" Joseph Fielding Smith, *Origin of the "Reorganized" Church and the Question of Succession* (Salt Lake City: The Deseret News, 1909), 3.

7   Brian Hales' Mormon Polygamy Documents, 71.040-71.045, https:// mormonpolygamydocuments.org/jsp-document-book-71/.

Joseph Smith III

after the Saints had settled in Nauvoo. Joseph put off the dreaded day as long as he dared. I recollect on a certain Sabbath, previous to the Apostles' return from Europe, of hearing my mother and others expressing their wonder and astonishment at what they had heard uttered that day by the Prophet, upon the restoration of all things, etc. His wife as well as others was quite excited over it. Seeing the effect that his sermon had upon his hearers in the afternoon, he consoled them by saying that the time which he had spoken of might be further off than he had viewed it; at all events the Lord would help them and carry them safely through it, if they were faithful.[8]

In her article, Helen published excerpts from letters between her father and mother, as well as a postscript from Sarah Noon, her father's first plural wife. Sarah had been sealed to Helen's father, Heber, by Joseph Smith while in Nauvoo. Helen went on to explain that she had experienced her own firsthand conversations with the Prophet on the subject—a demythifying fact in direct contradiction

8   Helen Mar Kimball Whitney, "Scenes and Incidents in Nauvoo," *Woman's Exponent* 10, no. 12 (November 15, 1881): 93.

to claims that Brigham Young was the originator of the practice. Her stated purpose was to establish Joseph Smith as the original revealer of Celestial plural marriage, and to clarify that Brigham Young and the Latter-day Saints who had emigrated west were simply following Joseph's direction. Turning her attention to Joseph Smith III, she challenged him for spreading the falsehood that suggested "polygamy"—the pejorative and inaccurate term he used—was not introduced until 1852, and that it was done by "wicked men," to "cover up their crimes."[9] Addressing the personal accusation he had hurled against many hundreds of her fellow Latter-day Saints, Helen spared no words in expressing her feelings:

> He must be blind not to see that his own tongue has condemned him, not only as an uninspired leader, but an unprincipled enemy to his own father's house. . . . A poor captain and soldier of the cross he would make to stand as his *father's representative* to carry out the purposes of the Almighty, for which the Prophet was willing to suffer with his people, and endure every kind of persecution, imprisonment and death, for the sake of the religion which his son Joseph, under the inspiration of the Evil one, has denied, and is now leagued himself with the worst enemies of his father to destroy the work for which he had to suffer so much and at last lay down his life.[10]

Helen reasoned that inspiration could only come with "honesty and sincerity of heart and purpose . . . subduing our *wills* and the pride of our hearts."[11] She also challenged Joseph III by quoting the teachings of his father, Joseph Smith Jr., and by appealing to scripture. She charged him with negligence for failing to follow in the footsteps of his father, reminding him that the Prophet Joseph had suffered much and been persecuted for his valiant defense of the Gospel. The course taken by Joseph III had led him far from the path his father had walked:

---

9   Helen Mar Kimball Whitney, "Scenes and Incidents in Nauvoo," *Woman's Exponent* 11, no. 1 (June 1, 1882): 2.

10   Ibid., 2; italicized in original.

11   Ibid., 2; italicized in original.

❧ The life of the Prophet Joseph was very different from that of his son's, who says, "'Mormonism' proper, as a religion, was at the option of any one to believe unmolested and undisturbed," etc., but if he was actuated by the same spirit he would certainly have had a similar experience. His father's life was similar to that of every true prophet; and every one who enlists in the true service of Christ, if he is valiant for that cause, may look for persecution, which will be just in proportion to his diligence in opposing the enemy of all righteousness and his agents.[12]

Defending Celestial Plural Marriage

Helen's responses to Joseph III were published in a detailed pamphlet titled, *Plural Marriage as Taught by the Prophet Joseph Smith*. Helen took time to refute claims that the Book of Mormon denounced plural marriage, she spoke of marriage in the days of the biblical patriarchs (Abraham, Isaac, and Jacob), and then, fueled with what seems to be righteous indignation, she defended the integrity of all women who have been plural wives under the direction of God. "What do we read about Hannah, Rachael, Ruth, Bathsheba and other holy women?" she questioned. "Were they in a shameful condition of legalized prostitution, or were they lawful and honored wives?"[13] Helen would later explain that Celestial principles of marriage had been revealed by God to offer hope for women who desired to be sealed to a virtuous man—women who despaired after the realities of life had revealed the sad truth that "real men are rare."[14] If any woman so desired, she had a right to a man who would respect, love, care for, and honor her integrity—a man honorable himself—a man

---

12   Helen Mar Whitney, *Plural Marriage as Taught by the Prophet Joseph* (Salt Lake City: Juvenile Instructor Office, 1882), 8.

13   Ibid., 28.

14   "Every woman was designed to be the glory of some man instead of being prostituted to administer to his wanton pleasures and to be bought and sold like goods and chattels. Those who have no regard for virtue and keep not the laws of God, fail to answer the end of their creation. It is useless to try to shut our eyes to the fact that 'real men are rare,' especially such as have souls sufficiently large to take upon themselves the responsibility of families. This being the case there are thousands of good women, among whom are those who have been born and nursed in the lap of luxury, who, under the present system of monogamy are denied the blessings of matrimony. They are deprived of their birthright and forced by this tyrannical and unjust law to live and die 'old maids.'" Ibid., 47-48.

who would never betray her for unbridled passions, sexual perversion, or lusts. God had provided a way for every woman to be treated with dignity, and no woman would ever have to settle for less. For Helen and many other women, plural marriage represented the redemption and elevation—*not* the subjugation—of women.

Helen also wrote of Levirate marriage, which God did not merely condone—but established as a *requirement* for Israelite families:

> **//** ... it was a law in Israel, and it was an express command of the Almighty that if a brother should die without offspring the surviving brother (no exception was made if he were married) should marry his widow. We read in the thirty-eighth chapter of Genesis that a certain son of Judah, who, according to this law, should have taken his brother's widow, was put to death by the act of the Almighty because of his wickedness in taking a course to prevent rearing offspring by this woman.

> The Savior was unsparing in His rebukes where merited. Both He and His apostles denounced the sins of hypocrisy and adultery, but they never rebuked any one for living in polygamy.

> If polygamy were so great a sin these holy men certainly would not have remained silent upon this subject; but we do not find a single passage within the Holy Bible which condemns it.[15]

Helen then turned her attention to arguments that suggested the Prophet Joseph Smith had fought polygamy by sharing her own, firsthand experience:

> **//** ... I have a personal knowledge that the Prophet did teach and perform every ordinance which has ever been administered by Brigham Young, or any of the Presidency of this Church, and that they were first administered by him, his wife, Emma, being a co-worker with him, notwithstanding all her statements to the contrary.[16]

Helen's narrative provided dates, facts, and other eyewitness testimony that Joseph Smith both taught and practiced the

---

15   Ibid., 28-30.
16   Ibid., 14.

principle of Celestial plural marriage in Nauvoo. She wrote that there were "hundreds" of Saints "aware of these things, [and that] it would be useless for me or any one to undertake to deny it even if we wished to."[17] She had had far more than just an occasional interaction with this principle and its practice: Her father-in-law had been in possession of the original copy of the very revelation in question—Doctrine and Covenants 132—as dictated by the mouth of Joseph Smith, and her own husband, Horace, had been assigned to make a copy. She referenced her parents' integrity, especially her mother, whom she described as having "never deceived nor taught her children an untruth."[18] Her father, she continued, was a knowledgeable witness—both in terms of his own experience in living it, and also in the role of mediator when Joseph & Emma experienced marital conflict:

// I know of the blessings received by my father and mother through this man of God, and of their daily associations with him and his wife Emma. When he could do nothing with her he would send for my father, for whom she had such love and unbounded respect that he could always make peace between them, and this was how he received the appellation of the "peace-maker."[19]

Emma's children and their followers denied that Joseph had expressed his desire—had even prophesied—that the Saints should settle in the Rocky Mountains; admitting this fact would immediately call into question their own failure to heed his counsel. Helen refuted their claims of this denial by providing excerpts from several of the well-documented sermons and statements given by Joseph Smith before his death that demonstrated his wishes for, and knowledge of, the Saints' settling in the West, in Utah—or Deseret, as the Saints preferred to call their mountain home. Why, she asked, would Brigham Young and the early pioneers choose this forbidding, "desolate, barren and out-of-the-way" desert, unless the Lord had directed them to settle there, just as Joseph prophesied?:

---

17   Ibid., 15.
18   Ibid., 16.
19   Ibid., 14.

II ... if he [Brigham Young] had not been led by some other spirit than selfishness and a desire to gratify his own worldly ambition he would have accepted the tempting offers held out to settle upon the Pacific coast, in a land of gold mines. If he had not allowed wisdom to lead and control his actions he would not have chosen the path that he did—struggling on for years with the untoward circumstances that met him in every shape, and the care of a great people dependent upon him and his brethren, not only for counsel, but many for food, raiment and shelter. If there was ever a great father upon this earth he was one, and if it had not been for the deep-rooted faith which they had in the revelations and predictions of Joseph Smith, and if they had not been of the true metal, they could never have endured and carried out the programme which he, by the light of revelation, had marked out.[20]

Three years after sparring with her sister-wife's son, Helen was returning to Salt Lake by train after a trip away from home, when two unknown men entered her car and sat down in front of her. One of the men gave Helen an odd feeling—the sensation that he was a "gentile" and her intuition suggested he was "one that would not hessitate to have several women at a time." What was her surprise when she later learned that that man was none other than Joseph Smith III:

II Between Juab & Nephi, Joseph Smith of Lamoni, and another man boarded the Car we were in, and sat in front of us—one seet between I didnt know this till after they'd got out at Nephi, where they were to hold a meeting. This we were told by a brother, who came to speak to my companion. How we regretted not knowing this, though I'd took a good look at him, & remarked that he must be a gentile, and I judged one that would not hessitate to have several women at a time—probably was an officer or one of our persecuters. If I had known him, I'd been more bold to criticise, & tempted to make myself known. The man on the next seet, who came with him bought a Tribune, & they seemed to enjoy it. It contained the news of the arrest

---

20   Ibid., 17.

of Apostle Lorenzo Snow as also the Morning Herald, which was also there for sail.[21]

Helen had been raised by and associated with men who she described as noble, honorable and virtuous, and her keen eye, along with her natural sense of discernment allowed her to easily detect a counterfeit. Helen had often expressed her wonder at why Joseph III would take so much interest in persecuting the Salt Lake Valley Saints, pointing out that if his mind was occupied in building God's work, surely he would have no time for "persecuting [his] neighbors . . ."[22] Why the obsession? What was the ulterior motive?

Throughout her life, Helen's ultimate priority was defending the doctrines of the Restoration and defending the Prophet Joseph Smith. She openly acknowledged that many inwardly base and vulgar men had abused Celestial plural marriage—creating a counterfeit 'polygamy.'[23] However, Helen Mar—the 14-year-old sealed to Joseph Smith—raised her voice in clear and unmistakable defense that the Prophet had never abused the order—that he was a man of honor, virtue, and integrity.[24] Her testimony, perhaps even more so than

---

21   Charles M. Hatch and Todd M. Compton, *A Widow's Tale: 1884-1896 Diary of Helen Mar Kimball Whitney* (Logan: Utah State University Press, 2003), 118.

22   Helen Mar Whitney, *Plural Marriage as Taught by the Prophet Joseph* (Salt Lake City: Juvenile Instructor Office, 1882), 25.

23   Helen observed, "If some have become degraded in the practice of this celestial order, it is because they were naturally low and depraved, and have occasionally dragged others with them into corruption. The Prophet said this order would damn more than it would save, because it was a holy principle that could not be trifled with.

"I have been a spectator and a participator in this order of matrimony for over thirty years, and being a first wife, I have had every opportunity for judging in regard to its merits. The scriptures declare, "By their fruits ye shall know them;" so I know that this system tends to promote and preserve social purity, and that this alone can remedy the great social evils of the present day. When lived up to as the Lord designed it should be, it will exalt the human family, and those who have entered into it with pure motives and continue to practice it in righteousness can testify to the truth of these statements. There are real and tangible blessings enjoyed under this system which cannot be obtained in any other way. Not only can the cares and burdens be equally distributed among the members of the family, but they can assist one another in many ways, and if blessed with congenial natures and filled with the love of God, their souls will be expanded, and in the place of selfishness, patience and charity will find place in their hearts, driving therefrom all feelings of strife and discord." Ibid., 27.

24   Many men have attempted to live plural marriage without proper authorization from God, or have not lived up to the standard of moral purity, sacrificial love, masculine honor, and exact integrity that God expects from men who are called, or who personally choose, to live this order. These failures have contributed

Brother Joseph, by David Lindsley

the Prophet's other wives, is one of the most compelling evidences in support of Joseph's character:

> *// The Prophet said this & he also said that it [Celestial plural marriage] would damn more than it would [s]ave because so many unprincipled men would take advantage of it, but that did not prove that it was not a pure principle. If Joseph had had any impure desires he could have gratified them in the style of the world with are less danger of his life or his character, than ... to do as he did. The Lord commanded him to teach & to practice that principle & for a great while he dared not to face the frowns which he knew that he was sure to meet, but the*

to familial disorder, heartbreak, and an abuse of this principle. Just as there are husbands and fathers who exhibit abuse within their monogamous marriages, there have been husbands and fathers who have abused their plural marriage covenants. Helen's husband, Horace, was a man of honor, a man who lived this principle with purity. Helen's father was also a man of unquestionable integrity and virtue. Thus, Helen's experiences stemmed from an environment where the men in her life were chaste, resulting in her experiencing blessings commensurate with such behavior. Helen speaks from the perspective that the only men who should be allowed to engage in this practice are those who are men of a caliber equal to her father or her husband. She understood that this was a Celestial principle meant to be lived by those working to achieve a Celestial standard of living—and not for those who are destined for telestial climes.

threats of the Almighty made him willing to lay down his life for the truth & no man could do any more tha[n] he has done & he will wear a martyr's crown.[25]

Helen's personal experience living plural marriage in Utah, and her position as one of Joseph Smith's plural wives, rendered her a unique authority as she mounted a vocal defense of the principle. This generated considerable interest, leading to letters of inquiry from across the country, as well as social calls from curious visitors. In 1884, she published *Why We Practice Plural Marriage, by a 'Mormon' Wife and Mother.* The pamphlet took an interesting approach by compiling a series of letters that passed between Helen and a non-member friend from outside the Utah area. This exchange allowed Helen to discuss many of the 'frequently asked questions.' Her first pamphlet, *Plural Marriage as Taught by Joseph Smith*, investigated the question of whether the doctrine originated with the Prophet Joseph Smith, and whether it was in accordance with the scriptural teachings contained within the Bible and Book of Mormon—whereas her second pamphlet focused more on the practical questions of *how* the Saints lived this principle and whether or not it was demeaning to the women.

Helen Mar Kimball's readers and visitors asked a variety of questions about the practical implementation of plural marriage. She set out to answer those in her informative pamphlets, *Why We Practice Plural Marriage*, and *Plural Marriage as Taught by the Prophet Joseph*. Because this institution of marriage is a part of Latter-day Saint history and doctrine (although not practiced today by The Church of Jesus Christ of Latter-day Saints), these questions still persist—a curiosity that modern media and critics have capitalized on. For those seeking with honest inquiry, Helen's publications offer valuable insight from a wife and mother who lived this principle firsthand. They contain answers to questions including:

25   Brian Hales' Mormon Polygamy Documents, 71.040-71.045, p. 47, https://mormonpolygamydocuments.org/jsp-document-book-71/.

- Why did women choose, of their own free will, to live plural marriage?

- Did living plural marriage cause a righteous man to lose love for his first wife? How could a man love two women without depriving one or the other?

- Was it possible for two plural wives to love one another sincerely? How did Helen and others deal with jealousy?

- Was it hard for Helen to embrace plural marriage?

- Was plural marriage really ordained by God to provide homes for valiant, unborn children?

- How did plural marriage offer hope for a culture where men in general were not living up to their potential?

- Did some women really welcome additional plural wives out of compassion and a sacrificial desire for other women to enjoy the privilege of marriage to an "honorable" husband?

- Is there justice for men who abuse plural marriage? How were men dealt with who attempted to use plural marriage as a facade for adultery?

- Did plural marriage encourage men to be promiscuous or pure?

- Why did the Lord ask His people to practice this 'peculiar' doctrine?

Copies of Helen's writings are available from the Joseph Smith Foundation, www.JosephSmithFoundation.org

"Physician, heal thyself!"

Helen was not afraid to speak boldly, even delivering painfully sharp rebukes toward the general lack of morality and candor among the collective population of the United States. The ever-increasing rates of adultery and licentiousness were the undeniable fruits of the general illegitimacy of faith and integrity. Helen found it ironic that many of the American men who were engaged in persecuting Latter-day Saint plural families—on the pretense of a supposed moral crusade—secretly harbored mistresses themselves, and regularly visited houses of vice and ill repute. In *Why We Practice Plural Marriage*, Helen recounted a conversation with an acquaintance who was not a member of her faith, who described with repugnance the depths of depravity that existed in American homes and in society generally:

// [The husband of Helen's friend] had been, for many years, the proprietor of a large hotel in one of the western cities, which had been her home from the time they were married. But she had seen enough of the hypocrisy and sin that prevail and are fostered in the midst of society. She related instances where married and unmarried ladies of wealth and influence came there closely veiled to meet clandestinely with men who were fathers and husbands. And this illegal and revolting practice, she said, was carried on day and night, among different classes, and, what was worse, they were mostly church-goers and very distinguished patterns of propriety, who desired so much to convert and bring the "Mormons" up (?) to their own level. Oftentimes those women, she said, were accompanied by their daughters, and even little children came with their mothers for a blind, and in this way were being led into the same path of vice by coming in contact with it. Being a mother herself and seeing the dangers that beset her own children, they had, long since, moved into a separate house.

. . . But to resume. The Rev. T. Dewitt Talmage, of Brooklyn, has given the world the benefit of some midnight explorations, showing what exists in the midst of those righteous (?) souls who are so fearful of contamination from a people afar off that are guilty of the awful crime of marrying all the women they live with and acknowledging them as wives. Says he:

"I could call the names of many of the frequenters of these haunts of sin—judges of courts, distinguished lawyers, officers in churches, political orators that talk on the Republican, Democratic and greenback platforms about God and good morals, until you might almost take them for evangelists, expecting a thousand converts in one night. I have something to tell you more astonishing than that the houses of iniquity are supported by wealthy people, when I tell you they are supported by the heads of families—fathers and husbands, with the awful perjury upon them of broken marriage vows; and while many of them keep their families on niggardly portions, with hardly enough to sustain life, have spent their thousands for the diamonds, and wardrobe, and equipage of iniquity. In the name of high heaven I cry out against this popular iniquity. Such men must be cast out from social life and from business relations. If they will not reform, overboard with them from all decent circles. I lift one half the burden of malediction from the unpitied head of woman and hurl it upon the blasted pate of offending man. By what law of justice does the burning excoriation of society pursue offending woman down off the precipice, while offending man goes kid-gloved into respectable circles, invited up if he has any means, forwarded into political recognition, and all the doors of high life opening to the rap of his gold-headed cane."[26]

Helen expressed her disgust with the hypocrisy exhibited by these pretended luminaries of society. She passionately chastened the United States for its corrupting tumor of abortion, for the subjugation of women, and for the enslavement and separation of white and black families. She called out the hypocrisy of the abolitionists who had "drenched the land with blood to free the African," and then in the same breath, refused to allow them to "mingle in the same society."[27] She was not alone in her condemnation of these reprehensible acts, and she found unity with other non-member social reformers who recognized the same glaring contradictions and duplicity, whose words she included in her own work:

// Young people coolly reckon on divorce in contracting marriage. A Vermont couple married on trial for six months, agreeing to get a divorce if either party did not like.

---

26   Helen Mar Kimball Whitney, *Why We Practice Plural Marriage* (Salt Lake City: Juvenile Instructor Office, 1884), 26-27.

27   Ibid., 34.

[Quoting Senator Brown] ". . . The Mormons may well turn to us and say, 'Physician, heal thyself.' Or, in the language of Him who spake as never man spoke, may turn and look us in the face, and may justly say, 'Thou hypocrite, first cast out the beam out of thine own eye, then thou shalt see clearly to cast out the mote out of thy brother's eye.'" . . .

A distinguished clergyman, of Brookyn, uttered the following:

"Why send missionaries to India when child-murder of daily, almost hourly, occurrence; aye, when the hand that puts money into the contribution-box to-day, yesterday, or a month ago, or to-morrow, will murder her own unborn off-spring?"[28]

The Republican party of 1856 adopted as part of its platform a dedicated effort to abolish "those twin relics of barbarism—Polygamy, and Slavery."[29] Helen was led to question their underlying motives because adultery and fornication ran rampant in the States, and the African Americans affiliated with those members of the Republican party were not treated as equals in society. She wondered: Why didn't the lifestyles and actions of these societal figures correspond with their silver-tongued rhetoric?

Bearing Strong Testimony

Hers was to be a lasting legacy—at the end of her life, the obituary of Helen Mar Kimball (Smith) Whitney noted that "These books [*Why We Practice Plural Marriage* and *Plural Marriage as Taught by the Prophet Joseph*] have gone the world over, and were often inquired after by strangers who were always delighted to see and converse with the woman who wrote them."[30] Modern historians also note that, "As an example of their impact, when Susa Young Gates[31] sent Leo Tolstoy books and pamphlets on Mormonism, she included a copy of Helen Mar's *Why We Practice Plural Marriage*."[32]

---

28   Ibid., 28-29.

29   *Republican Campaign Edition for the Million Containing the Republican Platform* (Boston: John P. Jewett and Company, 1856), 5.

30   "Helen Mar Whitney: Her Death—A Sketch of Her Personal History," *Deseret Evening News*, November 16, 1896, 2.

31   Susa Young Gates was the daughter of Brigham Young and Lucy Bigelow.

32   "Helen Mar Whitney: Her Death—A Sketch of Her Personal History," *Deseret Evening News*, November 16, 1896, 2.

Throughout her life, Helen felt called of God to defend the Restoration and Joseph Smith's teachings on marriage. One of many experiences that cemented the importance and magnitude of this mission in her mind occurred in April 1890 with the following dream:

❧ I dreamed this morn of bearing a strong testimony to the principle of plural marriage. There were persons talking of it— one testimony was that a house where it was honored prospered while one that did not dried up like a dead tree. I testified to its truth, & that my experience had proven it—When the head of the house, & all did right—blessings of a temporal nature poured in till I couldnt help acknowledging it. that the Lord blessed us just according to our works, and so much so that I marveled at it—This was a living fact—just as I dreamed it.[33]

Helen lived uprightly, and stood firmly rooted in the Gospel of Jesus Christ. The trials and toil of life refined and purified this valorous woman who employed the talent of her pen, and the power of her refined spirit, to stand courageously in defense of the faith she loved and lived. Helen Mar not only acknowledged her belief in the sanctity and eternal nature of Celestial families, but through her writings, she became one of its most vocal advocates—and she laid bare her own noble character in the enduring works she produced.

Today, as we look back across the landscape of Restoration history, we can begin to see the wisdom and sagacity of Him who raised up one such as Helen Mar Kimball to defend Joseph Smith's personal character and his teachings on marriage. Helen offered firsthand testimony that plural marriage was revealed and restored through Joseph Smith himself, and that the women in his life knew, personally, that the Prophet was an exceptional and rare example of masculine honor, integrity, courage, and virtue.

---

33   April 23, 1890. Charles M. Hatch and Todd M. Compton, *A Widow's Tale: 1884-1896 Diary of Helen Mar Kimball Whitney* (Logan: Utah State University Press, 2003), 400; underline in original.

CHAPTER 13

Through Great Tribulation

⌘

While living in the New World and nearing his final days in mortality, the ancient patriarch Lehi taught his son, "there is an opposition in all things. If not so . . . righteousness could not be brought to pass . . ."[1] Adversity and affliction will eternally arise to subvert the purposes of God—and Helen's life was no exception to this principle. During her mortal pilgrimage, she was often beset with loss and privation. She knew all too well the depths of personal heartache, and the sting of fiery darts determined to quell her testimony, both before and after she began her work as a female author. However, she also witnessed the promise fulfilled that while sorrow and "weeping may endure for a night,"[2] *joy* surely comes in the morning:

" Ye cannot behold with your natural eyes, for the present time, the design of your God concerning those things which shall come hereafter, and the glory which shall follow after much tribulation.

For after much tribulation come the blessings. Wherefore the day cometh that ye shall be crowned with much glory; the hour is not yet, but is nigh at hand.[3]

---

1 2 Nephi 2:11.

2 Psalm 30:5.

3 Doctrine and Covenants 58:3-4.

Losing Her Father & Mother

In October 1867, Helen's mother passed away, leaving her father devastated and mourning deeply. "I shall not be long after her,"[4] came his prophetic cry of distress—a foretelling that was all too soon fulfilled when Heber breathed his last a short eight months later.[5]

Losing both parents within such a short span of time left an intense, aching void in Helen's heart. She had traversed dark paths and celebrated life's greatest victories with these two dear friends—and now she was forced to bid them farewell. She shared a long, intimate relationship with her mother, and was known as one of her father's most ardent supporters. "Helen was in many respects very like her illustrious father, so much so that it has been said of her by one of his intimate associates, that she was his 'best living representative.'"[6] She often chose to include her maiden surname, 'Kimball,' whenever possible without creating an awkward length of title.[7] Now, with both of her beloved parents departed, she

---

4   Orson F. Whitney, *Life of Heber C. Kimball* (Salt Lake City: Kimball Family, 1888), 483.

5   Heber had petitioned the Lord in October 25, 1842, asking that he and Vilate not be separated long in death—but that they would live the "same length of time." This beautiful request, revealing their deep love for one another, was granted. "Oh my God! I ask thee in the name of Jesus to bless my dear Vilate and comfort her heart and deliver her from temptation, and from all sorrow and open her eyes and let her see things as they are, for Father thou knowest our sorrow; be pleased to look upon thy poor servant and handmaid and grant us the privilege of living the same length of time that one may not go before the other, for thou knowest that we desire this with all our hearts ** and then Father, when we have done with our career in this probation, in the one to come may be still joined in one, to remain so to all eternities, and whatever we have done to grieve thee be pleased to blot it out, and let us be clean and pure before thee at all times, that we may never be left to sin or betray any one that believes on thy name; save us from all this and let our seed be righteous; incline their hearts to be pure and virtuous, and may this extend from generation to generation, let us have favor in thy sight and before thine angels that we may be watched over by them and have strength and grace to support us in the day of our temptation that we may not be overcome and fall. Now my Father these are the desires of our hearts and will thou grant them to us for Jesus sake and to thy name will we give all the glory forever and forever—, amen." Helen Mar Kimball Whitney, "Scenes and Incidents in Nauvoo," *Woman's Exponent* 11, no. 4 (July 15, 1882): 26.

6   "Helen Mar Whitney: Her Death—A Sketch of Her Personal History," *Deseret Evening News*, November 16, 1896, 2.

7   "When I was married father told me to never drop my Kimball name, and for years I kept it up, but it made my name so lengthy that I have left it out, only when requested to add it, but I love the name, and I am oftener addressed by it than any other; I suppose it is owing to the striking resemblance between us." Helen Mar

Vilate Murray Kimball

found herself parsing reflectively the temporal artifacts they left behind. Helen recorded the bittersweet experience she felt while tenderly reviewing her collection of memorabilia:

❝ [My father] wrote me from Pittsburg, that was more than forty years ago; and though his letters are now worn and yellow with age, and the fingers that wrote them are laid under the cold and senseless turf, yet the sublime truths, though taught in simple words, will never perish, no, never; and often as I read them, I drop a silent tear and am led to say:

"I owe thee much. Thou hast deserved from me

Far, far beyond what I can ever pay."[8]

Kimball Whitney, "The Last Chapter of Scenes in Nauvoo," *Woman's Exponent* 12, no. 11 (November 1, 1883): 82.

8   Helen Mar Kimball Whitney, "Scenes and Incidents in Nauvoo," *Woman's Exponent* 11, no. 5 (August 1, 1882): 39.

The letter that evoked such heartfelt emotion was written shortly after Helen was sealed to the Prophet Joseph Smith on July 10, 1843. She published an excerpt of the missive in the *Woman's Exponent* on August 1, 1882:

// My dear daughter, what shall I say to you? I will tell you, learn to be meek and gentle, and let your heart seek after wisdom, and always speak kindly to your dear mother and listen to her counsel while you have her with you, for there is no one that feels the care for you that she does. My child, remember the care that your dear father and mother have for your welfare in this life, that all may be done well, and that in view of eternal worlds, for that will depend upon what we do here, and how we do it; for all things are sacred. God knows my heart and how I feel for my dear family.[9]

As Helen waded through the loneliness that accompanied her loss, sleep brought her occasional dreams—some revealing the depth of her heartache, others offering respite and hope. At times one can detect, perhaps, a longing to join her parents in their state of rest:

// Dreamed of a river which numbers of people were crossing in wagons and some on foot. I wanted to go too and Father—who was there sought to discourage, or hinder me—I felt hurt & thought I could go without troubling him or any one—the water not being so deep but it could be waded—about knee deep, & some were wading it—the streem was clear. & the bottom covered with stones & cobbles.—I take Father's unwillingness for me to cross with him and those people, as a good sign, and my not going as a sign that I'm to live on a while longer.[10]

Just one month earlier, Helen had dreamt of conversing with a deceased Latter-day Saint friend. During this 'interaction,' her friend left her with the comforting knowledge that "We are arround here and know every thing thats being done—they do nothing that we are not witness to—meaning a great many brethren besides

---

9   Ibid.

10   Charles M. Hatch and Todd M. Compton, *A Widow's Tale: 1884-1896 Diary of Helen Mar Kimball Whitney* (Logan: Utah State University Press, 2003), 326.

himself who'd died, but were busily engaged in this cause though not visable to the natural eye."[11] Through experiences like this and others, Helen felt that she was not alone—believing that those who have left this mortal clime and passed into the spirit world are still with us, continuing to minister to their families and loved ones in ways we do not recognize or comprehend.

Losing Vilate & Phebe

In mid-January 1870, grief descended on the Whitney home yet again when Helen's oldest child, 16-year-old Vilate, contracted a fatal disease—one of the most dreaded in her time: tuberculosis. The ordeal was painful, as her feet and legs began to swell with edema— the building up and retention of fluid in bodily tissue. As breathing became increasingly difficult, Helen had to prop her daughter into a sitting position allowing Vilate to labor arduously through each breath. Patiently she held her, supporting her through the anxiety that accompanied gradual asphyxiation. During her last night, the chill of death settled in as Helen held her daughter in her arms close to the warm fire, the young girl's arms wrapped tenderly around her mother's neck in a final embrace. Horace was absent, serving a mission, and thereby missed the opportunity to say goodbye to his beloved daughter. Vilate had drawn her last constrained breath on February 5 at 7:45pm—joining her deceased siblings, maternal grandparents, and paternal grandfather who had preceded her to the other side of the veil.

Helen grieved over the death of yet another precious daughter. One night, in a tender mercy sent from heaven, she was given a dream that communicated hope and peace to her bereaved mother's heart:

> I dreamed that I was walking along & I saw & heard father preaching and prophesying about the car[e]lessness luke-warm condition of <u>his</u> family and others. I walked right up to him all the time hoping that he would let me go home with him. I knew that he had come back from the spirit world & would return again He did not look at me but took my hand & held it untill he was through talking, when with out speaking a word to me he drawd my hand through his left arm & walked

---

11   Ibid., 321.

off, and I hoped & felt that I was going to his home, but did not like to speek & ask him We walked on swiftly, I thought that my Vilate's spirit was on his right side & Orson was at my left, & was rather slow I kept reaching out my left hand to him motioning for him to keep up with us. I thought I was dressed in my Mothers black silk, & black lace shawl (which she gave me before she died) we only walked a little way before we came to a house where there were many people, both old and young. We never stopped in the lower room but crossed it & father took me up a pair of stairs. Orson sat down near the foot of the stairs & took up a Book & began reading. I tried to catch his eyes that I could entice him to follow us, but he didn't look up & when we got to the top step a man stood there to whom father gave some pass-word before we could go on. There was no door & the room was filled with people, I met Br & Sister Woodruff, shook hands & spoke with them and expected to see my mother and daughter Vilate, but awoke without seeing any more. This dream at that time was a great comfort to me. I felt <u>sure</u> that I should soon be free from sickness & sorrow, enjoying their dear society and those of the righteous that had passed behind the Vail.[12]

Helen anticipated that the dream foretold her own approaching release to rejoin her loved ones on the other side of the veil, but the Lord still had a mighty work for her to perform—a work she did not fully comprehend.

Four years later, in the summer of 1874, Helen's youngest child—four-year-old Phebe Isabel—lost her battle with scarlet fever and, with a mother in deep anguish standing by, breathed her last on July 23.[13] Helen was devastated. The resulting heartache had a deleterious effect on her naturally delicate health. The following winter of 1875,

---

12   Helen M. Whitney reminiscences and diary, 1876, p. 6-7, Church History Library, https://catalog.churchofjesuschrist.org/assets/3d699b7f-4abd-43d1-b3fc-f05f20b64368/0/5; underline in original.

13   Helen wrote, ". . . my youngest child my little Phebe was Snatched from out our little circle which had grown <u>small enough we thought</u> after my oldest <u>my dear Vilate</u> was taken, but God knew best and I felt to kiss the rod, but little Phebe's death was so sudden, only sick twenty nine hours. Go where we would, we could see her little trinkets, her play house & every thing as she had fixed them two days before when she seemed well and the evening before she was attacked with scarlet fever she was playing and frolicking on the floor with Flodie." Ibid., 4; underline in original.

she contracted a serious cough that settled in her lungs. Helen suspected it was the final stage of 'consumption' (tuberculosis). Her doctor insisted she quit housework and unnecessary physical exertion, but when she was confined to bed rest, the thought of her children running the household sent her into a panic:

❚❚ My Girls [Elizabeth Ann "Lillie," 18; Genevieve "Gen," 15; Helen "Henty," 13; Florence "Flod," 8] had never done as much as to bake a loaf of bread nor did they know how to wash, or any thing much about home-keeping and the work coming so suddenly upon them made it very hard for them as well as for myself. They were weak & Jenny in particular who had been sick with Rheumatism, when she'd try to rub clothes on the wash board her hands bent under her wrists. . . . then was the time when my grace was hardly sufficient. I'd hear their troubles often one or the other, sometimes Lilla & Jenny both would cry because they were so tired & discouraged. I had to sit or lay & pray to the Lord for them & for myself that He would give me patience & grace to endure these trials. My feelings cannot be described I had (like the children) to give vent to them in teers. I became melancholy & I felt in my heart that I should soon follow my parents & children who were happy beyond this Vail of tears.[14]

With Helen's family in distress, she turned to scripture for comfort, and once again—as always—the Lord did not fail her:

❚❚ I read much in the Bible & found great consolation. The comforter drew near to me, & I felt at times very happy often. I'd lay awake in the night thinking of the goodness of God, and thanking Him that I was counted worthy to be among His people to walk the thorny path with the Saints of God. I felt all the time to acknowledge His hand in my trials, although my cup of sorrow, at times, would run over.[15]

Out of this trial emerged a hidden blessing in disguise. As a mother, Helen had been too often tempted to shoulder most of the housework and food preparation. She loved to cook, and it seemed

---

14   Ibid., 5-6; underline in original.
15   Ibid., 8; underline in original.

Horace Whitney

an unnecessary burden to expend the patience and energy to train and delegate this responsibility to her inexperienced children. However, her illness now forced her to step back and allow them the opportunity to develop skills and bond as a family. Helen learned that children could take on more responsibility than she had suspected:

> ... I loved to work and could do it to suit myself and there was generally enough for them to do to help me & I did not think them able to do any <u>more</u> but when I was <u>forced to let</u> them

work they learned to do many things which they could not, had they not been brought to it.[16]

The Lord uses trials for our benefit, to expand our abilities and mold our character in acquiring new skills and attributes—to change our very nature for the better. Helen was learning to be a better mother, and her children were being prompted to mature, stretch, and grow. Helen's tribulation refined her natural weaknesses, and gave her invaluable mothering experience she would carry into the eternities.

Left Alone in Widowhood

Four years after the publication of her first article in the *Woman's Exponent*, Helen's husband, Horace, fell ill—finally passing away on November 22, 1884.[17] Six months previous, Horace had stumbled home from work, struggling with shortness of breath. Determined to push through in spite of his weakened physical condition, he continued to work whenever possible to provide for his family. However, just four months later, his illness had progressed to the point that he was forced to quit. This man of vigor now found himself experiencing difficulty in breathing, swelling/dropsy, memory failure, rheumatism, likely a severe leg infection, and many other ailments. His earthly companion tenderly nursed him, even though this added burden endangered her own feeble health. As Horace's final moments drew near, Helen faithfully sat beside him— holding his hand, rubbing his legs and cleaning the sores festering there—taking occasional periods of rest while her daughter and others assisted. She remained calm and composed to the end of his struggle—but the morning after her husband's death, her strength gave way and she suddenly broke. A deep sense of immense loss struck her, causing her to flee from the breakfast table to "go out to give free vent to my feelings."[18]

Horace had faithfully fulfilled his duty as a loving husband to Helen—the complementary companion and protector she needed as she faced mortality. Their love, respect, and trust for one another had

---

16   Ibid.

17   November 22, 1884. Charles M. Hatch and Todd M. Compton, *A Widow's Tale: 1884-1896 Diary of Helen Mar Kimball Whitney* (Logan: Utah State University Press, 2003), 47.

18   November 24, 1884. Ibid., 48.

been profound, with only occasional disagreements amid common familial discord. A moving example of their loyal and committed relationship is evident in an undated letter found among Horace's personal papers. The note is a love letter from Helen to Horace in the wake of an unidentified conflict that had risen between them. Helen writes:

> *//* <u>My Dear Dear Horace</u>[,] I am grieved, if what I said has hurt your feelings for I spoke thoughtlessley, and did not realize, the afect it would have and I thought no more of it; for I never thought, you would take such foolishness to heart; but if it has hurt your feelings, I am ready to ask your forgiveness, and I hope you will not hold any hardness against me, I know, I am apt to speak impaishent words when I feel [indiscernible]; without thinking how it sounds, I am <u>sorry</u>. and I will try and remember this, and mend my ways hereafter, and think twice before I speak. <u>Horace you know I love you with all my heart</u>, and <u>now if you will forgive me</u>, we will have the settlement verbally. <u>I am your true and affectionate Helen, both now and forever</u>[19]

From the days of their early youth, socializing in Nauvoo, to their early married years in Winter Quarters and Utah, to the decades spent building a home together in the desolate west—raising children and establishing a Zion in the Rocky Mountains—Horace and Helen had shared a union of love and honor. Now she found herself alone.

Death had been a frequent visitor in Helen's life, and now she was widowed again at the young age of 56, with six surviving children. Horace also left behind another widow—his plural wife, Mary, who had seven minor children under her care at home.[20]

A few weeks before Horace's passing, Helen began a personal diary, maintaining it faithfully until her death 12 years later. Her entries offer a glimpse into the private mind and heart of this

---

19 Helen K. Whitney letter to Horace K. Whitney, Church History Library, https://catalog.churchofjesuschrist.org/assets/d6d3155f-2c82-4d48-b259-60dd3c30e1e8/0/0.

20 Mary Cravath Whitney's minor children consisted of Laura Maria, age 18; Lucy Helen, age 17; Mary Linda, age 12; Clark Lyman, age 10; Samuel Austin, age 7; Lafayette Talbot, age 6; (George Washington, Lafayette's twin, had died in his second month); Harriet, age 1.

dedicated heroine of the Restoration. Candidly, she spoke of her journey enduring widowhood, financial strains, chronic disease, life-threatening illnesses, and other low points in her life that brought bouts of discouragement. In the midst of suffering, however, these entries are offset by the miracles, dreams, and spiritual impressions that conveyed a sense of balance to her life—each event bringing her closer to honorably finishing her life's mission. One example of the insightful prose woven throughout her diary is the following entry, made shortly after Horace's death:

// Monday Nov [Dec.] 1st Feel no better, death has not let go its grip on my feeble frame, and my trials it seems are not to be made lighter, but heavyer—Am weighed down to the very earth—still, the Lord is my friend, & as I'm nearing the end of my earthly life I should not repine for "There is sweet rest in Heaven" awaiting me, and there I shall enjoy my "home sweet home" with naught to molest or make afraid.[21]

A little over a week later, on December 11, Helen wrote: "My Father has promised that I shall never want, & I never expect to."[22] And then again on December 18:

// . . . I told Orson, if I could get back my strength of body & mind to be capable of it. I feel still more that the Lord has remembered his handmaiden in the days of her affliction & that His promises will not fail—that my last days should be the best. My treasures are laid up in heaven, where, I've been told, that I should be enthroned in the presence of God, and also that here I "should be honored of God and by man," and no power should stay the blessings pronounced upon my head by my dear father in my Patriarchal blessing, & at various times. But O, how weak & unworthy I feel, and dependent upon His arm to lead me and to sustain me in the midst of this dark world of sorrow and disapointment.[23]

---

21   Charles M. Hatch and Todd M. Compton, *A Widow's Tale: 1884-1896 Diary of Helen Mar Kimball Whitney* (Logan: Utah State University Press, 2003), 50; underline in original.

22   Ibid., 52; underline in original.

23   Ibid., 54; underline in original.

Helen derived strength in looking forward with joyful anticipation to the fulfillment of her father's blessing she had received on May 28, 1843 as a 14-year-old young woman in Nauvoo, Illinois. This blessing outlined some extraordinary promises conditioned on her own faithfulness—a charge she endeavored to achieve throughout her life. She was assured a "numerous and great" posterity while being personally "honored of God and by man." She was given hope of a future "immortal glory ... enthroned with glory in the presence of the Lord," that she would receive "the blessings of Abraham, Isaac and Jacob," and be "crowned with ... intelligence." The blessing had also proclaimed that she would receive intellectual gifts, including an understanding of "things in heaven and on the earth, kingdoms, and all things by which the earth is governed," that her wisdom and understanding would "reach to heaven," for "[l]et thy mind be diligent in study ... no one shall excel thee." If she kept her covenants, "no power [would] stay these blessings from thee." And finally, she was granted the confirmation: "I seal thee up unto eternal life and thou shalt come forth in the resurrection and shalt have power to waft thyself from kingdom to kingdom where they increase forever."[24]

Painful Health Challenges

Helen wrote many memoirs while confined to her room due to persistent nervous attacks and the agonizing effects of unknown chronic disease—both, unfortunately, her constant companions. Modern professionals have reviewed the numerous symptoms and conditions that Helen recorded in her journals, endeavoring to provide a tentative diagnosis. Their suppositions include panic attacks, circulatory issues, diabetes, epilepsy, seizures, a muscular disorder, and perhaps a form of cardiac illness.[25] Helen's diary records a wide variety of ailments, from insomnia, chills, fevers,

---

24   Blessing given to Helen Mar Kimball by her father, Heber C. Kimball on May 28, 1843. Helen Mar Kimball Whitney papers, 1843, 1868, p.1-2, located in the Heber C. Kimball family collection, 1840-1890, Church History Library, https://catalog.churchofjesuschrist.org/assets?id=355f1771-8adb-439e-aba0-81a614be6bfa&crate=0&index=0.

25   Charles M. Hatch and Todd M. Compton, *A Widow's Tale: 1884-1896 Diary of Helen Mar Kimball Whitney* (Logan: Utah State University Press, 2003), 23.

painful sore points on her body,[26] coughing, pleurisy, "deathly spells,"[27] and recurring low moments suffused with tears and a longing for death to end her relentless suffering. In one entry from April 1889, she records:

> **//** So sick the forenoon—there having been no cesation night nor day—felt that <u>death would be a sweet relief.</u>—how much longer have I got to suffer? Prayed for grace to endure what's needful to make me perfect. They began to let up afternoon, & I soon felt better, & full of gratitude.[28]

Through each painful moment of her oft-recurring struggles, Helen endeavored to reach upward and keep her mind focused on the Savior—feeling that God was the only deliverer who could assuredly relieve her suffering or give her the strength to endure. Prayer was her comfort and support during the tedious nights of insomnia, as exemplified in the following entry:

> **//** February Thursday 5th. Spent almost a sleepless night—<u>sleep would not come to my relief</u>, till hours of prayer & struggling had passed. I arose late with head ache.—Wrote some of my feelings on paper. I hear that Heber is fast failing. David told me I would be the next one to go after Heber.[29] I presume I shall be glad to go when the time comes.

---

26 See for example, "After undressing my feet last night I discovered a sore place, nearly in the hollow of my left foot, I hit it as I got into bed & it was very sore and painful. I expected to find a pimple or fester, when looking at it in the morning, but not a sign of any thing could I discover—still the the spot is painful to the touch. What it can be I cant imagine." December 28, 1884. Ibid., 59.

27 Ibid., 21-22.

"A 'deathly spell' was an experience approximating death in some way—a psychic dislocation, a temporary loss of consciousness, perhaps a blacking out, combined with physical pain of some sort. Sometimes Helen referred to them as 'those awful spasms' (May 5, 1894) or 'spells of stagnation of my blood' (November 4, 1893). Once she called them 'strokes' (April 13, 1893)....

"The best account of a deathly spell may be that on April 12, 1886. After fixing a bed (physical labor often triggered the spells), Helen wrote, 'I commenced to feel faint so had to go & sit down, or I should have dropt on the floar—it was the most deathly sensation, and I could not stand up to undress but layed on the bed while unfastening part of my clothes.' Chills and fever followed." Ibid., 22.

28 April 19, 1889. Ibid., 353; underline in original.

29 Heber and David were both brothers of Helen, sons of Heber and Vilate Kimball.

... <u>Friday 6th</u>. I slept but little, & that in the latter part of the night, & awoke before daylight—felt broken hearted, but not discouraged.[30]

Helen was being completely weaned from any fallible support—from any reliance whatsoever on the arm of flesh. She was being taught—moment by moment, tear by tear, and prayer by prayer—how to rely entirely upon the Lord. No program, no strategy, no cleverly devised positivity statement could sustain her—the Lord *alone* was her unfailing relief.

Yet another entry offers a valuable insight into how Helen dealt with suffering. A stoic and determined woman of grit, she had always prayed for deliverance, but this account reveals her humility in pleading with the Lord to forgive her for her faults. Even in her suffering, Helen turned her desires to the Lord in seeking repentance and grace:

> I've never scarcely given way to weeping as I did last night and to day. I cried aloud, & besought the Lord to take cognisance of my sorrows and interceedings, & take off the weight from my shoulders that did not <u>belong</u> to me, and show me my own shortcomings, that I might have charity for the ones who wound me. Charly came into my room this afternoon & we had a good talk—He says he feels as though he did not want to mix again with the world & its follies—desires to go forth & preach the gospel—this being the higth of his ambition—This does my soul good. Would that there were more of his way of thinking.[31]

As a loving and concerned mother, Helen's prayers often turned toward her children. She was desperate for them to commit themselves to God and consecrate their lives to His service, and seeing them stray from the path of happiness caused her heart to ache with sorrow.

---

30   December 5-6, 1885. Charles M. Hatch and Todd M. Compton, *A Widow's Tale: 1884-1896 Diary of Helen Mar Kimball Whitney* (Logan: Utah State University Press, 2003), 68; underline in original.

31   Ibid.

Death still persisted in its unsolicited visits to her family with the passing of her 50-year-old brother, Heber, seven years her junior.[32] All this contributed to her distress—yet she found joy in the promises she received from the Lord:

// Sunday 8th. Spent a tolerable night a portion of it in prayer, to know the Lord's will concerning myself & family & what course to take to please Him. My eyes are a fountain of tears. I fasted to day—Gennie brought me coffee & food at 12 o'clock, which I partook of—but intended to fast till 4—the usual hour for Sunday's dinner. Lucy came in with a plate of sweet meats, sent me by Zine We had quite a talk on various things—Heber died this morning, at 11 o'clock. I almost felt home sick to go with the same escort that took him to father, mother, and others who would welcome me there, where no sorrow can enter.

Orson came into my parlor after we'd taken dinner, and we had a good talk. He was humble as a little child—told me how sad he felt to see me bowed down in sorrow, etc, etc, and many other things he said that took a weight from off my shoulders, & made my heart lighter—Though the Lord had already shown me that my prayers & offerings had been accepted & that He approved of my acts, and that as long as I did right I would rise triumphant over every power that sought to discomfort . . .[33]

Only those who have walked through similar trials can truly understand the depth of emotion in Helen's words—the pleadings of her soul for strength, wisdom, and comfort. Helen shed maternal tears as she supplicated the Lord for her children's welfare. Her anxiety frequently drove her to fast, even when her frail mortal frame dangled in the balance between life and death. All the while,

---

32 Heber Parley Kimball, born June 1, 1835, was the fifth child of Heber and Vilate Kimball. At 13 years of age, he traveled to the Salt Lake Valley in company with his father, Heber C. Kimball. At 21, he was one of the men who participated in the rescue of the Saints stranded in the frigid Wyoming winter of 1856 (rescues of the Willie and Martin Handcart Companies and the Hodgetts and Hunt Wagon Companies). In 1861, when he was 26, Heber served as captain of a later company of Saints who were emigrating to Utah or Deseret.

33 Charles M. Hatch and Todd M. Compton, *A Widow's Tale: 1884-1896 Diary of Helen Mar Kimball Whitney* (Logan: Utah State University Press, 2003), 68-69.

she stood firm in her convictions, as evidenced by the following entry regarding her 19-year-old daughter, Florence. Helen knew that compromising her standards would never save her children—that their only hope was in choosing to follow the Lord and their mother's voice was essential in communicating that message:

> [May] Sunday 23d [1886]. I fasted and prayed—that my children might come to feel as I do concerning things pertaining to the gospel and the necessity of doing as commanded. Florence gone to Gennings farm with Hen, & mother and others of the two families—Gennings & Dinwoodies. I opposed it last night, and this morning, & told them I washed my hands of it, and could not give my consent to her going contrary from what we were commanded—that I was grieved to think my words were treeted so lightly when I'd spoken so plainly about such things. She said she would not do so again, but had promised the folks, etc. Before leaving she came back to my room stating that Henry told her they would go to meeting to Farmington, a mile & a half from the farm—Also promised she'd read, & do nothing to break the Sabbath—I have fasted, prayed, read the Bible, & wept with a broken heart before the Lord that we might find favor in His eyes, & grace to enable us to keep the "word of wisdom" in its true meaning—[34]

Helen's life reminds us that in this world, the Lord allows his saints—especially his noble and great ones—to experience all manner of tribulations; it is their privilege to gain knowledge through struggle and perseverance. No true follower of Christ lives a life of ease. The message of the Gospel is not one of luxury—but of *overcoming*, of gaining victory during the darkest trials and lowest valleys of shadow. Suffering proves our integrity—it refines and reveals our true identity. Helen could scarcely have imagined that in some future time, women of her own faith would examine her diaries with interest, striving to overcome difficulties in their own day—searching for needed strength, and drawing it from her noble example.

---

34   Ibid., 158.

CHAPTER 14

Rolling Waters & Gifts from Heaven

❧

A s the Prophet Joseph Smith languished in Liberty Jail, the Lord revealed to Him a singular truth—that suffering for Christ and humbly enduring trials are the inescapable cost of obtaining sanctification and revelation. But for those who endure it well, no opposition, no foe, and no obstacle can restrain the Lord from opening the windows of heaven and pouring down knowledge upon His faithful children. Hearing the Prophet's cry of anguish in the midst of his crushing distress, the Lord comforted Joseph with the power and beauty of the most sublime language, saying:

❝ My son, peace be unto thy soul; thine adversity and thine afflictions shall be but a small moment;

And then, if thou endure it well, God shall exalt thee on high; thou shalt triumph over all thy foes.

. . . How long can rolling waters remain impure? What power shall stay the heavens? As well might man stretch forth his puny arm to stop the Missouri river in its decreed course, or to turn it up stream, as to hinder the Almighty from pouring down knowledge from heaven upon the heads of the Latter-day Saints.[1]

Helen learned this principle firsthand as she battled through a life fraught with heartbreak after heartbreak. However—just as Joseph had been promised of the Lord—in the midst of her trials, Helen

---

1 Doctrine and Covenants 21:7-8, 33.

recorded experiencing powerful gifts of the Spirit akin to those bestowed during the apostolic era of the early Christians; the Lord poured down knowledge from heaven upon her own head as she trod the refining path of a true Latter-day Saint. As one of the preeminent women of the dispensation, it is no surprise that Helen earned and exercised many spiritual gifts, including the gift of healing, the gift of dreams, and the gift of prophecy.

The Gift of Healing

Many times, Helen was the recipient of miraculous healings in the midst of chronic pain and intermittent illness. She recorded one such experience that occurred on September 21, 1889. She had become ill, suffering with a headache and severe pain in her left side after the brisk autumn air had chilled her during the night. Helen hoped for an elder to give her a priesthood blessing—but unfortunately, she was alone and physically incapable of mustering the strength to obtain the needed help by herself. Ever trusting in her Father's care and willingness to respond to her needs, she began praying earnestly for "the Lord to send an angel to administer to me," when suddenly she heard a knock at her door:

// T'was Orson—he didn't know I was sick, he said, but was impressed to come around. I took this as an answer to prayer, I believed that I'd been restored under his administration— rested pretty good through the night.[2]

The unexpected visit from Helen's son was a gentle reminder that God was aware and listening—He knew the secret pleadings of her heart.

On another occasion, Helen dreamt one night that she was sitting in a room, surrounded by her beloved sisters in the faith, including Eliza R. Snow. Brigham Young then entered the room, and Helen felt he was acting in the role of a physician as he gently voiced to Helen that "he thought he could help me."[3] This particular dream occurred nearly nine years following President Young's death. Helen was not alone in witnessing Brigham's intervention, as her daughter,

---

2   Charles M. Hatch and Todd M. Compton, *A Widow's Tale: 1884-1896 Diary of Helen Mar Kimball Whitney* (Logan: Utah State University Press, 2003), 375.

3   Ibid., 147.

back row, beginning left: Genevieve "Gen," and Florence "Flod"
front row, beginning left: Elizabeth "Lillie," Orson, and Helen "Henty"

Florence, also experienced a dream confirming that President Young—even from the other side of the veil—continued in his protection and support of her and her family.[4]

Helen recognized her dire circumstances—she knew her life was in the hands of the Lord, and she also recognized that assistance came as she prayed in faith. Sometimes the Lord was there, sometimes others were there, and sometimes He desired for her to exercise faith and act independently. There were occasions when no priesthood blessing was available, and when all medical innovation had failed. Yet Helen still

---

4   "Florence had a beautiful dream last night President Young paid me a visit, and she thought that he represented the Lord. He had come to see me the day before, & she asked me why he didn't come and see her. She thought our rooms joined each other, and were down in the ground. I told her maybe he would come the next day to see her—She told me she feared she'd be frightened to see him as he was dead She thought he came unto her room the next evening while she was on her knees praying for something. She turned & sat on the bed and talked to him, and he said 'The oftener you pray the oftener I'll come, and the easyer your prayers will be answered.' And told her that he represented the Lord. She said it made her perfectly happy. The spirit of it is manifest in her talk and appearence to day. She told me that that same peaceful spirit came over her a number of times while I was gone to Tooele, & she felt so happy under its influence; which was a striking proof to me that my prayers were being heard & answered, upon her head." Ibid., 143.

trusted in the deliverance promised by the Lord—as one experience from her journal on Saturday, March 27, 1886 demonstrates:

❧❧ My throat has been more or less sore from the first job that I did of this kind, and nothing seemed to help it till I began taking consecrated oil a couple of nights ago and praying in faith to the Lord, and the soreness & dryness that has afflicted me is all gone.[5]

Helen's gesture of faith is reminiscent of the woman with an issue of blood who whispered with a glimmer of hope, "If I may but touch his garment, I shall be whole."[6] The greatest barrier between ourselves and the Lord is our own doubt; how often is He merely providing us an opportunity to discover for ourselves whether we will follow Him in darkness, as well as light?[7] Helen strove to gain mastery over her doubts as she diligently sought to bridge that gap.

On June 10, 1891, Helen was lying sick with a cold, accompanied by rheumatism and headache, when she was pleasantly surprised by a visit from "patriarch father [William J.] Smith."[8] He administered to and blessed the ailing woman—reaffirming all she had been promised—and left her with a rekindled sense of hope through the assurance of:

❧❧ . . . a repetition of things that had been previously pronounced upon my head concerning the great work that I was to live to perform—He told me to rest my body and not let my mind be troubled, that my spirit could wear out a number of such bodies, etc. Said that the time had come for the Lord to favor me &

---

5   Ibid., 145.

6   Matthew 9:21.

7   Eliza R. Snow Smith taught, "The Spirit of God, never brings darkness, but light, joy, & peace. The Lord loves a cheerful heart. If we sometimes discover gloomy feelings creeping over us—we must arouse ourselves, & shake it off. God sometimes withdraws His Spirit from us, to try us—or we might think, it was something inherent with us, & God will try us & show us He is our strength. We must acknowledge His hand in all things. He will have a tried people—if we want all the glory we must be willing to endure the trials. We are gaining an experience which is our wealth beyond the grave; & why should we shrink from experience. Try to overcome every thing, that is not honorable in a Saint of God, watch over yourselves . . ." Twentieth Ward Relief Society minutes and records, 1868-1973, Volume 1, p. 27-28, Church History Library.

8   William Joseph Smith was a convert from England—and a good friend to Helen Mar Kimball—who lived from 1820-1897. He was ordained as a patriarch in 1879.

that I would recover my health, & many things besides . . . I cling to the promises that the Lord has made me—now—more than ever—[9]

The events surrounding this period deserve further mention. Helen had been feeling her "uselessness keenly," but felt that "when the Lord wished me to go forth again He'd give me strength to do so." A week passed following the patriarch's visit, but Helen's health continued to decline, her suffering exacerbated by the persistent headaches and "deathly spells." Finally, in anguish, she cried out in prayer, confessing in her diary that her feelings were "so sick & down hearted [that] I prayed in my heart that if bro. Smith, who'd visited and administered to me, was the man of God that he professed to be that he might be inspired to come again."[10]

Throughout the course of history, it has been observed that the God of Israel tends to work through 11th-hour miracles—intervention at the darkest hour, when all appears lost. This He does as an expression of love, to test the faith of His people, that they might know with certainty who He is—His true character. In a world with conflicting notions and divided opinions regarding the nature of God, true faith can only exist when we have a "*correct* idea of [H]is character, perfections, and attributes."[11] Coming to know God is the destination of the penitent—following a time-honored path that leads to testimony and conversion through divine, though difficult, experience.

Not long after Helen had finished her fervent plea for reassurance, she looked up to see the very man, Patriarch William J. Smith, entering her gate! ". . . not having thought of my prayer, after making it, I was a little startled, but I took it as in answer to my prayer . . ."[12]

In seeming coincidence, Patriarch Smith had been on his way to give Helen's brother Solomon and his wife a patriarchal blessing, and "why he'd just come to mine he hardly knew." But there he was

9   Charles M. Hatch and Todd M. Compton, *A Widow's Tale: 1884-1896 Diary of Helen Mar Kimball Whitney* (Logan: Utah State University Press, 2003), 452.

10   Ibid., 453-454.

11   Lectures on Faith, Lecture Three, found in Doctrine and Covenants, 1835, p. 36, The Joseph Smith Papers; italicized in original.

12   Charles M. Hatch and Todd M. Compton, *A Widow's Tale: 1884-1896 Diary of Helen Mar Kimball Whitney* (Logan: Utah State University Press, 2003), 453.

again, aptly prepared to give Helen another needed blessing. Shortly thereafter, Solomon arrived looking for the expected patriarch. Feeling impressed to give Helen a *third* blessing, Patriarch Smith and Helen's brother unitedly laid their hands on her head and proceeded to bestow the words impressed upon them through the Holy Ghost. The blessing "again gave me wise coun[sel] about taking care of my body, & resting my mind." In addition to the instruction regarding the care of her person, she was also admonished that—despite her physical pain—she should "go out among my sisters & brethren & let my voice be heard again." This injunction came with the promise that if she would exert faith and follow the counsel thus impressed by the Spirit, "I should be made equal to it, & grow stronger all the time."[13] Faith must precede the miracle,[14] and for Helen, this meant she would resolve to step out once again.

Three days later, and still ailing from her headaches and the pain in her left side, Helen forced herself to leave her bed upon learning that her ward's Relief Society was meeting that day. She fixed her mind on attending, "determined to go on my mission that I might claim the blessing."[15] After receiving yet another blessing that afternoon, she declared it was "calculated to inspire the heart of any one who has any faith—being glorious." Holding to the promise "that I'd grow stronger by going out that I'd begin to improve from this day," a determined and resolute Helen set out for her Relief Society meeting:

> When Sisters Horne and S. Kimball saw me they arose and greeted me—They were just singing. I was pretty tired, but enjoyed meeting, & spoke with great freedom—Told some of my experiences, & how I'd come there on the strength of the promises that were made me if I'd do my duty in this line, etc. Many sisters came & shook my hand. I was prayed for, at the morning session, Sister Horne told me. I walked to the Car on main street, & when I got home bandaged my head with wet cloth & flannel—it pained me worse as well as my body, but felt

---

13   Ibid.

14   Ether 12:12; Doctrine and Covenants 35:8-11.

15   Charles M. Hatch and Todd M. Compton, *A Widow's Tale: 1884-1896 Diary of Helen Mar Kimball Whitney* (Logan: Utah State University Press, 2003), 454.

better after laying down awhile & enjoyed dinner more than any meal eaten for some days.[16]

After spending the evening with her fellow sisters, Helen returned home and retired to bed. The next day, she recorded her pleasant surprise following a night of relative rest:

// Enjoyed my bed & rested better than at any previous time since I layed on my new one—over a month ago, & to day have not had any of that tired out feeling that I've been accustomed to at doing half that I've done to day, & my eyes & head haven't pained me though I've read more than usual. My side is very sore yet near my heart & painful at the least touch, but I've faith that it will go away with the rest of my ales.[17]

Truly, the Lord was refining Helen through her physical suffering—strengthening her faith and encouraging her patient and persistent submission to Him. The promises of the Lord had not guaranteed ease, nor an effortless healing—priesthood power is not a magic cure, and it carries with it no spell or charm. Instead, Helen was granted just enough strength and endurance to accomplish her divine calling. She lived, as it were, by daily gifts of spiritual manna. These were the miracles! But to answer the Lord's call required real faith—it required obedience to laws, personal growth, repentance, hard work, patience, and unfortunately, this path often included suffering. This principle was reaffirmed for Helen in 1886 during a blessing she received through another wife of the Prophet Joseph Smith:

// Saturday 20th. We arose early to go to attend to the washing & anointing of those sisters. Presendie[18] stayed to Sister De-la Mar's, where we found a room full of sisters. . . . Presendie anointed me & blessed me, asking the Lord to assist me, and heal me of all my ales, & that my right arm and hand might be healed & made strong; which had become lame & painful

---

16 Ibid.

17 Ibid.

18 Presendia Lathrop Huntington Smith Kimball was sealed as a plural wife to the Prophet Joseph Smith, and later married to Heber C. Kimball for time following the martyrdom. See Chapter 9, footnote 4, for additional details.

from much writing, etc, And that my mind brain, and all my powers might be renewed that I could perform all my duties and labors with ease, & many things were pronounced upon my head, being, at the same time anointed with oil.[19]

On this occasion—as well as many others during her life—Helen was given blessings of healing by righteous sisters in the Church. During the early days of the Relief Society in Nauvoo, the Prophet Joseph Smith had begun restoring ancient teachings regarding the far-reaching role and mission of women—tenets of the Gospel that had been lost during the Great Apostasy. Some of these teachings involved healing of the sick, and even the laying on of hands, by women, to exercise a blessing of faith.[20] Early Church leaders were very clear that these healing blessings were given based on the principle of *faith*, as opposed to priesthood authority. Speaking on this principle, Eliza R. Snow taught in 1883: "Women can administer in the name of Jesus but not by virtue of the Priesthood."[21] Women were taught that although they did not hold priesthood authority in

---

19   Charles M. Hatch and Todd M. Compton, *A Widow's Tale: 1884-1896 Diary of Helen Mar Kimball Whitney* (Logan: Utah State University Press, 2003), 142-143.

20   "Thursday 28 at Two o'clock after-noon met the members of the 'Female Relief Society' and after presiding at the admission of many new members. Gave a lecture on the pries[t]hood shewing how the Sisters would come in possession of the priviliges & blesings & gifts of the priesthood—& that the signs should follow them. such as healing the sick casting out devils &c. & that they might attain unto. these blessings. by a virtuous life & conversation & diligence in keeping all the commandments." Joseph Smith, Journal, April 28, 1842, p. 94, The Joseph Smith Papers.

"It is the privilege of those set apart to administer in that authority which is confer'd on them—and if the sisters should have faith to heal the sick, let all hold their tongues, and let every thing roll on. . . .

"Respecting the female laying on hands, he further remark'd, there could be no devil in it, if God gave his sanction by healing-that thre could be no more sin in any female laying hands on the sick than in wetting the face with water-that it is no sin for anybody to do that has faith, or if the sick has faith to be heal'd by the administration.

". . . you are now placed in a situation where you can act according to those sympathies which God has planted in your bosoms. If you live up to these principles how great and glorious!—if you live up to your privilege, the angels cannot be restrained from being your associates. . . . If you will be pure, nothing can hinder." Joseph Smith, Nauvoo Relief Society Minute Book, April 28, 1842, p. 36, 38-39, The Joseph Smith Papers.

21   Comments given on April 28, 1883. Morgan Utah Stake Relief Society minutes and records, 1878-1973, vol. 1, p. 93, Church History Library, https://catalog. churchofjesuschrist.org/assets/ded7e0ed-ee1c-4ce7-a6ea-18294bb07ca3/0/96.

themselves, there were opportunities to serve in conjunction with authority vested in their husbands, and under the direction of those holding proper authority.[22]

---

22   On October 6, 1880, the Quorum of the Twelve drafted a letter explaining: "It is the privilege of all faithful women and lay members of the Church, who believe in Christ, to administer to all the sick or afflicted in their respective families, either by the laying on of hands, or by the anointing with oil in the name of the Lord: but they should administer in these sacred ordinances, not by virtue and authority of the priesthood, but by virtue of their faith in Christ, and the promises made to believers: and thus they should do in all their ministrations." Quorum of the Twelve Apostles circular letter, October 6, 1880, p. 10, Church History Library, https://catalog.churchofjesuschrist.org/assets/6422529f-17ee-4061-9681-be7d596d4157/0/16.

Some teachings inferred that women were able to act under the authority of the priesthood of their husbands, if they were united and functioning under their leadership. However, leaders were clear that women do not hold the priesthood independent of their husbands.

Mary Ellen Kimball recorded: ". . . I thought of the instructions I had received from time to time that the priesthood was not bestowed upon women I accordingly asked Mr Kimball if woman had a right to wash and anoint the sick for the recovery of their health or is it mockery in them to do so.

"He replied inasmuch as they are obedient to their husbands th[e]y have a right to administer in that way in the name of the Lord Jesus Christ but not by authority of the priesthood invested in them for that authority is not given to woman. He also said that they might administer by the authority given to their husbands in as much as they ware one with their husband." Mary Ellen H. Kimball Journal, March 2, 1857, p. 12, Church History Library, https://catalog.churchofjesuschrist.org/assets/b56d5253-572e-4c95-b236-7890d8f36d5c/0/11.

"You [sisters] suppose that you receive the priesthood when you receive your endowments, but the Priesthood is on your husbands. Can you honor God and the Priesthood, and abuse your husbands like the Devil? How can you honor the Priesthood, except you honor the man you are connected with? I am talking about good men: I will not in this connection say anything about bad men. How can you honor the Priesthood, except you honor the one you are connected with?" Heber C. Kimball, "The Latter-Day Kingdom—Men not to Be Governed By Their Wives—Love to God Manifested By Love to His Servants," in *Journal of Discourses*, vol. 12 (Liverpool: Albert Carrington, 1869), 31. Discourse given on July 12, 1857.

". . . it is not the calling of the sisters to hold the Priesthood, only in connection with their husbands, they being one with their husbands." John Taylor, "The Order and Duties of the Priesthood, Etc.," in *Journal of Discourses*, vol. 21 (Liverpool: Albert Carrington, 1881), 367-368. Discourse given on August 8, 1880.

Joseph Fielding Smith taught:, "Does a wife hold the priesthood with her husband, and may she lay hands on the sick with him, with authority? A wife does not hold the priesthood with her husband, but she enjoys the benefits thereof with him; and if she is requested to lay hands on the sick with him, or with any other officer holding the Melchizedek Priesthood, she may do so with perfect propriety. It is no uncommon thing for a man and wife unitedly to administer to their children." Joseph Fielding Smith, "Questions and Answers," *The Improvement Era*, vol. 10, vo. 4, February 1907, 308.

During the 20th century as Church leaders began to standardize procedures and ordinances, they issued policies that increasingly discouraged women from giving blessings of faith. Initially, during the early 1900s, leaders counseled members to prioritize their requests for blessings by deferring to those holding the priesthood. Eventually, within a few decades, the policies were changed, resulting in the current stipulation that "Only Melchizedek Priesthood holders may administer to the sick or afflicted."[23] These changes contributed to a loss of doctrinal understanding and confusion about the role of women in the priesthood, as well as some of the principles underlying the priesthood. This misunderstanding has likely played a role in the organization of counterfeit movements that mimic sacred ordinances but do not follow the Lord's revealed pattern.[24] There are other examples of this pattern where cultural influences and general unwillingness of the Saints to live the higher laws and teachings of the Restoration resulted in a loss of understanding regarding the patriarchal order, consecration, priesthood, eternal sealings, the divine role of women, and so forth.[25]

---

23   "18.13.1 Who Gives the Blessing," *General Handbook: Serving in The Church of Jesus Christ of Latter-day Saints* (Salt Lake City: The Church of Jesus Christ of Latter-day Saints, 2021).

24   The authors feel that the 20th and 21st-century initiatives and movements behind 'Christ-centered energy healing' and 'energy medicine,' as well as the progressive Ordain Women organization are a few of many counterfeit ideologies that appear to mimic, or echo teachings of early leaders on the role of women exercising spiritual gifts. However, a closer examination of the teachings of the Restoration reveals many contradictions between the tenets adopted by these movements and the teachings of the Prophet Joseph Smith. This subject exceeds the scope of this book, but there are resources and materials produced through the Joseph Smith Foundation and other supportive groups that address this issue.

25   Alma 12:9-11. "And now Alma began to expound these things unto him, saying: It is given unto many to know the mysteries of God; nevertheless they are laid under a strict command that they shall not impart only according to the portion of his word which he doth grant unto the children of men, according to the heed and diligence which they give unto him.

"And therefore, he that will harden his heart, the same receiveth the lesser portion of the word; and he that will not harden his heart, to him is given the greater portion of the word, until it is given unto him to know the mysteries of God until he know them in full.

Helen Mar Kimball herself frequently participated in blessings with her sisters in the faith. For example, on May 24, 1888, Helen was assisting her daughter Lillie during a difficult labor. Lillie's water had broken at about 5am, but by the middle of the day, no further progress had been made. The doctor—likewise a man of her faith—soberly requested Helen to send for a priesthood holder to administer to the exhausted mother, "as the child's life was in danger." Helen recorded:

/ / Orson soon came and administered to her, & I laying on hands with him and the pains became more natural and effective. Sister Shipp manifested the greatest skill—with the assistence of her instrments the baby's life was saved, though every sign of life was extinct when it entered the world, & for a time its case seamed hopeless.[26]

Helen acquired faith, not because she believed in a theoretical or mystical hope—but because she had *seen* the Lord's hand; she had experienced the outpouring of His mercy, and had been privileged to take part as an active participant herself in many miracles. Helen had learned for herself what her dear friend Brigham Young once called the "difference between a professor of religion, and a *possessor* of religion."[27]

The Gift of Dreams & Visions

Like her father—and through her own personal faithfulness— Helen was endowed with many gifts of the Spirit, including the gifts of prophecy and dreams. In 1895, Helen experienced three dreams foretelling that someone near to her would soon be called home to the other side. A short time later, a fellow member, Brother Isaac

---

"And they that will harden their hearts, to them is given the lesser portion of the word until they know nothing concerning his mysteries; and then they are taken captive by the devil, and led by his will down to destruction. Now this is what is meant by the chains of hell."

26   Charles M. Hatch and Todd M. Compton, *A Widow's Tale: 1884-1896 Diary of Helen Mar Kimball Whitney* (Logan: Utah State University Press, 2003), 301.

27   Brigham Young, May 29, 1847, as recorded by William Clayton. *William Clayton, An Intimate Chronicle: The Journals of William Clayton*, ed. George D. Smith (Salt Lake City: Signature Books, 1995), 325; emphasis added.

Groo, passed away.[28] On another occasion, Helen was given a dream wherein she saw and conversed with numerous concourses of angels, and she took this dream as a sign of great and glorious prophecies being fulfilled:

❦❦ I had an interesting dream—Was standing with Orson in a place where there were large trees scattered about and green grass. Numbers of people were there. Suddenly I saw decending from the clouds above a groop of angels, & I said to Orson—"look". As they drew near they proved to be children of various sises, with a man in the centre. Every one had a beautiful wreath of flowers over their heads, just touching them, & the children were formed into a circle above 3 or 4 rows & reaching down to the man's feet. I thought, as they neared the earth, that he, maybe, was Joseph the Prophet—He'd turned half way to the right, and I gazed to see his face; but when he turned to us again I saw that it was a Scandinavian brother with a round fair countenence, who had died a short time before. And when they stept upon the ground I went up to him & enquired if he'd seen my father & mother? he said "yes". I asked him other questions, & also of one or two children. They answered only a few, & I forgot what they were. They scattered among the few people that were there till near night—they appeared to be preparing to leave. Orson & I took it as a sighn of the great & glorious things foretold us by prophets, that were beginning to come to pass, which filled us with joy.[29]

---

28 "Bro. Isaac Groo died last evening, & George Bourne came this eve to see if I'd like to go to his funeral with Helen, he'll get a Hack to take us—Orson told us Sunday that he'd been & administered to bro. Groo, whom we'd heard was very low, & he revived after it. I knew that some one near to us was going to die—three times I've dreamed of my house being cleaned & the earth by my house being dug up—in the first dream it was about the sise of a grave—next it was plowed by my house—The third I dreamed of a large celler being dug by the side of a new house I was having built, & I asked Sol, who was one of the workmen, if they'd wall up my celler, & he said 'yes.' This house was in a thinly settled place in the city, & I thought to myself would I like it as well as my present one? There was a broad platform being built at the back part of my new one & this was to cover the celler at my back doar." January 25, 1895. Charles M. Hatch and Todd M. Compton, *A Widow's Tale: 1884-1896 Diary of Helen Mar Kimball Whitney* (Logan: Utah State University Press, 2003), 643.

29 October 12, 1984. Ibid., 624.

Orson F. Whitney, dated March 21, 1873

Helen's dreams frequently included loved ones who had passed to the other side—family members and friends who brought her comfort, counsel, and encouragement to keep the faith. One of these included her adopted 'uncle' Joseph Young as a resurrected man,[30] and another included President Brigham Young:

/ / Dreamed Pres. Brigham Young visited me—I was in a large house & some woman with me—I was overjoyed to see him approaching me & ran to meet him & we embraced. his face looked just as it did many years before his death[.] I introduced him to the sister, telling her that he dandled me in his arms from my babyhood as an explanation for so warm a greeting.[31]

---

30   "Dreamed of Uncle Joseph Young coming & eating with a table full of Mary Whitney's folks & mine— When I saw him eating I said I knew by that that he had his resurected body. He had come to enquire for some one whom he wanted. I didn't know who it was." Ibid., 415; underline in original.

31   Ibid., 671.

The Gift of Prophecy

In 1890, Helen was given a dream foretelling that the Latter-day Saint people were on the "eve of a great move," and she saw a written command: "Israel up, arise"![32] Helen and other members felt that the prophecies of the ancient prophets were being fulfilled—both good and ill—and that the Latter-day Saints were playing a significant and fundamental role. She dreamed of battles and trials the Latter-day Saints would be called to pass through,[33] and felt that the time would come when persecution and economic difficulties would humble her people and prepare them to be willing to live the Law of Consecration and the United Order, as revealed by the Lord.[34] In yet another dream, she heard a terrible noise, and when word reached her of great destructions in American cities from storms and earthquakes, she felt they were confirmation of what would soon befall the Saints:

// When informed of the facts it was viewed as the fulfilment of the words of the prophets concerning the awful judgements upon the wicked in the last days. I had been reading the <u>News</u> and the account of Tornados in Missouri, Kansas & other portions

---

32   "The other night I dreamed that I saw in the D. News 4 or 5 paragraphs in fine print that struck me as containing a deep meening, & I wondered if the same had impressed others as it did me. I took it to meen that this people were upon the eve of a great move. But the remembrance of all but the first 2 or 3 words left me—something like a command—as 'Israel up, arise'—an event that is being hastened by the efforts of the would-be exterminators of 'Mormonism[.]'" Ibid., 393.

33   "Last night I dreamed that a battle was raging between the 'Mormons' & their enemies in the city, & word came from the Presidency that we were to go from there—south—to dwell in a place, I couldnt remember the name of it. I remarked to some who were at my house, that there we'd be on a par, that this people were now to be humbled—thought that we'd be in more humble circumstances, that we'd have to be satisfied with less house room, & conveniences there than what we were now accustomed to. The most of the dream went from me before morning." Ibid., 473.

"Visited at Cristeen Kimball's with several other sisters. Heard two visions read which pictured out the tereble destruction that is coming upon the works and the trials, etc, of the Latter-day Saints." Ibid., 140.

34   "Ed returned at night, has to go again in the morning. Special poliece called out—caused by the great strike that has affected our country & people as none other has done, which brings to our remembrance the predictions uttered by the Prophet Joseph & others, that were to come to pass in our day & generation, and is one of the things that will drive us into the United Order. The Lord works in a misterious way, etc." Ibid., 608.

of the States which caused such suffering. We shall soon hear of greater ones.[35]

Another dream Helen was given in 1885 seemed somewhat peculiar and vague, and involved two darkened pictures with white surrounding them, and a piece of meat curiously hanging alongside:

> I was struck by the strangeness of their being placed there, and asked Major Talbot, who was standing behind me what it meant He not answering—I looked at him, & his countanance expressed deep feeling. I said Tell me what does it mean? And I repeited it twice before he replied. He hated to tell me, but as I insisted he said, "It means the tearing up of the earth." I understood it to meen that our foes had placed these signs at different houses in our city as a warning of their intentions, and that was war.[36]

Helen's father had likewise been given spiritual prophecy relating to events that would befall the United States—and the world at large—in preparation for the building up of Zion, the gathering of Israel, and the impending Millennial reign of the Prince of Peace. Helen recorded one visit in which a friend shared one of Heber's prophecies with her:

> Bro. Crochron called and left me the book, which I'd asked him for. He told of 2 predictions made by my father concerning the trials that would befall the Saints after they had built up Salt Lake City—it then being little else than a baron waste—He said they would be brought into so tight a place that to the natural eye, there'd be no escape from being wiped from the earth but the pure in heart would be delivered, etc, And said this city would be perfectly surrounded by armies of the United States, and I've no doubt but that will soon be fulfilled.[37]

Outside her immediate family, Helen lived within a circle of family and friends who shared the benefit of her spiritual gifts, and

---

35   Ibid., 156; underline in original.

36   Ibid., 108.

37   Ibid., 129-130; underline in original.

who also expressed a desire for greater truth. Unlike many parties and amusements today that too often devolve into idle, light-minded, and improper usage of time, Helen's social gatherings and celebrations often resulted in deep gospel discussions and profound spiritual experiences. Helen knew the difference between frivolous and fleeting pleasure, and true, lasting joy. On February 8, 1895, Helen recorded another uplifting evening with her fellow sisters that involved the gift of tongues, and the bestowal of additional blessings and prophecies concerning her mission:

> We had a meeting after her supper was out of the way—every one spoke, & Sister Phelps, the last, spoke powerfully in her tongue, & in a lamanitish tongue—she came to me & poured out a great blessing upon me & afterwards proposed to have all lay hands on my head & rebuke my afflictions—they did so Nellie Taylor was mouth & offered up a prayer for my recovery. Sister Phelps said— among other things—that a year from this time I'd see that a great change had been wrought in my bodily condition, etc. I have not spoken with so much power & felt the Holy spirit upon me as I did there[38]

A Written Legacy on Tear-Stained Pages

Ultimately, Helen's trials and prophetic gifts were not endowed merely by chance, but with a divine purpose. It would seem that the Lord's design was to equip her with both the joy and the pain she required to faithfully execute the mission she had been set apart to perform—to bear a woman's testimony and witness to the truthfulness of the Gospel.

Helen's testimony did not flow effortlessly onto perfumed stationary from a pampered nib—but rather, it fell with anguish onto tear-stained pages, scrawled out during times of affliction and distress, and often while she was in considerable physical and emotional pain. Her writings are an enduring testament to commitment and faith, left by a woman who chose to let the light of her legacy shine in spite of the trail of tears through which she was required to pass. Even progressive historians—many of whom are

---

38   Ibid., 646.

openly critical of her belief in miracles and her support of doctrine revealed and taught by the Prophet Joseph Smith—are obliged to acknowledge her remarkable determination to share her testimony despite persistent adversity:

// Helen Mar devoted considerable labor to her editorials, which are her most topical and ephemeral writings. They are nevertheless interesting records of the polarized era before the Woodruff Manifesto. Her diary chronicles in detail the genesis, composition, and revision of *Deseret News* articles and indicates what a grueling physical ordeal writing could be for her. On the last day of 1884 she began an article, completing the rough draft on New Year's Day with her aching head bandaged in wet cloth and flannel. The next day her right arm ached and she felt "worn out." On the third, she battled a cough and general weakness as she made a copy of the article. She revised it again a week later, despite continuing to feel ill, and the next day showed it to Orson, who praised it. She made a final copy before giving it to Orson on the fourteenth to turn over to John Nicholson at the *News*. The article, "A Mormon Mother Presents Some Sensible Reflections for the Benefit of Whom It May Concern," discussed reasons for the persecution of Mormons and polygamy in Utah and was printed two days later.[39]

What kind of driving force would compel the expenditure of the energy Helen invested in her prolific writing? According to a journal entry from 1885, one motivation stemmed from the anxiety she felt to fulfill her mortal mission before it was time for her to depart this life:

// **February Thursday 12th.** This day spent copying from Horace's journal, at "Winter Quarters"—my arm & shoulder painful, from writing—caused by the great amount of writing previously done from time to time with pencil, etc. Have had to give up & lay down awhile, last evening, & this—being completely used up—Am so anxious to accomplish what I have on my mind to do, before I pass over to "the other side."

---

39   Ibid., 36; italicized in original.

Friday 13th. Wrote half the day, & found my strength gone.—
concluded that I must quit & go away, or I'll be sick in bed—
head aches & my back lame—[40]

In spite of daily opposition, Helen found an assurance and source
of continuing hope in knowing that God "had a work for me to
do, and with Him, I know that all things are possible."[41] And there
were also times of respite, when beloved friends buoyed her spirits.
A few months after her husband's death, Helen recorded:

// 23 of my beloved sisters came, loaded down with good things,
& with hearts filled with blessings & good cheer for me. Many
prophecies were given that I should get well & again visit my
sisters & attend meetings and use my pen etc., as I had done.
Testimonies were given of the good I had already accomplished
with my voice and pen.[42]

Helen's driving motivation was to do the Lord's work, to serve her
sisters, comfort the afflicted, and bear testimony to the world of the
Restoration of the Gospel—a testimony from which many women
for generations after her would draw strength. Helen summarized
her life and purpose in a biographical chapter published in 1876:

// I lost three babes before I kept any, (two boys and girl). My
first to live was Vilate, she grew to womanhood and was taken.
Orson F. was my next, who has been appointed Bishop of the
Eighteenth Ward. I had four more daughters, then a son, my
last a little girl who died at five years of age; being eleven in
all. My parents have left me and my heart has been wrung to
the utmost, yet I have said Thy will God, be done. Persons
have sometimes wondered at my calmness and endurance,
but I think they would not had they passed through the
same experience.

---

40   Ibid., 69.

41   Augusta Joyce Crocheron, *Representative Women of Deseret* (Salt Lake City: J.
C. Graham & Co.), 114.

42   Charles M. Hatch and Todd M. Compton, *A Widow's Tale: 1884-1896 Diary of
Helen Mar Kimball Whitney* (Logan: Utah State University Press, 2003), 65.

I have encouraged and sustained my husband in the celestial order of marriage because I knew it was right. At various times I have been healed by the washing and annointing, administered by the mothers in Israel. I am still spared to testify to the truth and Godliness of this work; and though my happiness once consisted in laboring for those I love, the Lord has seen fit to deprive me of bodily strength, and taught me to 'cast my bread upon the waters' and after many days my longing spirit was cheered with the knowledge that He had a work for me to do, and with Him, I know that all things are possible

... God grant that I may ... be able to labor faithfully with my sisters yet many years, in relieving and comforting the tried and afflicted, and enlightening the minds of those who are in darkness concerning the things of God and His people.[43]

Instead of prompting Helen to focus on herself, her writings repeatedly emphasize her deep desire to "labo[r] for those I love" and "labor faithfully with my sisters yet many years ...." This was her focus, this was the desire of her heart.

The Prophet Joseph Smith had been warned by the Lord: "Be patient in afflictions, for thou shalt have *many*; but endure them, for, lo, I am with thee, even unto the end of thy days."[44] None have suffered more on this Earth than the Son of God, and it has been said of the Prophet, "Joseph Smith, the Prophet and Seer of the Lord, has done more, save Jesus only, for the salvation of men in this world, than any other man that ever lived in it."[45] Joseph taught that a person's contributions required a sacrifice equal to their station. As a wife sealed to him in this last and final dispensation, it is no surprise that Helen would likewise be asked to walk through fiery trials that she might obtain the promised state of happiness and Celestial glory she so desired to share with those she loved. Both Joseph and Helen lived true to their testimonies. They fought the good fight, finished their course, and kept the faith.

---

43 Augusta Joyce Crocheron, *Representative Women of Deseret* (Salt Lake City: J. C. Graham & Co.), 115; underline in original.

44 Doctrine and Covenants 24:8; emphasis added.

45 Doctrine and Covenants 135:3.

Focusing on Eternity

In 1888, Helen dreamed of a magnificent building, constructed and outfitted with such thoughtful consideration and beauty that every want she could have imagined, and more, had been satisfied—a tender message from the Lord that He would see to her every need:

> I dreamed last night that I was having some building done, or a new kitchen built—As I stood looking it seemed to work into shape as if by magic more than by the efforts of the workmen who were engaged to build it—the thing was all accomplished similar to the wonders in <u>Alladden's Lamp</u> the windows, doars, & every thing took their place, & the thing that struck me most was <u>this</u>, and I said to a woman standing by me, "<u>Why look</u> if I had dictated the job I could not have thought where to place the doars & windows so nice and convenient as they are now—" I was perfectly delighted with it. I've concluded to fret no more over certain matters but leave all to the Lord believing He'll manage every thing to my advantage, & to those in my charge.[46]

Helen was determined not to allow the adversary to plant a permanent bitterness in her heart as a result of her many hardships. In 1883, she observed that she was willing to bear "all manner of crosses" to follow in the footsteps of Jesus Christ and become a "joint heir." She felt a great sense of gratitude for her blessed station in this life:

> Words cannot express the gratitude that I feel for being counted worthy to have place among the ones of whom the Lord has made a "peculiar people," which is the only Church ever established upon the earth since the one we read of in the days of Christ, who believe and accept the whole of the gospel as taught in the ancient scriptures, instead of choosing that portion only which agrees with our peculiar ideas and notions. The ones who do this are blind indeed.
>
> If Christ is truly our pattern, and He had to submit to bear all manner of crosses and sink below all things, that He might rise

---

46   Charles M. Hatch and Todd M. Compton, *A Widow's Tale: 1884-1896 Diary of Helen Mar Kimball Whitney* (Logan: Utah State University Press, 2003), 287.

above all things, how are we to become joint heirs with Him unless we have a similar experience in this life? This people have proven their willingness to submit to be persecuted and hated of all men for righteousness' sake; and where is there another people who have manifested such true Christian patience, and faith enough to trust in an unseen hand under all circumstances and still believe in and rely upon those promises made by our Savior, who also commanded that we should become one in all things, and said, "Unless ye are one ye are not mine."[47]

Helen understood that true joy could not come through a pursuit of comfort, ease, or self-gratification. Eliza R. Snow—a woman who certainly experienced her own share of heartbreak in this life—had taught the Twentieth Ward Relief Society in 1868:

// He will have a tried people—if we want all the glory we must be willing to endure the trials. We are gaining an experience which is our wealth beyond the grave; & why should we shrink from experience.[48]

And again in 1886, to the Sugar House Ward Relief Society:

// If we are called to suffer affliction, God will sanctify it to us for our good; if we want to be superfine flour we must stand still and let the mill roll on, he can overrule all things for our good.

It is necessary for us to taste affliction that we may learn to appreciate the blessings of our Heavenly Father.

If we have not as much of his spirit as we ought to have[,] live for it . . .[49]

While Helen may have suffered more than many Latter-day Saint men and women in our day, it would be difficult to identify a woman

47   Helen Mar Kimball Whitney, "Scenes in Nauvoo after the Martyrdom of the Prophet and Patriarch," *Woman's Exponent* 11, no. 22 (April 15, 1883): 170.

48   July 10, 1868. Twentieth Ward, Ensign Stake, Relief Society Minutes and Records (1868–1973), vol. 1, p. 28, Church History Library, https://catalog.churchofjesuschrist.org/assets/404600b0-b7cb-4350-9d7f-d1bfab625e0f/0/39.

49   July 29, 1886. Sugar House Ward Relief Society minutes and records (1860-1973), vol. 2, p. 13, Church History Library, https://catalog.churchofjesuschrist.org/assets/4e4f6dec-067d-4662-9fba-baa08fe9896a/0/0.

with more hope, foresight, and acute discernment of the Lord's dealings with His people. There is no doubt that Helen is numbered among those whom John the Revelator saw in vision—those arrayed in robes washed white through their suffering for Christ—who "came out of great tribulation":

> And one of the elders answered, saying unto me, What are these which are arrayed in white robes? and whence came they?
>
> And I said unto him, Sir, thou knowest. And he said to me, These are they which came out of great tribulation, and have washed their robes, and made them white in the blood of the Lamb.[50]

As a young girl, Helen was naturally averse to the pain of sacrifice, and hesitant to surrender ease in the interest of a higher calling. She built her "castles in the air" and lived the idyllic life of one doted on by loving parents. But this blissful childhood would not last forever. Helen would not live a picture-perfect life, and her mortal journey would take her far from the avenues of pleasure, comfort, and ease. Her true character was proven each time she faced difficulty— repeatedly choosing to lay down her life rather than to save it.[51] She trod a rough, uneven road of trial and error and perseverance that slowly ground and polished her doubts into resolute conviction. She battled the weaknesses of mortality—earnestly striving to overcome evil—and in her crucible she became the woman—the queen and prophetess—she was meant to be. The enduring gift and legacy Helen left behind is a story of faith and fortitude that we must never allow to sink into the obscurity of forgotten history. Her story should be preserved, told, and retold, for generations of Latter-day Saint women to come.

---

50   Revelation 7:13-14.

51   "26 And now for a man to take up his cross, is to deny himself all ungodliness, and every worldly lust, and keep my commandments.

27 Break not my commandments for to save your lives; for whosoever will save his life in this world, shall lose it in the world to come.

28 And whosoever will lose his life in this world, for my sake, shall find it in the world to come.

29 Therefore, forsake the world, and save your souls; for what is a man profited, if he shall gain the whole world, and lose his own soul? Or what shall a man give in exchange for his soul?" JST, Matthew 16:26–29; italicized in original.

CHAPTER 15

A Battle to Live the Word of Wisdom

❧

Helen understood that she was entitled to the blessings of God, but she also understood that those blessings were predicated on her obedience to certain laws and commandments. She had a pure heart—it was her sole desire to do the will of her Father in Heaven, even when the cost of such faithfulness meant enduring physical and mental suffering. One area in which she felt an acute struggle—particularly in her later years—was her occasional consumption of coffee as a means of alleviating almost unbearable physical pain. Despite her dependence on the substance, Helen pushed herself to the very brink of death several times in a desperate attempt to free herself entirely from any 'stimulating' drinks. She sought diligently to live by the principle that those who are called by the Lord to do His work—those who desire to participate in the great work of the Restoration—must strictly follow the requirements of God, just as the Savior so perfectly exemplified.

Understanding the Word of Wisdom in Helen's Day

The Word of Wisdom came by way of revelation to the Prophet Joseph Smith in 1833, but it was understood by the early Latter-day Saint leaders and members in terms of a series of *principles*, rather than a specific set of rules fastidiously dictating 'do's' and 'don'ts.'

An example of how this principle was adapted to various circumstances and needs can be seen five years after the Prophet had received the revelation, when the battered and destitute Saints arrived in Illinois after being driven from their homes in

Missouri. The swampy conditions of their living quarters caused many to succumb to malaria and the accompanying chills, fever, and ague that wracked their exhausted bodies. Men, women, and children were dying while their fathers, mothers, brothers, and sisters were too weak even to rise from their beds. To make matters worse, the Saints had been stripped of most of their bedding and clothing during the Missouri persecutions, leaving them almost completely unprepared for the night temperatures. While surveying the desperate conditions and realizing that their water was unfit to drink, the Prophet Joseph Smith began recommending and personally preparing tea, thus bringing some alleviation to the suffering of those he ministered to. Helen recorded:

// Brother Joseph, seeing the condition of the Saints, especially those on the bank of the river, where the water was unfit for drinking purposes and they were dying like sheep, his sympathies were so wrought upon that he told them to make tea and drink it, or anything that they thought would do them good; and he often made tea and administered it with his own hands. That was the commencement of their using tea and coffee; previous to this the Saints had been strict in keeping the Word of Wisdom.[1]

In addition to Joseph's administration of tea in 1839, there are several entries in the Prophet's history and journals indicating the use of 'hot drinks' for a variety of purposes.[2] Unfortunately, the malleability of this principle has proven to be a major concern—even a faith crisis for some members—both then and now. However, if we consider the *principles* behind the Word of Wisdom, rather than reading into it the idea of rigid regulations devoid of context, we learn that such concerns are unnecessary. For the Prophet, the Word of Wisdom was not an arbitrary, unbending regimen—rather, it was

---

1   Helen Mar Kimball Whitney, "Scenes in Nauvoo," *Woman's Exponent* 10, no. 4 (July 15, 1881): 26.

2   See for example, "Saturday March 11th. So cold last night as to freeze water in the warmest rooms in the city. river fillid with anchor ice—8 1/2 o clock. in the office Joseph said he had tea with his breakfast. his wife asked him if [it] was good.— he said if it was a little stronger he should like it better, when Mother [Lydia Dibble] Granger remarked, "It is so strong, and good, I should think it would answer—Both for drink, and food..." March 11, 1843. Journal, December 1842–June 1844, Book 2, p. 3, The Joseph Smith Papers.

Word of Wisdom Revealed, by Ken Corbett

counsel given by the Lord to be used and applied with prudence and wisdom. When coffee, tea, or even alcohol, were needed for medicinal purposes—and sometimes due to sanitary conditions, including the lack of a clean water source[3]—the Prophet voiced no objections.

Years later, in 1855, Joseph Smith's cousin, George, recalled that some members struggled to grasp the Prophet's purpose and intentions when it came to applying true doctrine and principles. He shared an example of one family apostatizing after Emma Smith offered them tea and coffee in her home following their especially long and physically taxing trip:

// I know persons who apostatized because they supposed they had reasons; for instance, a certain family, after having travelled a long journey, arrived in Kirtland, and the prophet asked

3 "Difficulties in assuring clean water supplies also make tea or coffee a sometimes wiser choice for health. Both coffee and tea are made from boiled water, which will kill bacteria. Even without boiling, the tannic acid in tea would kill the bacteria that caused such scourges as cholera, typhoid, and dysentery—all real risks on the American frontier." "Joseph Smith or other early members of the Church used tea and tobacco," FairMormon, accessed January 2, 2022, https://www.fairlatterdaysaints.org/answers/Word_of_Wisdom/Joseph_Smith_used_tea.

them to stop with him until they could find a place. Sister Emma, in the mean time, asked the old lady if she would have a cup of tea to refresh her after the fatigues of the journey, or a cup of coffee. This whole family apostatized because they were invited to take a cup of tea or coffee, after the Word of Wisdom was given.[4]

Another instance that remains challenging for some members comes from the historical testimony of John Taylor, wherein he mentioned that while incarcerated in Carthage Jail, he and the Prophet partook of some wine as a remedy to "revive us."[5] The *History of the Church* account describes the Prophet as "tasting" the wine before it was returned to the guards, who consumed the greater part of the bottle.[6] There was apparently no shame in relating this story during their day or by later Church leaders who saw this as merely a part of our history.[7] Additionally, a revelation

---

4   George A. Smith, "Gathering and Sanctification of the People of God," in *Journal of Discourses*, vol. 2 (Liverpool: F. D. Richards, 1855), 214. Discourse given on March 18, 1855.

5   According to John Taylor's firsthand account of the martyrdom, "Sometime after dinner we sent for some wine. It has been reported by some that this was taken as a sacrament. It was no such thing; our spirits were generally dull and heavy, and it was sent for to revive us. I think it was Captain Jones who went after it, but they would not suffer him to return. I believe we all drank of the wine, and gave some to one or two of the prison guards. We all of us felt unusually dull and languid, with a remarkable depression of spirits. In consonance with those feelings I sang a song, that had lately been introduced into Nauvoo, entitled, 'A Poor Wayfaring Man of Grief', etc." John Taylor, as recorded in *History of the Church*, vol. 7 (Salt Lake City: Deseret Book Company, 1950), 101.

6   John Taylor also recorded: "Before the jailer came in, his boy brought in some water, and said the guard wanted some wine. Joseph gave Dr. Richards two dollars to give the guard; but the guard said one was enough, and would take no more.

"The guard immediately sent for a bottle of wine, pipes, and two small papers of tobacco; and one of the guards brought them into the jail soon after the jailer went out. Dr. Richards uncorked the bottle, and presented a glass to Joseph, who tasted, as also Brother Taylor and the doctor, and the bottle was then given to the guard, who turned to go out. When at the top of the stairs some one below called him two or three times, and he went down." *History of the Church*, vol. 6 (Salt Lake City: Deseret Book Company, 1950), 616.

7   Another statement recorded in Joseph Smith's history confirms the Prophet's use of alcoholic drinks when he considered it necessary for health: "The Company moved on to Andover, where the Sheriff of Lee County requested lodgings for the night for all the Company. I was put into a room and locked up with Captain Grover, it was reported to me that some of the Brethren had been drinking whiskey that day in violation of the word of wisdom. I called the Brethren in, and investigated the case,

given in August 1830 includes a commandment from the Lord to consume wine only when "it is made new among you."[8] The Word of Wisdom revelation itself speaks of drinking wine as part of the ordinance of the sacrament, provided that it be "pure wine of the grape of the vine, of your own make."[9]

These are significant insights into understanding how Joseph Smith and those tutored directly under him interpreted and applied the Word of Wisdom. From their own history, it is clear that the Prophet and other leaders occasionally employed the use of alcohol, tea, and coffee to relieve suffering, for physical illness, for other unique purposes—generally medicinal—or when otherwise deemed prudent. It is interesting to note that the recommendation was against a persistent and addictive use of coffee, and not as a clear-cut prohibition. In some cases, such as during the pioneer trek west, the early leaders actually requested the Saints to bring coffee with them among their essential supplies.[10] The original revelation given from the Lord—and echoed by early leaders—was a warning against using those items recklessly or becoming dependent on them as stimulants. The Lord desired that his people should be free from addiction or reliance on *any* substance.

Women Warned of Relying on Stimulation

After the Saints' migration to Utah, Brigham Young became concerned about the inappropriate and liberal use of alcoholic and other cautionary beverages. He noticed that some Saints had failed to develop the necessary temperance and discipline required to overcome the appetites of the flesh, giving way to the indulgence of unhealthy cravings. These observations led him to realize that such a path would lead to an abuse of their liberty and freedom, and so he sought to apply a more easily defined approach:

---

and was satisfied that no evil had been done and gave them a couple of dollars, with directions to replenish the bottle, to stimulate them in the fatigues of their sleepless journey." June 27, 1843. Joseph Smith, History, 1838–1856, volume D-1, p. 1587-1588, The Joseph Smith Papers.

8   Doctrine and Covenants 27:3-4.

9   Doctrine and Covenants 89:6.

10   "Bill of Particulars For the Emigrants Leaving this Government Next Spring," *Nauvoo Neighbor*, October 29, 1845.

Painting of Brigham Young, by Ken Corbett

// I said to the Saints at our last annual Conference, the Spirit whispers to me to call upon the Latter-day Saints to observe the Word of Wisdom, to let tea, coffee, and tobacco alone, and to abstain from drinking spirituous drinks. This is what the Spirit signifies through me. If the Spirit of God whispers this to His people through their leader, and they will not listen nor obey, what will be the consequence of their disobedience? Darkness and blindness of mind with regard to the things of God will be their lot; they will cease to have the spirit of prayer, and the spirit of the world will increase in them in proportion to their disobedience until they apostatize entirely from God and His ways.[11]

---

11   Brigham Young, "The Word of Wisdom—Degeneracy—Wickedness in the United States—How to Prolong Life," in *Journal of Discourses*, vol. 12 (Liverpool: Albert Carrington, 1869), 117. Discourse given on August 17, 1867.

Helen and her sisters learned from President Brigham Young and others that they should not become reliant on 'hot' or stimulating drinks as a source of energy. Some women felt *dependent* on these beverages as a remedy for enduring the physically and emotionally taxing labor required to settle and tame the Utah desert. President Young encouraged the women that if they needed rest, they should sleep—not take stimulation.[12] He also pled with the sisters to carefully and conscientiously avoid passing on poor genetics and a "foundation of weakness" to their children through a careless and undisciplined diet:

// Many sisters think they cannot live without tea; I will tell you what we can do – I have frequently said it to my brethren and sisters – if they cannot live without tea, coffee, brandy, tobacco, etc., they can die without them. This is beyond controversy. If we had the determination that we should have, we should live without them or die without them. Let the mother impregnate her system with these narcotic influences when she is bringing forth a family on the earth, and what does she do? She lays the foundation of weakness, palpitations of the heart, nervous affections, and many other ills and diseases in the system of her offspring that will afflict them from the cradle to the grave. Is this righteous or unrighteous, good or evil? Let my sisters answer the question for themselves, and the conclusion which each and every one of them may come to is this, "If I do any injury to my child, I sin."[13]

President Young prophesied that it would be the *mothers* in Zion who would bring about the health and vitality promised during the Millennium. He taught that it was the mothers who lay the foundation for health—or for disease—in their children, largely

12 "I have said to my family, and I now say to all the sisters in the Church, if you cannot get up and do your washing without a cup of tea in the morning, go to bed, and there lie. How long? Until the influence of tea is out of the system. Will it take a month? No matter if it does; if it takes three months, six months, or a year, it is better to lie there in bed until the influence of tea, coffee and liquor is out of the system, so that you may go about your business like rational persons, than to give way to these foolish habits." Brigham Young, "The Word of Wisdom—Spiritualism," in *Journal of Discourses*, vol. 13 (Liverpool: Horace S. Eldredge, 1871), 278. Discourse given on October 30, 1870.

13 Ibid., 276.

by how they chose to eat. When they repented, he promised, health and longevity would return to the Earth, as they existed in the days of the ancient Biblical patriarchs:

// If the days of man are to begin to return, we must cease all extravagant living. When men live to the age of a tree, their food will be fruit. Mothers, to produce offspring full of life and days, must cease drinking liquor, tea, and coffee, that their systems may be free from bad effects. If every woman in this Church will now cease drinking tea, coffee, liquor, and all other powerful stimulants, and live upon vegetables, etc., not many generations will pass away before the days of man will again return. But it will take generations to entirely eradicate the influences of deleterious substances. This must be done before we can attain our paradisiacal state, for the Lord will bring again Zion to its paradisiacal state.[14]

This understanding and interpretation of the Word of Wisdom by President Young was shared by other early leaders, including President George Q. Cannon, who interestingly considered chocolate a stimulating drink, presumably because chocolate shares an attribute with both coffee and tea—the potential to become addictive:

// We are told [by Church leaders], and very plainly too, that hot drinks—tea, coffee, chocolate, cocoa and all drinks of this kind are not good for man. We are also told that alcoholic drinks are not good, and that tobacco when either smoked or chewed is an evil. We are told that swine's flesh is not good, and that we should dispense with it; and we are told that flesh of any kind is not suitable to man in the summer time, and ought to be eaten sparingly in the winter.[15]

The Prophet Joseph Smith, and those who followed his leadership example, taught correct principles and then encouraged the members

---

14   Brigham Young, "Privileges of the Sabbath—Duty of Living Our Religion—Human Longevity, &c," in *Journal of Discourses*, vol. 8 (Liverpool: George Q. Cannon, 1861), 63-64. Discourse given on May 20, 1860.

15   George Q. Cannon, "Word of Wisdom—Fish Culture—Dietetics," in *Journal of Discourses*, vol. 12 (Liverpool: Albert Carrington, 1869), 221-222. Discourse given on April 7, 1868.

to govern themselves.[16] They expected *agency* to define *application*, allowing leaders and members to adapt different interpretations as they strove to follow the guidance of the Spirit regarding their health and medical decisions. It was not until the 20th century, during the administration of President Heber J. Grant, that the Church institutionalized a more rigid interpretation of the Word of Wisdom. Coffee, tea, and alcohol began to be censored by rule, instead of by principle. Members have certainly benefited from the elimination of these drinks, but the loss of understanding and historical perspective regarding the *why* behind the Word of Wisdom has provided its own set of challenges.

Understanding the interpretation of the Word of Wisdom in Helen's day provides further insight into the reason why she occasionally partook of beer or wine, or used tea and coffee. Helen often made her own beer,[17] and she gave it away to children and friends in the Church as Christmas gifts. In fact, when she purchased her coffee, she did so from the Church's own store—Zion's Co-operative Mercantile Institution.[18]

Despite the usage of coffee by her fellow members, Helen understood the spiritual ramifications of her leaders' council, and she sought to free herself from a reliance on the drink. She had been introduced to the beverage in her youth, and as she battled life-threatening health challenges, coffee, it seemed, was the only remedy that could effectively relieve her suffering. And yet, she agonized over this quandary terribly. She wanted to obey the Lord, but what could she possibly do? Around 1884, Helen mustered all of her strength and— through sheer determination—absolutely refused to drink even a

---

16   John Taylor, "The Organization of the Church," *The Latter-day Saints Millennial Star*, vol. 13, no. 22, November 15, 1851, 339.

17   Although Utah had a thriving liquor industry and a number of breweries in the Salt Lake Valley during the 1800s, the beer made in the home included a wide variety of lightly fermented drinks, such as ginger beer, apple beer, etc. Naturally occurring alcohol was present as part of the living fermentation process.

18   Helen recorded purchasing coffee from the Co-op on August 10, 1885: "Did not finish my article till this morning. I took it to Em. Went to Co-op for coffee— returned home . . ."

December 29 1885: "I took back two glass pepper boxes to Co[-]op, which I got Christmas—ten cts a piece. Got Coffee and a bar of soap, in return." Charles M. Hatch and Todd M. Compton, *A Widow's Tale: 1884-1896 Diary of Helen Mar Kimball Whitney* (Logan: Utah State University Press, 2003), 97, 128.

drop of coffee. For five or six weeks she battled on, but the exertion nearly killed her, and she was compelled to return to drinking an occasional cup when her strength utterly failed her. Two years later, she still lamented her physical limitations relating to her use of coffee, though she continued to avoid it whenever possible. This often led to moments when her head was "nearly distracted with pain":

// Wednesday 24th. Fasted this fore noon, that I may gain faith, & be able to keep the commandments and control my family—or lead them to the Lord. that the Word of Wisdom may not be lost on us. I took no stimulants to day & my head has been nearly distracted with pain, till I hardly know what course to take. I prayed the Lord that my head might get better if I was doing my duty, or if I was not required to leave off my cup of Coffee for breakfast, that He would give me a testimony of the same, that I might act wisely this time, and not bring bodily suffering upon myself, as I did two years ago, by going without tea or Coffee for 5 or 6 weeks, which came very near ending my life. The Lord knows my heart.[19]

It was not so much the coffee itself—but rather, it was the effect coffee had on her system that was Helen's primary concern. It was the 'stimulant' effect of the coffee that was the cause of her misgivings. After all, it was this dependency that Church leaders had warned the Saints about. Her diary entries from 1884 reveal several emotive descriptions of her struggle:

// [December 1884] Thursday 18th—Sat up too late trying to knit—till I felt sleepy—couldn't sleep till nearly midnight—woke this morning wild with nervous head ache—couldn't rise till I took some toast & coffee—got up as Juliette had come to finish my dress—Went to bed again—pain grew worse Orson came in my room, at noon—found me distracted with my head—offered to administer to me—I told him I'd be glad to have him. He did so anointing my head with oil—I am now able to sit up & write, thank the Lord.[20]

---

19   Charles M. Hatch and Todd M. Compton, *A Widow's Tale: 1884-1896 Diary of Helen Mar Kimball Whitney* (Logan: Utah State University Press, 2003), 144.

20   Ibid., 54.

[December 1884] <u>Monday 29th</u>. Felt sick this morning—cough worse through the night—couldn't sleep only by snatches—late before I closed my eyes—was taken with awful distress in my right breast—up into my throat—caused by wind—got up and fixed soda in water, which gave relief—I had to go back to bed before eating breakfast—head was bad—had tea brought & my coffee taken away, & every thing, but bread & a little sauce. My head felt relieved by the tea.[21]

Sincerely conscientious, Helen pled and wept before the Lord over her dilemma, a subject she often noted in her diary:

// [March 1886] <u>Thursday 25th</u> I have taken Coffee for breakfast—after praying and strugling to be able to leave it off. I could not get any testimony only that my body could not be sustained without this little stimulous. I have felt sad all day over this & the thoughts that crowd themselves upon me concerning my children, and the necessity of living up to the principles of the Gospel.[22]

[May 1886] <u>Sunday 23d</u> . . . I have fasted, prayed, read the Bible, & wept with a broken heart before the Lord that we might find favor in His eyes, & grace to enable us to keep the "<u>word of wisdom</u>" in its true meaning—[23]

As she wrestled inwardly with her unwanted dependency, Helen's journal also reveals a mother's concern about the example she was setting for her children. Her children seemed to feel compassion and understand her struggle as well:

// [August 1886] <u>Friday 27th</u>. . . . I was sick, & grew worse till nearly noon, my pain was so excruciating & so much like that that was brought on me the other time I tried to break off drinking Coffee I concluded to take some Tea—It relieved me & I felt better every way, but not able to walk being very weak in body—Flod went and asked her Uncle Joshua to take me at six o'clock. My countenence shows the suffering that I've passed through in the <u>struggle</u> to <u>keep the word of wisdom</u> . . . I feel sad, & almost

---

21 Ibid., 59.
22 Ibid., 144.
23 Ibid., 158.

discouraged, as I desired so much to put away everything that prevented me from receiving the blessings promised by our Father to those who obeyed the word of wisdom. Orson had felt to rejoice over our attempt in this direction, and I [k]now I'm not able to accomplish it—The girls all want me to take coffee, & promise that they will abstain—all but Lillie whom they also think ought to have it—I asked to be administered to after Mr Hall was, and Bro. C. Stainer previously asked the cause of my ales. I told him—He thought it would be wisdom for me not to break off too short, but take a cup of coffee, or Tea for a while—do it more gradually—then maybe I could accomplish it. I was administered to & blessed after Bro. Hall was—We had an interesting time—conversed upon the two powers, who were working for the victory, & related incidents of faith, the power God and the Evil one, & struggles which we had experienced in our own lives—Orson asked me to tell some of my experience & others with the evil spirits, which I did. We had a very interesting meeting . . .²⁴

Then, one year later on July 29, 1887, Helen recorded a disturbing and unpleasant dream that she felt the Lord had given to her as a loving warning:

// [July 1887] Friday 29th . . . I had a terible dream Wednesday night about myself—My hair was filled with some kind of insects similar to musquetoes, raising my hair an inch or two, & the feelings I had were most appalling. Some person combed out small bits of my hair but did not clear my head. Some man was standing by me, and I told him that this was "one of the scourges which had been predicted would come upon those who did not keep the Word of wisdom". I thought there were scores of others who were afflicted in the same manner as I was. I have felt ever since that I would stop taking my cup of coffee for breakfast if the Lord would only help me. & have prayed for some time. continually to that effect—I sorely regret that I did not quit it when I had youth & strength on my side. I thought when so sick yesterday from the pain in my head, that

---

24   Ibid., 183-184; underlined in original.

my dream was fulfilling—"Obedience is better than sacrefise", did we but know it.—Would that my girls could realize this.[25]

Helen's diary fell silent for over a month following this experience. Then, with the effects of her dream still weighing heavily on her mind, she broke the silence in her journal with an entry that revealed she had become "dangerously sick with Typhoid fever" but had only doubled in her resolve to be free from the shackles of any addictive substance. She had finally regained the strength to go outside, but was disappointed when she caught a cold and found herself forced to return to bed—setting the stage for her to reflect on her dream from July:

⫽ September the 7th. Have been dangerously sick with Typhoid fever since writing the above—had on my clothes the 3d day of this month—The 4th George Bourne got a Hack, & Helen & Bro. Farington helped me to it. rode an hour & repeeted it Monday & Tuesday. Took cold 1st day out & had fever Monday—felt quite sick all day—The warning given me in my dream I never lost sight of, & was set & determined that I would not drink coffee nor tea. After I'd lain for some days growing worse & not knowing what ailes me Orson asked me if I had not better have the advise of some Dr, & proposed Dr Joseph Richards. I said yes, & he was sent for. Among other things he said I must take was Coffee & must have it twice a day. This roused me & I emphatically told him I would not drink it.[26]

A battle ensued between Helen, the doctor, and her friend, Lucy W. Kimball, who had taken the liberty of acting as Helen's nurse. Helen's refusal to drink as the doctor had ordered caused him to turn to Lucy, pressing her with the instruction that Lucy should "pay no attention to what I said & I was like a child."[27] But this time, being compelled by her attendants to drink the coffee she had so ardently refused brought about a strange reaction in Helen's body—*it* was rejecting the drink, and by the third unwanted administration of the coffee, she began to vomit. Helen took this as a sign from the Lord that, at last, He had answered her prayers and recognized her sacrifice:

---

25 Ibid., 253; underlined in original.
26 Ibid., 253-254; underlined in original.
27 Ibid., 254.

// ...that decided the matter with me that the Lord had heard my humble cries, & did not intend that Coffee should have the credit of my recovery. This was a comfort to me in the midst of my sadness & suffering that He had heard my cries. I felt that dejected over my unworthiness that I hardly felt deserving of anything at His hands, although I was administered to, & blessed almost daily, by elders, & prayed for by various circles.[28]

Despite this tender mercy, her recovery was neither swift nor easy—and for the next two weeks, Helen hovered by a hair's breadth between life and death:

// After a fortnight or more of terible suffering a sudden change came over my feelings. Previously I had clung to life but there seemed to me as though I could feel the presence, & in imagination see a throng of the departed hovering around waiting to welcome me into their circle. I longed to be set free, & could not help expressing it. I felt that there was little to hold me here, that my mind as well as body was wrecked, & I was weary of this struggle with lifes cares & sorrows.[29]

In terrible pain and suffering from severe insomnia, Helen felt the withering effects of sleep deprivation, and when she did finally sleep, it wasn't always restorative. One morning, she awoke suddenly, feeling "more dead tha[n] alive—the most death-like sensation which I could not discribe. the only thing I remember that morning was that I felt like a worm that might role up with the dust and go out of sight." As delerium overtook her, she slipped in and out of consciousness. Finally, she was given another blessing—and then suddenly, her long-anticipated healing began to take effect. That night, Helen slept through the entire night—her struggle had reached a turning point, and in her own words, "the prayers began to prevail ..."[30] Healing would take time, and—according to her son Orson—it required frequent priesthood blessings:

---

28   Ibid., 254.
29   Ibid., 254.
30   Ibid., 254.

❞ One morning after I had been so often relieved by being administered to he (Orson) came & finding I'd had a suffering night he took the oil & came to my bed & annointed & prayed for me, though he was feeling very miserable himself he afterwards said, & didn't know whether his administration would benefit me or not. But I was better all day, & that evening he brought bro. Stainer with him, both being filled with the Holy Spirit & annointed & blessed me after kneeling first & praying Bro. Sol made a practice of coming and praying evenings, & Orson mornings till I was better—. Orson said he saw that I must be adminis- tered to every day or I seemed to fail. I certainly owe my restoration to the <u>power of faith</u> & not to the power of man. only as far as they exercised it in my behalf.

There was one brother named Patterson from Payson who heard of my sickness at Sister E. R. Snow's nearly at the start & came over with a bottle of oil to administer to me—this seeming to be his mission—and he gave me the promise of life, & health & predicted great & mighty things that I was to accomplish [in] this life. I laid hold of his words and believed the Lord dictated them until I found my sufferings did not lesson, & my mind became weakened with my body—Through it all I never lost sight of my first determination that I'd <u>keep the "word of wisdom"</u>.[31]

Helen's resolve was put to the test once more when pressure came from another member of the Church who informed Helen's daughter and namesake, also Helen, that three doctors had specified the proper necessity of administering coffee to patients recovering from typhoid fever, insisting "that there was something peculiar in Typhoid feever which required Coffee to bring them up & there was nothing so good."[32] In determined protest—and typical of Helen— she turned to the Lord for wisdom:

❞ I laid the case before the Lord & prayed that I might be actuated by the right spirit & if I was acting unwisely that He would show me, but if I was not that He would come to my assistance

---

31 Ibid., 255; underlined in original.
32 Ibid., 255.

& raise me up from that sick bed. I immediately felt revived & was better from that time.[33]

In many ways, Helen's experience had been a test of obedience, as well as an opportunity to nurture her trust in the Lord. Throughout the succeeding years—as a result of extremely painful, chronic health conditions—Helen occasionally required a little coffee. Nevertheless, she continued to battle against her physical dependence until the day she died. Her story reveals the nuances many faced when striving to understand and live the Word of Wisdom during the early days of the Church. In view of her health challenges, natural frailty, and advancing age, it had proven impossible for Helen to gain complete freedom from the substance—but she never gave up the fight; she persevered with unquestionably rare tenacity, and a willingness to endure intense pain in the process. Helen would only give her very best effort for the Lord.

The abiding message Helen left for her children was one of warning and earnest pleading to live the Lord's laws of health from their youth. It was also her personal desire to see a generation of children in Zion who would never experience her struggle and pain, because they were reared in a pure environment. Truly, the sacrifices these early pioneers made to adopt the revelations of God should serve as a sober reminder—and a call to action—for each of us. Perhaps we should ask ourselves: Are we making the necessary sacrifices to live clean and holy lives today? Are we closer to achieving Zion today than we were yesterday? Will our posterity inherit a better world because of our personal and collective contributions as Latter-day Saints? *How can we do better?*

---

33   Ibid., 255.

CHAPTER 16

Charity Never Faileth

~ᴏ⦵~

In spite of her many struggles—or perhaps *because* of them—
Helen maintained a gentle heart, ever flowing with compassion
and Christlike charity. Rather than wallowing in her own self-pity,
she labored constantly to meet the needs she saw around her, and to
bless the lives of her children, neighbors, strangers—and even those
who may have injured her in the past.

On January 27, 1885, a 56-year-old Helen received a surprising
visit from a woman she referred to merely as "Em. Evans" in her
diary—a woman she had not seen for over 20 years. This woman
came to her with a request that would test both Helen's mettle and,
apparently, her spirit of forgiveness. In an unheralded turn of events,
Sister Evans expressed her desire to be sealed to Helen's late husband,
Horace, who had passed away only three months previous. Helen
wrote of this unexpected visit in her diary:

// She desires to cling to Horace—Said her brothers had always
told her she ought to have been his wife. I've heard that she had
acted in a way to forfeit her right to ones charity. But I told her
if she was sincere she could be seeled to Horace. She said she
was, but this is yet to be proven. I gave her one of my books on
plural marriage.[1]

The entry in her journal provides no further details regarding the
actions that "forfeit[ed] her right to ones charity,"[2] and little is said
about the woman, leaving historians to concede that—beside this

---

1   Charles M. Hatch and Todd M. Compton, *A Widow's Tale: 1884-1896 Diary of
Helen Mar Kimball Whitney* (Logan: Utah State University Press, 2003), 66.
2   Ibid.

Helen Mar Kimball Whitney

brief entry—"Em. Evans has a mysterious connection to Horace Whitney. Almost nothing is known about her."[3] What is clear from this entry, however, is the gracious spirit exemplified by Helen throughout her life.

Not everyone within Helen's circle embodied her gift of compassion. She recorded an incident involving her brother Solomon one Sunday

---

3   Ibid., 738.

afternoon when he became exasperated with her because, "I didn't fall into line with the common herd in condemning a poor woman of whom I knew nothing, except through reports," adding that he "told me he 'had no patience with me', & left in disgust."[4] Helen recognized the injustice, and felt that misinformation was too often spread through gossip—and that meant she kept her lips sealed, and expressly refused to take part.

One cold day in January 1888, a needy sister paid Helen a visit to ask "if I had any old shoes or clothes, as she'd numbers of children—& her husband had been unable to find work." Helen requested that she return at a later time, and when the woman arrived, she had one of her little girls in tow. Helen generously opened her family's closets to provide relief for the family in need:

❝ I found her quite a bundle of things—Gave her my Satteen basque, & skirt, which had not been washed but once—a thick coat once belonging to Gen—a pair of good warm kid gloves with fur on the wrists, which were left here by some one long ago—a basket full of stockings and socks that would do to cut down, & some still good enough to wear—a black skirt of fine cloth— once Flods, & a petticoat—A pound of butter for cooking, & over half I had of good table butter, etc, which she appeared grateful for—[5]

Helen did not merely offer a charitable gift of clothing; she also saw to it that the family was fed—even offering to hire the woman's husband to cut wood for her:

❝ When I asked what they had to eat, etc, she said only bread & a piece of bacon, so I gave her the butter telling her how I had known want of things that I could eat, etc, & knew how to feel for others. They had been here only a year—She took off a thin shawl & put on the coat which made her look more comfortable. Wealth & want has no busines to go side by side in the midst of "Zion"[6]

---

4   Ibid., 559.
5   Ibid., 280.
6   Ibid., 280; underlined in original.

A week later, another sister came to visit, to whom Helen gave a small stove, an "old lounge & a large pile of clothes & things." This time, the woman had been selling butter, but had no more to offer. Helen, seeing her plight, once again felt her heart move with compassion, and she determined to provide what she could to ease the suffering of this desperate family as well:

> I felt so for her—she having told me that she sold all the butter she made—that their home was morgaged, & their children were destitute, etc., that I gave her a two dollor order on the T.O. & told her I had some old things, which she asked me if I'd save for her till she could call for them next Saturday—I promised I would. I've about cleaned out my half worn old clothes, & things that I had on hand—to relieve the poor who've come to me—[7]

Helen's predisposition to care for her fellow brothers and sisters demonstrated that she was a true reflection of her benevolent father. "My heart aches to think of the suffering—& humanity—so hard to find among the rich, the proud and heartless," she wrote in her diary. "Some professing to be saints turn a cold shoulder to the poor in Zion but thank the Lord their time is measured."[8]

Balancing Justice & Mercy

Helen's open heart and giving spirit once prompted her brother to lightheartedly accuse her of being *too* compassionate. After a visit from her brother, Solomon, in 1893, Helen recorded a mirthful exchange, revealing her ever-present willingness to advocate and care for the weak and downtrodden:

> Sol has been here since & told me that he'd told Orson he thought had I been present when Lucifer was cast out that I'd taken his part—I replied that "I <u>was</u> present at that time & if I'd been on his (the devils) side I'd been cast out with him, etc," instead of being where I am—that I was like our mother, towards the poor and the friendless, I wouldnt join those who

---

7   Ibid., 281.
8   Ibid., 281; underlined in original.

Heber C. Kimball children at Kimball family reunion, June 14, 1887.
Helen is seated in middle row, third from the right.

were trying to crush another under their feet. This was said in good humor . . .⁹

While Helen could not turn away a brother or sister in need, she also recognized that compassion must be balanced with wisdom and justice. On one occasion, she received a letter from "Bro. Charley" that she determined was "full of affection but not much 'Mormonism'." When she wrote about Charley's letter, she expressed concern that instead of Christlike love, he seemed to indulge in a counterfeit—a dangerous tolerance for error:

// . . . [Charley is] liberal to all people though he says his heart and sympathies are always with his people, etc. Those who become so <u>liberal</u> toward all sects remind me of Lucifer—who was going to save every body—none should be lost if Father would send him down—but He wanted to give every one their agency, so sent the one who was wiling to do His bidding.¹⁰

From her writings, it is clear that Helen understood this multifaceted principle: how does one love their enemy without

---

9   Ibid., 559-560; underlined in original.
10   Ibid., 218; underlined in original.

condoning or supporting evil? In our modernist world today, this concept is perhaps more widely misunderstood—and more pertinent—than ever before. What is the difference between 'loving our enemies' and progressive tolerance/political correctness? In 1882, President Joseph F. Smith offered this helpful counsel in a discourse given to the Saints:

// Do you love these slanderers, these liars, these defamers, these persecutors of the innocent and of the unoffending—do you love them? [several voices, No, no.] I can scarcely blame you. [Laughter.] But that is not according to the law of God. I want to tell you how I feel towards them. I love them so much that if I had it in my power to annihilate them from the earth I would not harm a hair of their heads—not one hair of their heads. I love them so well that if I could possibly make them better men, convert them from the error of their ways I would do it, God being my helper. . . . yet I detest and abominate their infamous actions and their wicked course. . . . I do not love them so that I would take them into my bosom, or invite them to associate with my family . . . nor would I share with them the inheritance that God, my Father, has given me in Zion; I do not love them well enough for this, and I do not believe that God ever designed that I should; but I love them so much that I would not hurt them, I would do them good, I would tell the truth about them . . . There is a difference between the love we should bear towards our enemies and that we should bear towards our friends. . . . But we do not love to associate with our enemies, and I do not think the Lord requires us to do it. . . .

We should keep ourselves aloof from the wicked; the dividing line should be distinctly drawn between God and Belial, between Christ and the world, between truth and error, and between right and wrong. We ought to cleave to the right, to the good, to the truth, and forsake the evil.[11]

President Smith's words of more than a century ago continue to stand as sound guidance in a divisive contemporary culture with

---

11   Joseph F. Smith, "Love for and Forgiveness of Enemies," in *Journal of Discourses*, vol. 23 (Liverpool: John Henry Smith, 1883), 284, 285; brackets in original. Discourse given on October 7, 1882.

bigotry and hate on one side, and over-tolerance, falsely labeled as 'love,' on the other. Backed by scriptural authority, he called on the Saints—then and now—to heed the word of the Lord on the matter:

Joseph F. Smith, by Ken Corbett

// I am going to read a little scripture upon this subject, lest our friends or this congregation should feel that counseling the Latter-day Saints to keep aloof from the wicked and ungodly, to not divide their inheritances with them, etc., is unwarranted by the scriptures. I will read a little scripture on this very point . . . Now, here is the law of God upon the subject; it is the word of the Lord: "Come out from among them and be ye separate, and touch not the unclean thing."[12] What affinity can we have for them? Let them alone, let them go their own way. Help them to all the happiness that it is possible for them to obtain in this world; for it will be all that they will ever get, unless they repent of their sins, and forsake their wicked ways.[13]

12   "Be ye not unequally yoked together with unbelievers: for what fellowship hath righteousness with unrighteousness? and what communion hath light with darkness?

"And what concord hath Christ with Belial? or what part hath he that believeth with an infidel?

"And what agreement hath the temple of God with idols? for ye are the temple of the living God; as God hath said, I will dwell in them, and walk in them; and I will be their God, and they shall be my people.

"Wherefore come out from among them, and be ye separate, saith the Lord, and touch not the unclean thing; and I will receive you.

"And will be a Father unto you, and ye shall be my sons and daughters, saith the Lord Almighty." 2 Corinthians 6:14-18.

13   This entire discourse is highly recommended. Joseph F. Smith, "Love for and Forgiveness of Enemies," in *Journal of Discourses*, vol. 23 (Liverpool: John Henry Smith, 1883), 285-286. Discourse given on October 7, 1882.

Helen and her family truly lived the command to "love your enemies"[14]—a remarkable feat considering the trauma and terrible persecution of their past. Even as she reached the final stretch of her mortal run, Helen continued to push her own spiritual progression forward, to reach for an even higher standard. She embraced forgiveness with such sincerity that she could not take the sacrament in peace without "forgiving all those who'd wronged me." A few months before she passed away, this woman of charity bared her soul by sharing the following dream during a fast and testimony meeting in 1896:

// I related part of a dream I had last night—after speaking a few words—I felt it to have been given by the Holy Spirit—it being a lesson I hoped to profit by. I was shown how far I was from the mark laid down for the Saints who expected to win a Celestial glory—that though I thought I'd laid aside the hardness & unsaintly feelings, forgiving all those who'd wronged me, that my conscience might not sting me when taking of the sacrements but I was shown the deep humility that I had got to bring myself to—that I could feel as gentle & tenderly towards all as I did towards those whom I'd loved—as worthy of my best affections.[15]

Forgiveness of one's fellow man—particularly one's enemies—can be extraordinarily difficult, stretching the heart's embrace far beyond its perceived limits. But it was a duty Helen would not forsake. Helen noted that she was able to forgive because she cultivated humility within herself—she purposely focused on her own repentance, continually refining her character until she could not help but feel "gentle & tenderly" toward all her fellowmen.

However, there was another level. When Helen faced the moors of raising her children in mortality, this journey required a new level of charity—a learning experience entirely of its own.

---

14   Matthew 5:44.

15   Charles M. Hatch and Todd M. Compton, *A Widow's Tale: 1884-1896 Diary of Helen Mar Kimball Whitney* (Logan: Utah State University Press, 2003), 697.

CHAPTER 17

Faithful & Wayward Children

MOTHERING IN ZION

The Son of God taught, "Greater love hath no man than this, that a man lay down his life for his friends."[1] For a parent, this verse is often filtered through the lens of fatherhood and motherhood. In a very real sense, righteous fathers and mothers lay down their own lives, giving entirely of their strength, and investing their fondest hopes and dreams in their children. On the one hand, it can be a source of great joy to witness one's posterity choosing to live in the faith—on the other, fathers and mothers can experience terrible anguish if children rebel, a heavy burden that must often be borne in prayerful silence. Such a mother was Helen Mar Kimball.

Helen loved her children—she loved having them around her and sharing in their lives, sometimes even dreaming when they were separated of how deeply she missed them.[2] Helen also worried for the

---

1   John 15:13.

2   [December 7, 1888] "I . . . had troublous dreams—thought Gennie & baby were with me, & I'd got a large tub full of fresh beef and other things to keep house with—expecting her to live with me, when behold Ed sent for her & though he was in the place never came himself—I was heartbroken, & said to Gen over, & over, '<u>I can not live without you You must not leave</u> me, & <u>you shall not go</u>'. But go she did though she felt sad to leave me The next day they both came back—& I thought to stay as Ed was putting his wagon & horses in my stable but they left again that evening, & I passed through another agonising scene. I gave away, & sold my meat, & other things, as I had no body—ever Lilly had gone away—to keep house for . . ." Charles M. Hatch and Todd M. Compton, *A Widow's Tale: 1884-1896 Diary of Helen Mar Kimball Whitney* (Logan: Utah State University Press, 2003), 334-335; underlined in original.

[November 12, 1890] "Dreemed that Flod had been away to school & just came home—And Charley had been off to work & had come home but not to stay. He was sitting at my right with his face near mine. I said '<u>Charley you must not leave us again, I can not stand it to have you away</u>'. He smiled & looked at me & looked the

spiritual welfare of her sons and daughters—often fasting, praying, and exhorting them, as it were with all the feeling of a tender parent,[3] to consecrate their lives to God. On March 19, 1885, she recorded:

// Thursday 19th Gennie coughed some in the night—kept me awake—feel poorly but concluded, last evening, to fast to day and am doing so, that I may get faith & power over darkness, & gain strength to come up to my duties, in public and in private life, among my household—The Lord only knows my anxiety in behalf of those, whom He has placed under my charge.[4]

The heart of this stalwart and attentive mother—ever anguishing over the temporal and eternal welfare of her children—found a moment of reprieve when, on April 8, 1886, Helen received a special blessing under the hands of a fellow Church member, Brother Donolson. This blessing revealed to her that the Lord was intimately aware of her fears for her children, and that He had heard her prayers of intercession:

// . . . Bro D. gave me a blessing, and revealed such great & marvalous things to me concerning myself, & made such promises, & predictions of things present, and things to come, and what I should accomplish in this life that I felt that the Lord had heard my petitions, for I'd been praying and weeping over the things that were weighing me down—The slackness of my girls, in living for any thing but the present, and yearning for the spiritual gifts and blessings neccessary to make me adequate to accomplish my mission that with my bodyly ales, caused me to pray more fervently than usual last evening, and the evening before, that I might be able to do my part, and that my house

---

most pleasent & natural that I've seem him in a dream." Charles M. Hatch and Todd M. Compton, *A Widow's Tale: 1884-1896 Diary of Helen Mar Kimball Whitney* (Logan: Utah State University Press, 2003), 422; underlined in original.

3   1 Nephi 8:37. "And it came to pass after my father had spoken all the words of his dream or vision, which were many, he said unto us, because of these things which he saw in a vision, he exceedingly feared for Laman and Lemuel; yea, he feared lest they should be cast off from the presence of the Lord. And he did exhort them then with all the feeling of a tender parent, that they would hearken to his words, that perhaps the Lord would be merciful to them, and not cast them off; yea, my father did preach unto them."

4   Charles M. Hatch and Todd M. Compton, *A Widow's Tale: 1884-1896 Diary of Helen Mar Kimball Whitney* (Logan: Utah State University Press, 2003), 76; underlined in original.

might become a fit place for Holy angels to dwell, instead of the opposite. And when we were sitting talking this morning I thought of my prayer, and that with all the glorious things spoken to me overwhelmed me with gratetude to the Giver of all that is good & exalting.[5]

A few months later, Helen, with Horace's plural wife, Mary, gathered all of their children together for a family picnic. As the festivities began, her oldest son Orson took the initiative to stand up and plead with his siblings. Like Nephi of old, he encouraged them to reform their lifestyle—particularly by keeping the Sabbath Day holy and following the Word of Wisdom. One can only imagine the joy that filled his mother's heart as she listened to her son—standing forth in boldness as a leader among his siblings—beseeching them to fulfill the very desires of her heart:

... we had a glorious time—one never to be forgotten. Orson opened with prayer–then addressed us, and his teachings were sharp & to the point—He made a prophecy, at the close, that if we would turn over a new leaf, & obey God, honor His priesthood—keep the word of wisdom, etc, we should be able to stop the destroyer from this time, etc. But if we continued to break over His laws, & did not keep the Sab. day holy, etc. we would have something worse than Charley's death, and these things he prophesied in the name of Jesus Christ.[6]

The occasion was a bittersweet event—joy at seeing her oldest son so fully engaged in the Gospel, but accompanied by the painful sting of wounds still fresh after the tragic loss of her 21-year-old son, Charles. 'Charley,' as he was endearingly called, had committed suicide only weeks before—and the family had been caught entirely unprepared. The uncertainty surrounding the cause of his sudden passing brought a very somber tone to the family's outing.[7] Two

---

5 Ibid., 148; underlined in original.

6 Ibid., 182; underlined in original.

7 Helen's diary details the anguish she experienced after learning of her son's suicide, and her struggle to find peace. "When on my couch alone tears came to my relief, and I vented my anguish. How often I silently cried from the depths of my soul—My God—My God—My God, why is this and what have I done to merit so bitter a punishment at thy hand?—have mercy and help me to bear it and to 'kiss the Rod'.—Oh that I could know that my boy was worthy to be among the sanctified I would not utter a murmoring word.'

additional family members spoke, each sharing how Charley's recent death had prompted contemplation "of these things, & how much more he had been united, & associated, with those outside of his father's family than with his own brothers & sisters, etc." For Helen and her family, this gathering proved to be a unifying event to turn their hearts toward the Lord and one another in a newly awakened sense of familial love:

> ❙❙ I [Helen] was the next one called to speak . . . I gave some heartfelt expressions concerning our duties to ourselves and—to one another, & to our religion with some of my experience, etc and told them that I wished to remove every thing that stood between me & my God, that I might feel that he was near to me, & I asked to be forgiven of all that I had ever done to hurt the feelings of any of them—that I knew we'd got to become one in all things & to do this we must make due allowence for one another, etc.[8]

Helen's message as a mother was one of loyalty and union between siblings, patience, Christlike love, and humility. Helen was not afraid to humbly acknowledge her own faults and to seek earnestly for forgiveness. At the end of the day, her children knew her heart,[9] and they knew that it was committed to her God:

"Sleep came to my relief towards daylight. But when I saw the form of my Charley stretched in death, in an instant I was overwhelmed, & cried aloud—This was the first time and the last, though my sorrow has been deep and unspeakable. And yet with all I have been blessed and felt that the Lord had not forsaken me—Friends by hundreds have given me their prayers, & words of consolation have poured in as a healing balm—and the greatest of all my children that are left me have repented and confessed their sins & that this has brought them to see how far they were from the Lord, & that He had chastened them for this cause—How little I thought <u>how</u> they were to be chastened, when I was predicting it. I felt for a time that I would pray only the 'Lords Prayer' in the future. But 'the Lord works in a misterious way his wonders to perform.' Every one acquainted with Charley testafy to his purity of mind, and that he was unconscious at the moment he killed himself. This fact is bourn out by his turning to the Lord & being more attentive of late. to his spiritual duties—even when too sick to go & advised not to by friends he persisted in going to the evening meeting at the Chapel and be administered to, on Sunday—the 1st of August. & the very day, within a few moments of committing the tereble act he was talking of & urging B. Young to intercede for him to go as his companion on a mission to New Zealand." Ibid., 177-178; underlined in original.

8   Ibid., 182.

9   A few days after Charley's suicide, Helen recorded the following in her journal, revealing the deepest desires of her heart as a mother: "Another earthly prop

// I testified to the rightiousness of the plural wife order, & that I had known it from my youth, & dared not rebell against it for the Lord would punish all who did it.—Orson & Sold [Solomon] had born the same testimony & warned them to never do it, etc, etc I told them that the greatest exaltation would come through obedience to and honoring this Celestial order & many more things were said which I might write had I the time—We had Ice cream after the meeting was over, and every one expressed themselves as greatly pleased, and hoped we'd have more of the same kind of reunions, or meeting of the family. Mary met me after the meeting & kissed me, & asked my forgiveness for every thing she had ever done to hurt my feelings. May this spirit continue and spread among this people is my prayer.[10]

This memorable family picnic and council was a well-timed opportunity to address the need for family harmony, which would be unexpectedly tested just a few days later. Conflict erupted when Genevieve—Gen as they called her—admitted to having accepted an engagement to a young man who was not a member of the Church. Helen's motherly intuition had warned her that something was amiss, and she sensed with uneasiness, as she prayed for her daughter, that "she is losing the taste of the Holy spirit . . ."[11] Gen had previously assured her family that she was not pursuing a relationship with the non-member fellow, Ed Talbot, with whom she had been spending time. However, when her mother confronted her on the insensitivity of her accepting his attentions, "fooling him

---

removed—Why and wherefore is all unknown, only to Him who giveth and taketh away:—blessed be his name—He knows my heart, & that I have asked for nothing so much as the eternal salvation of my children; that before they should be left to do any thing that would cut short their glory He would take them to Himself—And that I have held them upon the 'Alter' that nothing should stand between Him & me, whom I will love though He slay me—" Ibid., 176; underlined in original.

10   Ibid., 182-183; underlined in original.

11   August 27, 1886: "Friday 27th. I am troubled in mind over Gen's running so much with the unbelieving fearing she is loosing the taste of the Holy spirit that she had gained since the chastening rod has fallen heavily upon us. I was reproving her this morning & warning her of the evil that would come upon her as sure as she did not repent & listen to counsel. I was urged last eve. to let her go again to the Lake with Ed. She came & kissed me when she left this morning and she made a promise to do my bidding in the future & to apologise to Hall for bad treetment." Ibid., 183; underlined in original.

along" when her intentions were non-committal, Gen shocked her mother by announcing their recent engagement.[12]

Helen was nearly broken by the disheartening news. In an instant, dreams of her beloved daughter enjoying the blessings she herself had known in being sealed to a righteous priesthood holder under the proper authority—and the subsequent raising of an eternal family unto the Lord—now seemed cruelly dashed before her face. Yet, her never-ending faith in the Lord's sure promises is evident in her thoughts regarding this trial, as well:

> I was dumbfounded, & heart broken & returned to my room— there I prayed and wept the best part of the day to the Lord that He would have mercy on us, & help me to acknowledge His hand in this as well as all other things, & to show me whether it was for a punishment for Gen's disobedience or if it would turn out as blessing, by Ed's joining this Church, & become, as Sol thinks maybe he will, a savior to his fathers house. Gen came to my room & put her arms around me & cried bitterly saying she wished she'd died when she was so sick since she saw how I took it, and begged me not to feel so. But my bitterness she cannot know, nor the doom that awaits those who sever themselves from this Church & its blessings, of which I have warned her of[.] She has been keeping the word of Wisdom and is prayerful. & gone every Sunday to meeting ever since Charley's death, & before, nearly every Sab. Oh, how long have I prayed that the Lord would send some man to her that she could love & respect, & would be truly a savior on Mount Zion, and why should my prayers be in vain? I feel that I am a mourner indeed.

---

12 "I was as much astonished at this as I was at the news of Charley's committing Suicide never having an idea that her feelings could change so towards Ed, whom she had always looked upon as nothing but a boy—When it was once rumored, by his brothers, that Ed was her admirer she appeared disgusted—I had told her last winter that I was satisfied what his feelings were toward her since he'd been so attentive and given her a book as a Christmass present—This was a surprize, & sickened her of him. She told me that his letters, which came too often, were not worth replying too. When he came up again from the mine he found Mr Hall here from Dacota, and took him to be an admirer of hers, and quit coming entirely. This made Gen feel sorry for treeting him so, and she has been going to Talbots oftener ever since. But it never entered my mind that she could ever come to like him, only as a friend—till she told me to the contrary Sun. morning. I asked her when such a change came over her—She Said She did not know, though it must have been gradual. He asked her last Thur. the evening they went home with Lile Lewis—" Ibid., 184-185; underlined in original.

But though my <u>sorrows are keen</u> the <u>Lord will not</u> withold His <u>mercy</u> from me when I've <u>tried so hard to serve Him</u>—and <u>to bring my children to His feet</u>—[13]

The following day brought with it another vexing period of "lementation & my eyes are sore with weeping." A distraught Helen turned to her son, Orson, for counsel:

// I told Orson how I felt & how I had prayed that the Lord would show me & him whether <u>His</u> hand was in this or not—that if it <u>was right</u> He would soften Orson's feelings towards Ed & make <u>me</u> reconciled.

He said he'd felt better since Sol talked to him about Ed's "being a good boy & that they might make a Latter-day Saint of him," & told me to treet them both kindly, but to inform them that we would not consent to their union untill he had first received the gospel & became a member thereoff. etc. This I had done—He also told me to set the facts before Gen. & what the Lord had said concerning the everlasting doom of those who married outside of the Church, that she might not go into it blindly—He said I had cleared my skirts, & this might work out <u>Gen's</u> salvation, and <u>perhaps Ed's</u>—"We must leave the rest to the Lord." I called G. into my bed room this afternoon & questioned her about her intention[s], & told her what her fate would be if she married out of the Church, & the awful trouble & sorrow that would be her portion when she came to see what she had brought upon herself through disobedience unless Ed would investigate & make up his mind to join this Church. She thought she had a good deal of influence with him, & maybe she could get him to look into this work, though the only thing that made her feel sad was that I felt so badly over it.[14]

Ever dutiful, and in customary charity, Helen accepted Orson's advice to show the young couple kindness, while also exhorting her daughter to consider the weighty spiritual consequences of her decision. Helen knew that she must speak plainly to her children: holding a high standard, teaching them the Gospel at every

---

13   Ibid., 185; underlined in original.
14   Ibid., 185-186; underlined in original.

opportunity, and "reproving betimes with sharpness, when moved upon by the Holy Ghost." But she also lived in expression of the scriptural command to show "forth afterwards an increase of love toward him whom thou hast reproved, lest he esteem thee to be his enemy." Helen strove to develop and exercise the gift of charity, as well as an uncompromising stance for truth—thereby equipping her to parent in the Lord's way. She would not be afraid to say 'no,' and she would not whitewash the consequences of sin—her "faithfulness [was] stronger than the cords of death."[15]

Even in the midst of debilitating health challenges, mounting financial pressure, and other familial and temporal demands, Helen exerted every last ounce of her strength in an effort to benefit and spiritually fortify her children. On one occasion, in 1888, Helen was seized upon by a "dreadful spasm" that caught her off guard, and then another later that night. Still undeterred, she used the 'respite' between to have a gospel discussion with her children:

> We were attending prayers—by the urgent request of Flod I was mouth, & when nearly through had to close—a dreadful spasm taking me, & then another before getting into bed. During the respit I had questions—on principles applied by Hen, & Flod, which I answered to my best ability, & tried to make Flod understand that we could make little or no progress in spiritual things [in the next life], or gain that faith, & knowledge that enables us to rise above the weeknesses of the flesh, to see into the future, & endure what the Lord in His wisdom & tender mercy—sees fit that we shall pass through to make us capable of filling an exalted position in His presence here—after, & that that was my greatest ambition, & desire, & to have my children walk in the path of obedience—that in doing this they'd find it much easyer, & their lives much happyer, than in rebelling, or "kicking against the pricks".[16]

One can be sure that Helen's children did not need words to explain that their mother's life and dedication was serving God—she *lived* that passion fully.

---

15   Doctrine and Covenants 121:43.

16   Charles M. Hatch and Todd M. Compton, *A Widow's Tale: 1884-1896 Diary of Helen Mar Kimball Whitney* (Logan: Utah State University Press, 2003), 333.

Answers to Prayers

Ultimately, Helen knew it was only the Lord who had power to soften the hearts, change the minds, and convert the souls of her children. She understood her role as a mother to be a friend they could trust, a source of gospel strength upon which they could rely, and one to whom they could turn for counsel when they were divinely prepared. On March 3, 1891, Helen's son, Orson, paid a visit to his dear mother, unloading the burdens that weighed upon his soul, and pouring out his heart as he sought for her inspired wisdom:

// Tues, 3. Felt about the same, but more humble in spirit, & solemn— Orson came & spent some time . . . He poured out his feelings, & told how he'd been tried and tempted in many ways, & was now sick & his mind weakened with his body so he was not able to write history nor anything and felt dejected. I could enter into every feeling particularly the latter. I talked & admonished him as I havent for years. I told him I'd seen him in a dream some time back, & I'd felt to pray more earnestly for him, knowing his nature, & that there was something that caused my feelings to be wrought upon in his behalf—that there was no being that felt like a mother, etc. He thanked me for my interest. I felt glad of the talk, & I think he was comforted.[17]

In refreshing bursts of encouragement and confirmation of her faithful efforts, Helen's prayers were often answered on behalf of her children. On one occasion, she received a letter from her daughter, Florence, who shared a remarkable dream the Lord had given her:

// Monday, 25th Received an interesting letter from Florence, telling a dream she'd had of the Savior. She thought I revealed Him to her— pointed to a beautiful drapery before us bade her look. As she did so the vail was drawn, & she saw the almost lifeless body of our dear Savior thrown as it were across a chair. He seemed to have just been taken from the cross. "He wore the wreath of thorns, & huge drops of blood droped from His brow & gushed forth from the wounds which I could plainly see in His hands, feet & side. And His face I shall never forget

---

17   Ibid., 436.

the expression of anguish & yet perfect resignation it bespoke. I closed my eyes to shut out the dreadful sight & opened them once more when you bad me look for the 2nd time, what a glorious sight I beheld, there He stood as after His resurrection His form clad in a simple yet apparently costly garment of a deep wine coler. His face turned to me while His finger pointed I thought to His Father's Kingdom. Such a hallowed light shone over His face and this time the expression was so beautiful as it had seemed terrible before. After gasing fascenatingly for some time, you or some one arroused me by saying, "Well, are you satisfied now? I replied oh yess I can never doubt now, then some one said or the thought came to me—Others have seen more & yet have doubted, then I began to tremble & fear that I might & how great would be my condemnation if I should turn from the truth, and the thought saddened me, & with the tears gushing forth (I could feel them distinctly on my face) I begged to see no more that my condemnation might be less providing I did turn away. Then all vanished, even you & I either wakened, or dreamed no more". She says "I feel this is to be an important dream, though I cannot comprehend it quite—"does it mean that I shall not prove faithful? Heven forbid"! No! it does not.[18]

Florence's grandfather, Heber C. Kimball, as well as her mother, had both experienced inspired dreams, and it seems this gift was passed on to Helen's children. Perhaps one of the more well-known spiritual experiences shared among members of the Church is the touching dream her son Orson had of the Lord in the Garden of Gethsemane. Although many members have become acquainted with this story, we find additional insight by pondering the circumstances 'behind the scenes,' as a loving mother fasted and offered repeated prayers on behalf of her children. Helen was surely a significant impetus behind the Lord's intervention—an intervention designed to persuade Orson to change his life's direction. Originally, Orson had intended to pursue a career in acting—but a series of roadblocks seemed to mysteriously arise, pointing him instead in the direction of serving a mission. Although he acquiesced, his mind and heart were distracted, and he struggled to maintain focus on his missionary

---

18   Ibid., 653-654; underline in original.

labors. Dreams of literary fame and ambitious business opportunities crowded his thoughts, leaving both God and faith tucked away in the dusty, cobwebbed corners of his mind—almost forgotten. All would suddenly change when, one night, he had a dream that would forever change the course of his life:

❦ I thought I was in the garden of Gethsemane. I saw the Savior and his Apostles, Peter, James, and John, enter from the direction to my right, and, leaving them there in a group, praying, He passed to the other side and also knelt down. He seemed to be in great mental distress and His face, which was turned towards me, was streaming with tears. He prayed to the Father: "Let this cup pass from me; nevertheless, Thy will, and not mine, be done." Finishing He arose and crossing to where His Apostles were, shook them—for they had fallen asleep—and rousing them up, reproved them for neglecting to watch and pray. He then returned to his former place and kneeling down prayed again. Unseen of them I watched their movements from behind a tree. My heart was so full of sympathy for Jesus and His sorrow that I wept in unison with Him and my whole soul as if melted, went out to Him. Pretty soon He arose and beckoning His companions to Him, seemed about to take His departure. The whole circumstance of the dream then changed, though the scene remained the same. The only difference was in time; instead of before the crucifixion, it was after, and the Son of God, having made the sacrifice required, was about to go to the Father, taking the three disciples with Him. I could stand it no longer, and rushing out from my concealment fell down at His feet, clasped Him about the knees, and begged Him to take me with Him also. He gazed upon me with inexpressible tenderness, then stooped and lifted me up into His arms and embraced me with all the affection of a father or an elder brother. I could feel the beating of His heart and the warmth of His bosom against mine. With a voice full of sweetness and compassion and slowly swaying His head in denial, he said: "No, my son; your work is not finished yet. These have done their work and they can go with me, but you must stay and finish yours." These words uttered in all kindness only made me more anxious to go, though I did not repeat my request, but clinging to Him besought him further:

"Well, promise me that I will come to you hereafter." Again He shook His head and sadly and sweetly said: "That will depend entirely on yourself." I awoke with a sob, and it was morning.

I was profoundly impressed and related the dream to Brother Musser. He told me it was from the Lord. Of this I had no doubt, for the lesson it taught was full of wisdom and warning, and it was stamped upon my mind eternally. I could not forget it and hope I shall always profit by its instruction.[19]

At times, it may have seemed to Helen that her prayers had been left unanswered—that her faith was failing, and the Lord had forgotten her. But God never failed to honor her sacrifices as a wife and mother—and through her perseverance, she proved and will prove a savior on mount Zion to her children. Her sentiments are beautifully expressed in one of her many writings:

// The highest aim and ambition of my life have been to see my children accomplished in the true sense of the word, that their appearance may be pleasing, not only at home but abroad, and in the society of the educated, the noble and refined of the earth. My aspirations, however, do not end here: they reach to a higher sphere. The true Latter-day Saint desires above all other things to become a fit subject for the kingdom of God, that he may dwell and associate with the nobility of heaven.[20]

Helen Mar Kimball was more than an author, she was more than a Latter-day Saint, and she was more than a vocal defender of the Gospel—she was first and foremost an eternal *wife & mother*,[21] and it was that legacy that she most honored and sought to take with her into the next life—to forever secure the treasures of her posterity in heaven.

---

19   Dennis B. Horne, *The Life of Orson F. Whitney: Poet, Historian, Apostle* (Springville, Utah: Cedar Fort Inc., 2014), 31-32.

20   Helen Mar Whitney, *Plural Marriage as Taught by the Prophet Joseph* (Salt Lake City: Juvenile Instructor Office, 1882), 43.

21   "It was from him [Joseph Smith] that I learned that the highest dignity of womanhood was, to stand as a queen and priestess to her husband, and to reign for ever and ever as the queen mother of her numerous and still increasing offspring." Parley P. Pratt, *The Autobiography of Parley P. Pratt* (Chicago: Law, King & Law, 1888), 329-330.

CHAPTER 18

Wrestling Against Principalities & Powers

∽

F or Helen, her God—the God of Abraham, Isaac, and Jacob—
was one of living flesh and blood—an actual corporeal being.
At the same time, she believed the adversary—Lucifer, the enemy of
Jehovah—was, although disembodied, just as real and tangible. In
her diaries, Helen recorded experiences that she described as spiritual
threats, intended to impede her and her work. On December 30,
1884, Helen recorded one such hostile encounter:

// Last night, when taking my first nap, I had an awful struggle
with a woman. (there seemed to be a man near by.) She was
trying to convince me that I could not get out from under her
power—that I had given myself to the powers of darkness, and
they now claimed me. I thought it something like witchcraft,
and wondered in my mind, while the contest was going on
between us, if I had done any—such thing, and given them any
claims upon me, but I never yealded an inch to her. I fought till
I conquered, and the coast was cleared, when I thought, Well,
if I had given way to that doubt, and yealded to her instead of
struggling on, she would have had me. The place seemed to be
in a forest. This is another good omen for me—the Lord heard
my prayer last night, and these dreams are to encourage and
increase my faith, which is not all that I desire it to be, or I
might be healed I think.[1]

---

1   Charles M. Hatch and Todd M. Compton, *A Widow's Tale: 1884-1896 Diary of
Helen Mar Kimball Whitney* (Logan: Utah State University Press, 2003), 60.

Helen's determined resistance to any resemblance of compromise is reflected in several dreams in which she recounts fighting "like a tiger" with weapons. These dreams illustrate her determined resolve to defy subjugation to those "in league with the powers of darkness."² Helen recorded memories of dark messengers who appeared as spirits, snakes, or dangerous men. Each time, Helen refused to be intimidated.³

As Helen read the scriptures, she found the accounts of many prophets who recorded experiences that paralleled her own. Jacob had wrestled with a spirit before receiving his endowment.⁴ Joseph

---

2   Helen's diary records on December 30, 1884: "I had an awful struggle in my sleep, with a man who, I felt, had insulted me by his familiarity. I caught a gun, & Horace, who was there, and an another man took guns & tried to fire at this man, but they wouldn't go off. I pointed mine into his face, & had the same trouble. Some person told me to pull the trigger. I did so and fired, shooting him through the face. The shot appeared fatal for a moment, when he revived and took from his neck a tie, which he threw at me, or to my feet, when it began to show symptoms of life like, a serpent. I took my large knife, or it was more like a sword and cut it into several pieces, & there was filth ran out on the floor. This trick of the man gave me to understand that he was a wizard and in league with the powers of darkness, being determined to hold me in subjection to it. But I was quite as determined on my part, and fought like a tiger till I awoke. He was fleshy, with good features, and well dressed but a devil incarnate. I thought (in my dream), after firing the gun, that I'd shown pretty good nerve for one that had never before fired off a gun or a pistol." Ibid., 63.

3   Helen's journal entry of March 18, 1890 records: ". . . dreamed of 2 snakes coming into my dining room—the 1st a large & long one spit venom but was demolished by members of the family—the 2nd was shorter but of equal thickness, & its head was just entering my bed room under the door when I caught up a big slab and thrust the end of it upon its neck—Some woman was about to take part as I was doing it, & I told her not to. I thought they'd been in the upper part of the house probably, as it seemed thus when I awoke. They were destroyed without doing any harm." Ibid., 396.

Helen's diary records on July 15, 1890: "One night last week I dreamed of being up by the Mill. Horace & some woman were there—A Snake was laying on this side of the Aquaduct reached from there to opposite my place—Its head right near us I was startled, but Horace got something & struck it, cutting its head in two, & two more pieces off—It was of a lightish collor . . ." Ibid., 408.

4   Genesis 32:24-32. The question has often been asked who Jacob wrestled with. According to Andrew Skinner, "It is not entirely clear from the Bible the nature of Jacob's experience. The Hebrew word used to describe the patriarch's visitor is simply 'ish, meaning 'man,' without overt reference to divine status." Andrew C. Skinner, "Jacob: Keeper of Covenants," Ensign, March 1998, 54.

Joseph Fielding Smith taught: "To think he wrestled and held an angel who couldn't get away, is out of the question. The term angel as used in the scriptures, at times, refers to messengers who are sent with some important instruction." Joseph Fielding Smith, Doctrines of Salvation, vol. 1 (Salt Lake City: Bookcraft, 1992), 17.

Genesis 32 seems to indicate that this sacred experience was likely akin to Jacob receiving his endowment. Great spiritual experiences in scripture are often preceded

Smith's First Vision accounts speak of facing a thick darkness, and a terrifying enemy "who had such marvelous power as I had never before felt in any being."[5] Jesus, Himself, spoke of a face-to-face confrontation with Lucifer, who attempted to dissuade Him from His mission after He had fasted for 40 days and 40 nights.[6] Helen found plenty of experiences and teachings on spiritual warfare as she studied the Bible—the foundation of her Christian faith.[7]

For Helen, her manifold dreams and experiences often carried specific meaning, including warnings of impending danger. One such occurrence happened in 1887, when she recorded that a message was communicated to her through a dream, warning that the adversary was scheming to destroy her. However, the dream also conveyed that the Lord was aware of these subversive designs, would thwart the attacks, and ultimately preserve her:

// I had a peculiar dream this morning, as I slept late— Thought I overheard some woman telling something to three or four others about me, but not understanding it, asked her to repeat it—which was something like a revelation from the Lord— this being the substance of it. She had been informed that Satan was intending to lay a deep plan for my destruction but that the Lord was going to take me to Himself just in time to thwart him—I have had many dreams that lead me to think that I am not going to get well, though I have put them away from me, & clung to every promise that has been made me . . .[8]

Helen believed her sometimes harrowing experiences taught that the adversary posed a very real threat, but no power could overcome those who are faithful to and supported by the Lord. Even during her dreams, Helen found herself praying fervently, and with intensity— exerting mighty faith to pierce the veil:

---

by struggles with the adversary. A logical conclusion could be reached that Jacob wrestled with opposition before receiving his new name and covenant blessings.

5   Joseph Smith—History 1:16.

6   Matthew 4:1-11.

7   See Ephesians 6:11-13, James 4:7, Job 1:6-12, 1 Peter 5:8-9.

8   February 7, 1887. Charles M. Hatch and Todd M. Compton, *A Widow's Tale: 1884-1896 Diary of Helen Mar Kimball Whitney* (Logan: Utah State University Press, 2003), 219.

I Saw a Light, by Jon McNaughton

❝ Dreamed of praying, & as I prayed my faith became so powerful that I felt astonished—being so unusual—& in a moment the vail was removed and right by me were two girls—one was grown, & the other small—sitting at her feet—the large one arose, & it seemed that she went to do something for me, but the next thing was a strugle with an evil power, & I awok[e]—with nightmare.[9]

Helen's experiences paralleled those attested to by the Prophet Joseph Smith, who spoke frequently of contests with the adversary. Prior to his receiving the First Vision—a transcendently glorious experience that stands as the greatest recorded vision in the history of the world—the young 14-year-old Joseph was beset by a calamitous, dark, and paralyzing satanic force:

9   April 24, 1889. Ibid., 354.

// After I had retired to the place where I had previously designed to go, having looked around me, and finding myself alone, I kneeled down and began to offer up the desires of my heart to God. I had scarcely done so, when immediately I was seized upon by some power which entirely overcame me, and had such an astonishing influence over me as to bind my tongue so that I could not speak. Thick darkness gathered around me, and it seemed to me for a time as if I were doomed to sudden destruction.[10]

As the strangling weight of darkness neared its climax, young Joseph's reaction was not one of cowering surrender—but rather, a valiant exertion of faith:

// But, exerting all my powers to call upon God to deliver me out of the power of this enemy which had seized upon me, and at the very moment when I was ready to sink into despair and abandon myself to destruction—not to an imaginary ruin, but to the power of some actual being from the unseen world, who had such marvelous power as I had never before felt in any being—just at this moment of great alarm, I saw a pillar of light exactly over my head, above the brightness of the sun, which descended gradually until it fell upon me.[11]

In like manner, Helen's diaries document her perspective regarding the power of the Lord versus the power of the adversary. Both she and the Prophet recorded their personal feelings that it was only through the intervention of Jesus Christ that their lives were spared—time and time again. In 1890, Helen recorded:

---

10 Joseph Smith—History 1:15.

11 Joseph Smith—History 1:16. Joseph Smith's 1835 account of the First Vision records: "... I made a fruitless attempt to pray, my toung seemed to be swolen in my mouth, so that I could not utter, I heard a noise behind me like some person walking towards me, I strove again to pray, but could not, the noise of walking seemed to draw nearer, I sprung up on my feet, and looked around, but saw no person or thing that was calculated to produce the noise of walking, I kneeled again my mouth was opened and my toung liberated, and I called on the Lord in mighty prayer, a pillar of fire appeared above my head, it presently rested down upon my me head, and filled me with joy unspeakable, a personage appeard in the midst, of this pillar of flame which was spread all around, and yet nothing consumed, another personage soon appeard like unto the first, he said unto me thy sins are forgiven thee ..." Joseph Smith, Journal, 1835–1836, p. 23-24, The Joseph Smith Papers.

❭❭ I had a dream the other night that there was an evil power hold of me pressing something acrost my neck—& down at each side, from which a something—I cant describe, arose, and knowing it to be the power of the evil one I tried to rebuke it—& made the 4th effort before I could do it—When I rebuked it in the name of Jesus Christ, I was awake when I did it.[12]

Helen and Joseph were not alone in describing adversarial attacks on their persons. Helen's father and mother recorded their own struggles, after which they sought out the Prophet to gain greater understanding. Helen wrote of these occurrences in a July 1, 1880 publication for the *Woman's Exponent*. In her account, she shared a firsthand experience with her mother one night while the family was living in Nauvoo:

❭❭ ... we were awakened by our mother, who was struggling as though nearly choked to death. Father asked her what was the matter, when she could speak, she replied, that she dreamt that a personage came and seized her by the throat and was choking her. He lit a candle and saw that her eyes were sunken and her nose pinched in, as though she were in the last stage of cholera. He laid his hands upon her head and rebuked the spirit in the name of Jesus, and by the power of the holy priesthood commanded it to depart. In a moment afterwards, some half a dozen children in other parts of the house were heard crying, as if in great distress; the cattle began to bellow and low, the horses to neigh and whinnow, the dogs barked, hogs squealed, and the fowls and everything around were in great commotion, and in a few minutes my father was called to lay hands on Sister Bently, the widow of David Patten, who lived in the next room. She was seized in a similar manner to my mother. They continued quite feeble for several days from the shock.[13]

According to his diary, Heber approached the Prophet Joseph, seeking to learn more, and sharing at the same time another dark

---

12   November 4, 1890. Charles M. Hatch and Todd M. Compton, *A Widow's Tale: 1884-1896 Diary of Helen Mar Kimball Whitney* (Logan: Utah State University Press, 2003), 421.

13   Helen Mar Kimball Whitney, "Life Incidents," *Woman's Exponent* 9, no. 3 (July 1, 1880): 18.

experience he had undergone while serving a mission in England. He recorded the insight gained from this visit in his diary:

// He [Joseph Smith] took me [for] a walk by the riverside and requested me to relate the occurrence at the Bozier house. I did so, and also told him the vision of evil spirits in England on the opening of the gospel to that people.[14] After I had done this,

---

14   Heber's account of an experience that occurred while first bringing the message of the Restoration to the British Isles can be found in his biography, written by Helen's son, Orson F. Whitney:

"'Saturday evening,' says Heber C. Kimball, 'it was agreed that I should go forward and baptize, the next morning, in the river Ribble, which runs through Preston.

'By this time the adversary of souls began to rage, and he felt determined to destroy us before we had fully established the kingdom of God in that land, and the next morning I witnessed a scene of satanic power and influence which I shall never forget.

'Sunday, July 30th, about daybreak, Elder Isaac Russell (who had been appointed to preach on the obelisk in Preston Square, that day,) who slept with Elder Richards in Wilfred Street, came up to the third story, where Elder Hyde and myself were sleeping, and called out, "Brother Kimball, I want you should get up and pray for me that I may be delivered from the evil spirits that are tormenting me to such a degree that I feel I cannot live long, unless I obtain relief."

'I had been sleeping on the back of the bed. I immediately arose, slipped off at the foot of the bed, and passed around to where he [Elder Russell] was. Elder Hyde threw his feet out, and sat up in the bed, and we laid hands on him, I being mouth, and prayed that the Lord would have mercy on him, and rebuke the devil.

'While thus engaged, I was struck with great force by some invisible power, and fell senseless on the floor. The first thing I recollected was being supported by Elders Hyde and Richards who were praying for me, Elder Richards having followed Russell up to my room. Elders Hyde and Richards then assisted me to get on the bed, but my agony was so great I could not endure it, and I arose, bowed my knees and prayed.

'I then arose and sat up on the bed, when a vision was opened to our minds, and we could distinctly see the evil spirits, who foamed and gnashed their teeth at us. We gazed upon them about an hour and a half (by Willard's watch). We were not looking towards the window, but towards the wall. Space appeared before us, and we saw the devils coming in legions, with their leaders, who came within a few feet of us. They came towards us like armies rushing to battle. They appeared to be men of full stature, possessing every form and feature of men in the flesh, who were angry and desperate; and I shall never forget the vindictive malignity depicted on their countenances as they looked me in the eye; and any attempt to paint the scene which then presented itself or portray their malice and enmity, would be vain.

'I perspired exceedingly, my clothes becoming as wet as if I had been taken out of the river. I felt excessive pain, and was in the greatest distress for some time. I cannot even look back on the scene without feelings of horror; yet by it I learned the power of the adversary, his enmity against the servants of God, and got some understanding of the invisible world. We distinctly heard these spirits talk and express their wrath and hellish designs against us. However, the Lord delivered us from them, and blessed us exceedingly that day.'" Orson F. Whitney, *Life of Heber C. Kimball* (Salt Lake City: Kimball Family, 1888), 143-145.

I asked what all these things meant and whether or not there was anything wrong in me. "No, Brother Heber; at that time when you were in England, you was then nigh unto the Lord. There was only a veil between you and Him, but you could not see Him. When I heard it, it gave me great joy, for I then knew that the work of God had taken root in the land; it was this that caused the devil to make a struggle to kill you." Joseph then said, the nearer a person approaches the Lord, a greater power would be manifest by the devil to prevent the accomplishment of the purposes of God. He then gave me a relation of many contests that he had had with Satan, and his power had been made manifest from time to time since the commencement of bringing forth the Book of Mormon.[15]

The early Latter-day Saints felt that there was, and is, a dark opposition at work, furiously seeking to destroy the Kingdom of God on earth—a power raging tirelessly in its relentless attempts to extinguish even the smallest flicker of the light of Christ throughout every corner of the world. The eternal conflict between these two opposing powers—the war between good and evil, light and darkness—comprises the forces waging battle over the souls of men. When Helen had occasion to bear her testimony, she did not feel she was repeating a blind adherence to the beliefs or expectations of others. She recorded her personal experiences through the hardships of life—she had lost infants and older children, had battled physical illness, had been afflicted with spiritual warfare, and she had also experienced doubt.

All great men and women will inevitably experience opposition and tribulation enough to test them beyond their own fleshly capabilities in this life—pushing them to call upon the light, goodness, and mercy of Him who has power to subdue all things under His feet. Is it possible to be neutral in this war between darkness and light? Is it possible to stand idly by, disengaged in the eternal conflict? For Helen, the answer was a resounding "*No!*" and she clearly declared her allegiance. She stood for God and Christ, she stood for the Prophet Joseph Smith, and she kept that faith burning brightly to the end.

---

15   Helen Mar Kimball Whitney, "Life Incidents," *Woman's Exponent* 9, no. 3 (July 1, 1880): 18.

CHAPTER 19

The "Wife of a God"

༼࿇༽

Although Helen did not live as a wife to the Prophet in mortality, she never disavowed her sealing—she regarded herself as a wife of the Prophet Joseph Smith to her last breath. Eliza R. Snow and others who were also sealed to the Prophet shared this great legacy with her. Helen cherished this sacred and eternal connection with Joseph Smith deep within her heart, and in 1886, while attending the temple with Lucy Walker Kimball,[1] she noted the "greatness of the responsibility" she carried as a queen in this last dispensation:

---

1   Lucy Walker Smith Kimball was sealed to the Prophet Joseph Smith in 1843. After the Prophet's death, she married Heber C. Kimball for time. The Prophet Joseph did not approach Lucy at first, but instead asked her brother for permission to present the subject. Lucy's brother, William, remembered:

"I went to Joseph Smith's, and was made welcome. I learned that mother was living on the island in the Mississippi River, and that it was dangerous to cross because of so much ice running. The next morning the Prophet invited me to hitch up my horse with one of his, in a buggy, and ride with him. We were riding all day through the city and county making a number of calls on business [and] pleasure combined. On this occasion the subject of celestial, or plural marriage, was introduced to me. As we returned home he remarked, 'If there was anything I did not understand, to hold on a little, and I would understand it....'

"In the spring of 1843, my father, being away on a mission, the Prophet asked my consent, for my sister Lucy in Marriage. I replied, that if it was her choice: that if she entered into the celestial order of marriage of her own free will and choice, I had no objection. This of course was in contrast with my former education and traditions. It also was altogether different from the course to[o] generally pursued by monogamists. Instead of taking a course to deceive and prostitute and bring about her ruin, he took a straight-forward, honorable, and upright course, in no way depriving her of her agency.

"When father returned from his mission, the matter being fully explained in connection with the doctrine, received his endorsement and all parties concerned received his approbation." William Holmes Walker reminiscences and diary, p. 7-11, Church History Library, https://catalog.churchofjesuschrist.org/assets/3157f95e-d577-4b2b-882f-e5940796dcd7/0/0.

II ... I went there [to the Temple for washings and anointings] at one o'clock—I was first baptized for my health—then for Elizabeth Ford Sikes Whitney, & Lucy Blocksom Kimball Whitney²—then was washed & anointed by Sister's Richards & Clark. The latter, afterwards addressing me, & Lucy Walker Kimball, who were standing there—as "the wives of a God"³— meening the Prophet—and a number of things she said—by the power of the spirit, that were calculated to make us feel the greatness of the responsibility resting upon us, to carry ourselves

---

Lucy recorded her testimony as follows: "When the Prophet Joseph Smith first mentioned the principle of plural marriage to me I felt indignant and so expressed myself to him, because my feelings and education were averse to anything of that nature. But he assured me that this doctrine had been revealed to him of the Lord, and that I was entitled to receive a testimony of its divine origin for myself. He counselled me to pray to the Lord, which I did, and thereupon received from him a powerful and irresistible testimony of the truthfulness and divinity of plural marriage, which testimony has abided with me ever since." Lucy Walker, Affidavit, December 17, 1902, Church History Library, https://catalog.churchofjesuschrist. org/assets/13f8c8d0-5102-4d85-9fca-3e63d3477fb7/0/0.

2   Elizabeth and Lucy Whitney were sealed to Helen's husband, Horace, before his death. Helen's conscious effort while attending the temple to do work not only for herself, but also for these women, illustrates her thoughtful nature, no doubt contributing to her success in living and maintaining her personal testimony of plural marriage.

3   The early Saints did not worship Joseph Smith, but they did recognize him as the priesthood leader over this final dispensation. President Brigham Young explained, "Joseph Smith holds the keys of this last dispensation, and is now engaged behind the vail in the great work of the last days. I can tell our beloved brother Christians who have slain the Prophets and butchered and otherwise caused the death of thousands of Latter-day Saints, the priests who have thanked God in their prayers and thanksgiving from the pulpit that we have been plundered, driven, and slain, and the deacons under the pulpit, and their brethren and sisters in their closets, who have thanked God, thinking that the Latter-day Saints were wasted away, something that no doubt will mortify them—something that, to say the least, is a matter of deep regret to them—namely, that no man or woman in this dispensation will ever enter into the celestial kingdom of God without the consent of Joseph Smith. From the day that the Priesthood was taken from the earth to the winding-up scene of all things, every man and woman must have the certificate of Joseph Smith, junior, as a passport to their entrance into the mansion where God and Christ are—I with you and you with me. I cannot go there without his consent. He holds the keys of that kingdom for the last dispensation—the keys to rule in the spirit-world; and he rules there triumphantly, for he gained full power and a glorious victory over the power of Satan while he was yet in the flesh, and was a martyr to his religion and to the name of Christ, which gives him a most perfect victory in the spirit-world. He reigns there as supreme a being in his sphere, capacity, and calling, as God does in heaven. Many will exclaim—'Oh, that is very disagreeable! It is preposterous! We cannot bear the thought!' But it is true." Brigham Young, "Intelligence, Etc.," in *Journal of Discourses*, vol. 7 (Liverpool: Amasa Lyman, 1860), 289. Discourse given on October 9, 1859.

straight in this life, to be worthy of that which is awaiting us in asmuch as we hold out to the end. Oh how grateful I felt that I had been to the Temple ...[4]

Over five years earlier, in 1881, Helen signed her name to a letter she penned for her children, sealing up the document that would convey her dying words—her last legacy—a generational message she hoped her posterity would never forget. Helen's words were written with the fervency of a mother who desired her children's welfare and happiness above all else. She prayed that God would cause her message to be preserved in their behalf:

// Now, my children, I ask Him to bless and preserve these lines that my children & my grandchildren & their children's children may read them & may they all live so as to accomplish th[e] designs of our Maker

Before they have broken this seal the writer of these few lines will most likely have passed onto another stage of action. but I shall live until I have finished my Earthly mission and rejoice in the day of salvation & may all my loved ones enjoy these blessings is the prayer of your affectionate mother.[5]

Inside this priceless letter, Helen recounts the story of her sealing to the Prophet Joseph Smith by writing of her father's desire for their family to be united with the Prophet eternally. She speaks plainly of the challenges this decision naturally compelled her to embrace, openly acknowledging her mother's "bleeding heart" struggle to live plural marriage and introduce the same to her precious daughter. Perusing the soul-baring prose of this mother and grandmother, one learns the answer to the question: *Was it easy for Helen?* Without a doubt, the answer is: *No.* Life rarely is. Helen wrote of her own "bitter price," but her message was never one of despair. Instead, it bore the impartation of ultimate triumph and victory! The spirit of the letter makes it clear that she exulted in the glorious "crown" she had been shown in vision. Her testimony that God had accompanied them, as

---

4   Charles M. Hatch and Todd M. Compton, *A Widow's Tale: 1884-1896 Diary of Helen Mar Kimball Whitney* (Logan: Utah State University Press, 2003), 205.

5   Helen M. Kimball Whitney papers, 1881-1882, p. 5, Church History Library, https://catalog.churchofjesuschrist.org/assets/2c0cb6bb-493b-417a-8bd5-dce48180827f/1/4.

if with shafts of light in their walk through the clouded and dreary valleys of sorrow, and that she and her family stood as "monuments of God's mercy," gave her the determination to persevere:

❧ I am thankful that He has brought me through the furnace of affliction & that He has condesended to show me that the promises made to me the morning that I was sealed to the Prophet of God will not fail & I would not have the chain broken for I have had a view of the principle of eternal salvation & the perfect union which this sealing power will bring to the human family & with the help of our Heavenly Father I am determined to so live that I can claim those promises.[6]

Should Helen's children forget everything she had taught them—everything she had lived for—she desired for this one message to stand the test of time, remaining as clear and vibrant in their memory as the rising sun: Helen was proud and deeply *thankful* that she had been sealed to the greatest man to walk the earth, excepting the Son of God—the Prophet Joseph Smith.[7] She now understood *why* she was destined to stand as a queen of the Restoration. She had awakened to the deepest desire of her heart, realizing where she felt she truly belonged. She was grateful for the thorns by which she had been pierced and bled in mortality, and she wanted her children to know that she knew it, that God knew it, and that she would *never* deny it. Critics could mock and scorn, future readers could puzzle over 'why,' but for Helen, she knew who she was—her true identity—and she felt it an honor to claim it. Helen signed the letter, "Helen Mar Kimball Smith Whitney."

Helen's Connection with the Prophet

In 1894, Joseph F. Smith—nephew of the Prophet, and son of his beloved brother, Hyrum—counseled the Latter-day Saints to hold in remembrance and celebrate the Prophet Joseph Smith's birthday.[8]

---

6   Ibid.

7   Latter-day prophets have taught that no greater prophet in character or mission has lived on the earth than Joseph Smith, excepting Jesus Christ. See article, "Latter-day prophets testify of the Prophet Joseph Smith's greatness," Latter-day Answers, https://ldsanswers.org/latter-day-prophets-testify-prophet-joseph-smiths-greatness/.

8   President Joseph F. Smith taught: "I should like to see introduced among the Latter-day Saints ... the practice of celebrating or commemorating the birthday

Apparently, this tradition had already been adopted by some of the Saints, as multiple entries in Helen's diary demonstrate that she and others observed the day:

// [1889] At last—there's found to be no help only from God—Fast day with the Saints—that the plans of these wicked persecuters may be thwarted, etc. This is the birth-day of the Prophet Joseph Smith. chosen as appropriate for this fasting and prayer—from 5 o'clock Sunday eve—till 5 today.[9]

[1890] Em proposed my being administered to. I went into her room & Apostles D. H. Wells & Franklin Richards administered to me. The spirit of prayers & blessing rested upon the latter he being mouth, to a great degree. This is the 8[blank] birthday of the Prophet Joseph[10]

[1894] This is the birthday of the Prophet Joseph—the 89th, & will be celebrated in several Wards in the city this evening.[11]

During her life, Helen was given several dreams wherein she saw and conversed with the Prophet Joseph Smith. She observed his birthday on December 23, defended his teachings, delighted in bearing testimony of his role and mission to numerous visitors, and

---

of the Prophet Joseph Smith. It is now over fifty years since he was martyred; and during those fifty years, we have never had to my knowledge more than a small private gathering occasionally, in honor of the birthday of the man who was chosen of God and designated by His voice to be the mouthpiece of God Almighty to the inhabitants of the earth in the dispensation of the fullness of times. The only exception I recall was when, on the 23rd of December, 1892, a general fast was proclaimed and observed among the Latter-day Saints, preparatory to the final completion and dedication of the Salt Lake Temple in April following.

"We celebrate what is supposed to be the birthday of our Lord and Savior Jesus Christ, but we get a long way off from His birthday; so that now, instead of celebrating the real birthday of our Lord, which was on the 6th of April, we celebrate the 25th of December in each year. And it is a proper thing that we should hallow His birthday, above all others. And in my judgment—and of course I may be a little biased in regard to this matter—in my judgment the next birthday celebration to that of our Lord and Savior Jesus Christ should be that of Joseph Smith, to this entire people of the Latter-day Saints." Brian H. Stuy, ed., *Collected Discourses*, vol. 5 (Burbank: B.H.S. Publishing, 1987-1992), 5.

9   Charles M. Hatch and Todd M. Compton, *A Widow's Tale: 1884-1896 Diary of Helen Mar Kimball Whitney* (Logan: Utah State University Press, 2003), 386.

10   Ibid., 426.

11   Ibid., 636.

she clung to the fragments of memorabilia she had acquired from his past, including a letter in the Prophet's own handwriting.[12]

In May 1889, Helen dreamed that the Prophet came with other brethren to administer to her daughter, Lillie, who had been suffering from an unidentified affliction. In the dream, he turned to Helen, saying: "'No body has ever understood her case'—meening that no one had known her ales, or what they should do for her.—He emphasised with his hand as well as his voice, and then resumed his prayer, & blessed her."[13] For Helen, the Prophet's tender, *personal* interest and concern for her children in the dream gave her a glimpse of his attentive and fatherly nature. According to early Restoration teachings concerning sealing ordinances, Helen likely felt that, spiritually, her children were Joseph's and, even from the other side of the veil, he was advocating for their welfare. As a mother, Helen may have felt that choosing to be sealed to the Prophet had provided her children with a realm of protection and hope—blessings that they and their descendants after them would assuredly need to weather the last days, far into the future.

In 1885, Helen recorded another dream, wherein, "by faith" she saw "Joseph—the Prophet." In the dream, she knew he was present, but saw only his hand, reminiscent of the brother of Jared's experience on Mount Shelem.[14] Helen wrote:

---

12   Helen's diary records on August 11, 1889: "I showed him some letters found among Horace's papers yesterday—directed to "General Joseph Smith, Nauvoo Hancock Co—Illi"—and one written by him concerning the selling of the "Maid of Iowa" (steem boat) This Sol wanted, but I thought too much of it, this being the only scrap in his hand writing, excep his signature, that I possessed. He asked to take it, which I consented to.—these letters were brought to this country by Bp N. K. Whitney." *Ibid.*, 368.

13   Helen's journal entry on May 22, 1889 records: "Near morning I dreamed of being in a company where Joseph Smith & Emma were—Joseph looked very nice—had on a black beaver hat. I dreamed of him & other brethren administering to Lily—in the midst of it he turned to me—as I stood behind him—& said something like this. "No body has ever understood her case"—meening that no one had known her ales, or what they should do for her.—He emphasised with his hand as well as his voice, and then resumed his prayer, & blessed her. There was a fine Coach & horses waiting for him.—Emma came to me & told me of some one offering her some pecuneary assistance & smiled as she told it, & that she had an abundence—She told me that she owned the place where Ab. Kimball now lives, & that I might have it to live in—I expressed my gratefulness saying that I could now rent my own house—but I thought that house was as it was when father owned it having but one or two rooms." *Ibid.*, 357.

14   Ether 3:1-10.

// [I] only needed faith to see him, which I exercised till I saw his left hand and part of his body. I grasped his hand in mine, & said "This is his hand." I knew it from recollection—his hand being plump and fair. I could not remember much when I awoke.[15]

Helen and many of Joseph's other wives anticipated the foretold return of the Prophet—prophecies many early Saints held in high regard.[16] As Helen and the others strove to build up Zion in the mountains of Deseret, she recorded conversations with those who had been intimately associated with the Prophet Joseph Smith. Now, they desired to share his teachings—to keep his legacy alive:

// Sister [Mary Elizabeth Rollins] Lightner[17] came in the forenoon— met Bro. Joseph Kingsbury here to have a talk about her letter sent by him to Bro. Woodruff. It was an interesting interview. She—by my request related a number of incidents of her life, & a vision that she had which preserved her in the faith. Joseph said among other things that he heard the Prophet Joseph say that he (the prophet) would be the man who—like Moses—would lead this people out of bondage, & that this would take place in 1890[18]—just 3 years, which is according to my belief, & a

---

15 Charles M. Hatch and Todd M. Compton, *A Widow's Tale: 1884-1896 Diary of Helen Mar Kimball Whitney* (Logan: Utah State University Press, 2003), 66.

16 Joseph Smith promised the Latter-day Saints that he would one day return (as a resurrected being) to finish his mission and to "lead" his people again. Brigham Young, Heber C. Kimball, and other early leaders prophesied that the Prophet's work as dispensation head was not finished, and that, in the future, he would fulfill every promise made to him in his priesthood blessings. For quotes and historical sources, please see the documentary, *The Prophet Joseph: More than we know* (DVD), as well as the Latter-day Answers article, "What can we learn from Joseph Smith's patriarchal blessings?" June 27, 2018, https://ldsanswers.org/what-can-we-learn-from-joseph-smiths-patriarchal-blessings.

17 Mary Elizabeth Rollins Lightner was sealed to the Prophet Joseph Smith in March 1842. Mary was one of the teen girls who bravely saved pages of the Book of Commandments when mobs were destroying the printing press in Independence, Missouri. She and her sister hid in a cornfield until the mob had given up searching for them. Mary Elizabeth recorded several spiritual experiences, including the visitation of angels and one experience where she was visited in the spirit by Heber C. Kimball as well as Joseph and Hyrum Smith.

18 Many early Latter-day Saints anticipated that Joseph Smith would return in the year 1890—the result of their personal interpretation of Doctrine & Covenants, 130:15 which reads: "Joseph, my son, if thou livest until thou art eighty-five years old, thou shalt see the face of the Son of Man; therefore let this suffice, and trouble me no more on this matter." Many interpreted this verse to mean 1890, but the Prophet

great many more who are looking forward to that time— and we expect the Temple to be finished in that time—the place where it has been prophesied that I should meet him, & the Savior, & work for the dead, & living.[19]

Being a member of Joseph Smith's family meant inclusion within a circle of men and women who contributed abundantly to the work and spirit of the Restoration with their varying gifts and talents. Helen often spent time with and enjoyed the companionship of inspiring women who were sealed to the Prophet Joseph Smith, as well as those sealed to her father and his close friend, Brigham Young. On one occasion, Helen wrote of an uplifting experience at a meeting when Sister Mary Elizabeth Lightner was "filled with the Holy Spirit—bore a powerful testimony to the truth of this work, and especially Celestial marriage."[20] A few weeks later, Helen was invited to a meeting of sisters where she heard Eliza R. Snow speak in tongues, prophetically blessing and personally encouraging her:

// When I arrived at Em's [Emmeline Wells] the room was filled, and they said they'd waited for me. The meeting commenced— Sister E. R. Snow being the first to speak Sister Elmina Taylor presided, & called on us to speak. Sister E. R. then spoke in tongues & addressed each one separately. It was said to me (the interpretation being given by Sister Zina) that she spoke as with the voice of my mother to comfort & encourage me—that my mind had been troubled over things, which she would not now mention, but that I need not be troubled over these matters— for all would turn out right, etc, etc—Spoke of the work that I'd done with my pen, being greater than I had thought of, & blessings that would be mine, that my "Spirit was mellow, & like Mary, the mother of Jesus, I leaned upon the cross". I could

---

Joseph Smith himself expressed doubts concerning the true meaning: "I was left thus, without being able to decide whether this coming referred to the beginning of the millennium or to some previous appearing, or whether I should die and thus see his face. I believe the coming of the Son of Man will not be **any sooner** than that time." Doctrine and Covenants 130:16-17; emphasis added.

19   Charles M. Hatch and Todd M. Compton, *A Widow's Tale: 1884-1896 Diary of Helen Mar Kimball Whitney* (Logan: Utah State University Press, 2003), 262.

20   Ibid., 162-163.

not doubt the spirit by which this was spoken as they did not know my inward thoughts only by the spirit.[21]

Not only was this a group of beloved, choice friends—this was a *family*, knit together through profound adversity, trial, and faith. Each had a sacred role that transcended this passing, mortal phase of eternity, and the possession of this knowledge bound them together as sisters and family. In June 1895, when the Kimball family assembled to celebrate Heber C. Kimball's birthday, Lucy[22] requested that the day be set apart as a fast specifically for Helen's health:

// Friday, 14th This is my fathers birth-day set apart by Lucy Kimball as a fast for the recovery of my health—The sisters at the Temple, many of them fasted & brethren too—also other sisters who were invited to fast made about 19—but 16 came to my house, some having prior engagements, bringing a picnic, flowers &c.

---

21   Ibid., 168. Helen's description of receiving a comforting message from her deceased mother, through the gift of tongues, should not be confused with the occult practice of Spiritualism and channeling of spirits. Elder Parley P. Pratt delivered a discourse in 1853, describing the difference between "... the lawful and the unlawful mediums or channels of communication—between the holy and impure ..." He reminded the Latter-day Saints that true revelation only comes through repentance, through the name of Jesus Christ, and through authorized priesthood channels:

"... how shall we discriminate between those who seek to Him, and those who seek the same by unlawful means?

"... it is impossible for us to seek Him successfully, and remain in our sins. A thorough repentance and reformation of life are absolutely necessary, if we would seek to Him.

"Thirdly, Jesus Christ is the only name given under heaven as a medium through which to approach to God. None, then, can be lawful mediums, who are unbelievers in Jesus Christ, or in modern revelation; or who remain in their sins; or who act in their own name, instead of the name appointed.

"And moreover, the Lord has appointed a Holy Priesthood on the earth, and in the heavens, and also in the world of spirits; which Priesthood is after the order or similitude of His Son; and has committed to this Priesthood the keys of holy and divine revelation, and of correspondence, or communication between angels, spirits, and men, and between all the holy departments, principalities, and powers of His government in all worlds." Parley P. Pratt, "Spiritual Communication," in *Journal of Discourses*, vol. 2 (Liverpool: F. D. Richards, 1855), 45. Discourse given on April 6, 1853.

22   Lucy Walker Smith Kimball was sealed to the Prophet Joseph Smith in 1843. After the Prophet's death, she was married to Heber C. Kimball for time.

We had a rich feast of the spirit, & I was lifted up by the comforting things said, & promises that the Holy Spirit inspired them to pronounce upon my head, & among them was the restoration of my health & usefulness. The spirit was poured out, especially upon Sisters Phelps & Barney to say things to me which gave me new hope, & faith that I would live and do more work in this generation. Words of consolation were spoken by the Holy spirit concerning my Charley[23] & the great work he is doing in the spirit world. backing up [w]hat Orson is doing on this side, etc, etc. The speaker was Dr Barney. The Sisters all spoke expressing their regards for me & for my father & mother telling of their words of kindness to them numbers told of his prophicies to them with their fulfilment. My table was filled with good things, & the room was hardly large enough for the table & guests.... I feasted more on the spiritual feast than the temporal.[24]

A Sacred Calling to Testify

Identity defines *mission*. Helen's personal identity defined her character, her faith, her strength, her life decisions, and her hope. Throughout her life, Helen felt a sacred calling to speak and bear testimony, as is evidenced by numerous entries in her diaries: "Bro. Gensen called to see me—wants me to write up incidents of my life as soon as I can," she recorded in June 1887. "I gave him a few incidents of Flora Gove's life who was a wife of Joseph Smith–"[25] In the dream where Helen's eyes were opened to see and grasp the Prophet's hand, there was another scene that appeared to symbolically commission her to speak and bear testimony:

// I had swallowed, as food, a great quantity of fine Cambrie needles till my throat was pricked and choaked with them, and I had to work to get my throat cleared of them—throwed up enough so

---

23   Helen Mar Kimball's son, Charley, committed suicide in 1886. See Chapter 17: Faithful & Wayward Children.

24   Charles M. Hatch and Todd M. Compton, *A Widow's Tale: 1884-1896 Diary of Helen Mar Kimball Whitney* (Logan: Utah State University Press, 2003), 665.

25   Ibid., 246.

that I felt relieved. I interpret this—that I shall become so full, that I'll be forced to give utterance to obtain relief.[26]

Helen frequently received visitors who were anxious to hear her firsthand, eyewitness experiences. On May 28, 1886, Helen was busy writing when she was visited by two women—one from Wisconsin and the other from Washington. Both came armed with tough questions, ranging from 'polygamy,' to blood atonement, to the Mountain Meadows Massacre—all of which Helen handled with proficiency, grace, and poise:

〃 They were deeply interested in the history of the "Mormons"— thought it a wonderful thing—This "Mormonism"—I was asked numerous questions—among them—whether there was such a thing as "blood atonment"—"destroying angels" etc—& about the M. M. Masacre. I answered them all, & explained the meening of "blood atonment"—also some of our religious principles, which I was asked about— Mrs Hoit said they were precisely like those of the church she belonged to—They both paid me a high complement for the manner in which I explained things, etc—A thing so foreign from my thoughts that it surprized me—I told them I had a very poor delivery, & there were many of my Sisters far more competant . . . . I handed them the D. News—to read the testimony of Joseph F. Smith and Wm Clayton—to the Prophet's recieving, and practicing plural marriage—I gave each the book—"Womens Protest"—and the Apistle of the Presidency and also my pamphlet on Plural Marriage—They gave me their address, and I gave them mine.[27]

When Helen and her visitors at last bade farewell, the hearts of these two women had been softened and they parted as warm friends:

〃 There was a warm feeling in my heart towards Mrs Hoit. And she had manifested the same towards me. We kissed at parting, and I told her I believed we were kindred spirits before we came on this planet & that we might not meet again in this life, but soon, there would be no other place in the outside world that

26 Ibid., 66.
27 Ibid., 158-159.

they could find peace—that this would be a refuge for the honest who desired to dwell in peace—They appologised for troubling me, and a number of times for asking what I might think impertenant questions, but I told them they need not, I was pleased to answer them, and was in my element when talking of my religion—this being my theme—²⁸

Helen received many visitors who expressed great curiosity concerning Joseph Smith's practice of plural marriage. She had adorned the mantle over her fireplace with a portrait of the Prophet which sometimes evoked welcome questions from visitors, opening a dialogue she was always eager to engage in:

// Had an agent call afternoon . . . she seeing a picture of Joseph Smith on my mantle, made inquiries many having admired his looks previously It led on till I gave a discription of much of his, & people's experience, and of my own—how I was convinced of this being the Lord's work, etc, etc. My body & spirits were benefitted by this conversation.²⁹

Helen's visitors often arrived carrying the baggage of strange misinformation and preconceived judgments she patiently corrected. Her natural gift for charity allowed her to appreciate and value each individual's heart. During Helen's lifetime, the Reorganized Church—led by Emma Smith's sons—violently opposed plural marriage. Their missionaries claimed Brigham Young instigated the practice for his own scandalous purposes, and that the Prophet Joseph Smith never lived the order. Helen, of course, knew this was not true from her own firsthand experience, and she stood as living proof. Her diaries are sprinkled throughout with references to visits from the "Josephites," as they styled themselves. One entry from October 9, 1891 read: "Forgot to mention Zula's sister coming here this morn to hear my testimony. She being a Josephite."³⁰ On another occasion, November 1889, Helen noted in her diary:

---

28   Ibid., 159.
29   Ibid., 475.
30   Ibid., 472.

// Last eve, E. B. Wells & Zina Young called with a young man from Cal, who wanted a testimony from me, & others of the Prophet Joseph's wives to show to his sweetheart's father, who'd dissmissed him from his house for declaring that Joseph had a plurallity of wives—the father— being a member of the Newly organized Church.[31]

On June 16, 1894, Helen received a visit from a man who had followed the leadership of James J. Strang after the Prophet's death, and who was "very anxious to see me." In opposition to President Brigham Young, Strang had proclaimed himself the rightful successor of Joseph Smith in 1844, and for 12 short years, served as a "prophet" to his followers—even professing to translate ancient plates, and reigning as a monarchical "king." After Strang was murdered in 1856 by disaffected members of his own church, most of his followers supported Joseph Smith III, the son of the Prophet Joseph Smith, who had taken up residence in Lamoni, Iowa. Helen was well aware of the antagonism directed at the Saints who had come west with Brigham Young—especially against those who stood in full support of the principles the Prophet Joseph Smith had taught, including Celestial plural marriage. Helen bore her testimony to the visitor:

// I'd told him how I knew this to be the true Church ... I gave him one of my first & second publications in defence of Plural Marriage & he said he'd send me some books—Some of my ideas he said were exactly his own. One was that those chosen to perform the greatest works were the most beset by the advisary & had the greatest faults & weaknesses to grapple with, but when they'd conquered they were the best & firmest in the cause of truth.

"After he'd gone I felt so sick bandaged my head in a wet cloth & laid down—I forgot to mention his telling me that he'd like to ask me some questions. I told him I would answer any that he desired me to. He wanted the testimony of the Prophet Joseph's wives, which he should believe if they said they'd been seeled to him, & would use it, when he met Joseph of Lamoni, as a weppon—that they'd flung some pretty sharp shots at each

31   Ibid., 383.

other. I told him that our testemony—wouldnt be accepted by him, as he'd had it before & rejected it.[32]

As an experienced plural wife, Helen was uniquely qualified to share personal insight. She spoke frequently at Relief Society events around the territory of Deseret,[33] and she published her public defense of plural marriage, as well as her written testimony concerning the Prophet's character.[34] At the end of her life, the summation included in her obituary made mention of her frequent witness of the sacred calling of the Prophet: "It was a pleasure and satisfaction to her to bear testimony of the divine mission of those two great leaders [Joseph Smith & Brigham Young]."[35]

Helen consistently defended Joseph Smith's character

If Helen had experienced any kind of impropriety from the Prophet Joseph, or if she had been aware of any dark blots on his character, she certainly had ample time and opportunity to expose any alleged wrongdoing, even in the slightest degree. However, her writing and her testimony remained consistently positive throughout her entire life. In every opportunity given her—even when convenience could have induced her to recant—she declared without hesitation or question her personal knowledge of Joseph Smith's Christlike character, and she bore her testimony of—even her love for—the doctrines he espoused, including Celestial plural marriage.

---

32   Ibid., 605.

33   Helen's diary records on April 27, 1892: "Spent afternoon at Rachel Simmons—with the Sisters of Relief Society of the Ward—E. B. Wells was there to dinner & till after meeting was called, & spoke, then left. I spoke quite lengthy upon one or two subjects introduced by E. B. W. particularly upon the Celestial order of marriage as taught me by Joseph Smith & bore my testimony to its truth, &c. There were but 3 or 4 who did not speak—& bear a similar testimony. The President asked me to open the meeting by prayer and also close it. I was surprised at this as well as dashed somewhat at the 2nd invite—" Ibid., 499.

34   Helen's journal entry on November 31, 1891 records: "Received a letter from G. Q. Cannon & Sons Co— requesting my name & Post Off. Address, & asking certain questions—of my birthplace, where I first met the Prophet Joseph Smith What were my 'impressions concerning his appearance & Character,' etc. And to give my testimony of him, & relate any incidents I 'may recollect in regard to any of his sayings or doings', etc, 'not on record.'" Ibid., 475.

35   "Helen Mar Whitney: Her Death—A Sketch of Her Personal History," *Deseret Evening News*, November 16, 1896, 2.

Return with Honor

As one gazes across the vibrant mural of Helen's life, her defining characteristics come to the forefront: her divine gift for charity, her sacrificial love for her children, her meek submission to ordained trials, and her remarkable zeal in using her life for good. Perhaps most notably, she kept her perspective aligned with an eternal, *hope-filled* future. If every woman followed Helen's example, Zion would truly be filled with holy women, as Eliza R. Snow envisioned:

// It is the duty of each one of us to be a holy woman. We shall have elevated aims, if we are holy women. . . . There is no sister so isolated, and her sphere so narrow but what she can do a great deal towards establishing the Kingdom of God upon the earth.[36]

Helen's life echoed the testimony of her righteous forebears and continues to stand as a beacon, calling for every Latter-day Saint man and woman to lift up their torch and become a holy people, both individually and collectively. Those who personally knew Helen Mar Kimball Smith Whitney recognized her as "a true heroine," as reflected in an account written by her dear friend and associate, Emmeline B. Wells:

// Volumes might be written of Sister Whitney, her life and experiences in the Church. She was a woman of noble character and attributes and possessed of the most true womanly virtues, and in abundance that beautiful charity "that thinketh no evil." And her compassion for the weak and erring partook of the sublime nature. She was a true heroine in every sense of the word; her sterling integrity to the Gospel and her zeal in the cause of truth were often strikingly exhibited. Her writings were forcible and telling, and she had a natural gift for heroic composition. . . . She possessed great mentality and spirituality, and was intensely poetical, prophetic and patriotic in her nature; and excelled most women in certain lines of writing. . . .

---

36 Eliza R. Snow, "An Address," *Woman's Exponent* 2, no. 8 (September 15, 1873): 62.

Sister Whitney was for many years prominent in the Relief Society and her testimonies to the truth will never be forgotten.[37]

Helen's well-deserved rest came on Sunday, November 15, 1896, as she lay surrounded by some of her immediate family. Just before drawing her last breath, at about ten minutes past 2pm, "she raised her eyes, with a look of surprise, as though the room was full of people." Emmeline shared what all who were present felt—that "no doubt her escort was there":

// She discharged every duty and responsibility placed upon her, whether temporal or spiritual, faithfully. She was a devoted Christian mother and trained her children in the love of the Gospel. Her love for her friends was true as steel, whether in prosperity or adversity. We who remain are bereaved indeed, but we know she was beloved of God, and therefore we say "Thy will be done."[38]

Helen lived a remarkable life that touched those of countless others, leaving many friends, family, and acquaintances to shed heartfelt tears at her passing. Her legacy was truly that of one who endured to the end and did not falter. She lived a life of sacrifice so that her children and fellow Saints—including those who would follow many generations later—could build Zion. In Doctrine and Covenants 25, the Lord counseled the women of the Church to "lay aside the things of this world, and seek for the things of a better."[39] Helen reserved her treasures in heaven—living with her eyes and heart set on eternity. She was indeed "a true heroine in every sense of the word."[40]

While those on this side of the veil mourned her passing, one can only imagine the glorious greeting Helen experienced when she reunited with her eternal husband, Joseph. No doubt there were tears of joy—this daughter of Zion had returned with honor! She

---

37   "Helen Mar Whitney: Her Death—A Sketch of Her Personal History," *Deseret Evening News*, November 16, 1896, 2.

38   Ibid.

39   Doctrine and Covenants 25:10.

40   "Helen Mar Whitney: Her Death—A Sketch of Her Personal History," *Deseret Evening News*, November 16, 1896, 2.

had fought the good fight, she had kept the faith—and she had at long last returned home.

And yet, Helen's story is not finished. For Helen, and all other Saints who choose to tread the stony path of discipleship, the joyous rest that each will reap during the Millennium will far outweigh past trials and heartache. What will be Helen's role, her position, and her influence, then? The final measure of her work, and the summation of her reward is yet to be seen—indeed, the true chronicle of her life, here and in the eternities, is yet to be written.

Helen's Latter-Day Call

If Helen Mar Kimball were here today, what would she have to say to us? If she were to pass again over the land of her beloved Deseret—now filled with bustling cities, highways, offices, schools, shopping malls, warehouses, and neighborhoods—what would she observe? How would she assess our culture, our faith, our families, our businesses, and our conduct? Would she favor and approve of our standards? Would she praise our choices in entertainment and leisure?

Or might she weep over the thousands of Latter-day Saints—especially our struggling youth—caught in the grip of sin, addiction, worldliness, and spiritual blindness? The outlook is bleak, when, by the assessment drawn from inside sources, we may be losing as many as 75% of Millennials in the Church today.[41] Imagine how Helen

---

41   Personal correspondence with multiple sources confirm the essential accuracy of this statistic. Granted, *definitions* are important. What does "losing faith" mean? When is faith lost? What age groups are being considered? Are the statistics accurate? Regardless of how optimistically we approach the research, there is unquestionably an increasingly serious problem. Our purpose is not to debate statistics. It seems to be clear that we are in the midst of a serious crisis.

Jana Riess has a more positive outlook with 'only' "four or five of every 10" losing faith during their youth: "According to the most recent wave of research in that same study, published earlier this year [2020], 61% of the participants who were Mormon as teenagers still claimed that religious identity as adults. That finding is consistent with other national studies from Pew, the General Social Survey, and the Public Religion Research Institute, in which the Latter-day Saint retention rate in recent years has ranged from a high of 64% to a low of 46%. Losing four or five of every 10 young Latter-day Saints is not something to whitewash . . ." Jana Riess, "Jana Riess: Controversial Latter-day Saint book pulled from publication," *The Salt Lake Tribune*, September 8, 2020, https://www.sltrib.com/religion/2020/09/08/jana-riess-controversial/.

Riess also explained in 2019: "In 2007, Pew found that Mormons had an overall retention rate of 70%, which is quite good. By 2014, this had dropped to 64% for

might feel after learning that—for the first time in Church history— roughly ¾ of the age group between 25 and 35 are in some stage of leaving—even renouncing—their faith. It's a staggering statistic, and a foreboding sign of the times.

Furthermore, would Helen mourn to see the character of Joseph Smith disparaged in best-selling biographies presenting the Prophet as a prideful, bumbling, treasure-seeking product of his culture—a groveling, weak man who should be removed from the pedestal erected by past presidents of the Church?[42] Would Helen cry out with indignation at the brazen attempts to cast Brigham Young as a tyrannical, racist autocrat—or even worse—as a murderer and a traitor? What would she say to those who despise and reject the principles she, herself, defended and held so dear? Perhaps one might ask: Were the scriptures she read riddled with errors? Was the history she lived so flawed that it required a progressive reinterpretation? Or did she, instead, live her life as a testimony of the marvelous work and wonder in the latter days—does her voice still herald a call to remain true to the Gospel of Jesus Christ?

---

all generations combined, and to 62% among Millennials.... A less rosy picture emerges from the General Social Survey ... With Generation X we start seeing a drop (62.5%) [retention rate], and with Millennials the drop becomes sharper: for those born after 1981, the GSS finds only a 46% retention rate." Jana Riess, "How many Millennials are really leaving the LDS Church?" ReligionNews.com, March 27, 2019, https://religionnews.com/2019/03/27/how-many-millennials-are-really-leaving-the-lds-church.

42   Many are unaware that there is a growing movement among members and scholars in the Church to change our history. Publications such as *Rough Stone Rolling* promote a progressive interpretation of Joseph Smith as a man who was involved in ritual magic, who used "peep stones" to find treasure, who suffered from "treasure-seeking greed," "anger," and "easily-bruised pride," who possessed "outrageous confidence," "[f]rom time to time drank too much," and grew up with an "oft-defeated, unmoored father"—a father who "partially abdicated family leadership." Excommunicated member John Dehlin and others have cited *Rough Stone Rolling* as one of the most influential works leading members into a personal faith crisis. The Joseph Smith Foundation has produced books and resources to refute this reconstruction of Latter-day Saint history. For more information, visit www.JosephSmithFoundation.org.

You may also be interested in *Faith Crisis, Volume 1: We Were NOT Betrayed!* & *Volume 2: Behind Closed Doors*, which document the organized objective to rewrite Latter-day Saint history from within, unbeknownst to the general Church membership, during the 20th and 21st centuries. These volumes detail Richard Bushman's close friendship with Leonard Arrington, and his work as an outgrowth of the movement Arrington advanced—the New Mormon History undertaking to rewrite the character of the Prophet Joseph Smith, and remove him from 'off his pedestal.'

We truly live in a pivotal moment in world history—we were born for this day of decision. Our future will be defined by *our* decisions and *our* priorities—these truly are 'times that try men's souls.' Today, as prophesied, the characters of the Prophet Joseph Smith and his loyal companions are under vicious attack. The message of the Restoration is under constant assault by critical voices sounding from all directions. No one can afford to stand idly by. Every truly converted member has a sacred, covenantal responsibility to remain true to the Restoration and the faith of their fathers—a duty to advocate for truth.

Helen willingly enlisted to lead her fellow sisters by example—to inspire women who share a critical role in standing alongside their fathers, husbands, brothers, sons, and friends:

// Every principle which the Lord reveals for the exaltation of mankind may be perverted which leads to degradation and even to everlasting damnation. There always has been and always will be those who pervert the ways of the Lord. The Tares must grow with the wheat until the harvest. . . .

The conflict is between them and our God, who has never forsaken His people; but He does not expect us to sit quietly down and fold our hands in idleness, while our enemies are publishing their outrageous falsehoods to blind the eyes of weak and credulous to the most glorious truths of heaven and to throw ignominy and dishonor upon our people, more especially the women and the innocent children, who are as much farther advanced in the ways of God and the order of Heaven, as our slanderers are on the road to perdition, but to use every honorable means to defend ourselves against their vile attacks.[43]

No one is too insignificant or too ill-equipped for this cause—"who knoweth whether thou art come to the kingdom for such a time as this?"[44] Helen Mar Kimball, as a young woman, the 'infamous 14-year-old,' was raised up by the Lord to defend Joseph's character in both her day and ours—especially regarding the confusion and

---

43   Helen Mar Kimball Whitney, "Scenes and Incidents in Nauvoo," *Woman's Exponent* 10, no. 13 (December 1, 1881): 97.

44   Esther 4:14.

condemnation surrounding the Prophet's revelation on Celestial marriage. She was physically weak, and she was only an inexperienced girl when she began her remarkable journey. Her life was fraught with affliction, and she suffered great loss. But she was righteous, she was faithful, and she endured. She was one of the "weak things . . . those who are unlearned and despised," called upon by the Lord "to thresh the nations by the power of my Spirit."[45] Her example stands as a testimony to Joseph's character. She fulfilled her mortal journey, leaving us to follow in her footsteps as champions of a sacred quest to defend the Restoration today.

The faithful legacy of Helen Mar Kimball Smith Whitney must never be forgotten. Where will you stand?

"If I one soul improve, I have not lived in vain."[46]

Helen Mar Kimball Whitney Smith

---

45   Doctrine and Covenants 35:13.

46   Helen Mar Kimball Whitney, "Life Incidents," *Woman's Exponent* 10, no. 2 (June 15, 1881): 9.

APPENDIX

Did Joseph Smith Marry a 14-year-old?

Originally published on LDSAnswers.org, December 17, 2016.
Reprinted here with minor edits.

To many Latter-day Saints, Joseph Smith's sealing to 14-year-old Helen Mar Kimball in 1843 is one of the most 'troublesome' aspects of early Latter-day Saint Church history. Discovering this fact has shocked many Latter-day Saints, leading to confusion and inner conflict.

Who was Helen Mar Kimball?

Helen Mar Kimball was the daughter of Joseph Smith's steadfast and loyal friend, Heber C. Kimball. According to the Prophet:

> Of the first Twelve Apostles chosen in Kirtland and ordained under the hands of Oliver Cowdery, David Whitmer, and myself, there have been but two, but what have lifted their heel against me, namely Brigham Young and Heber C. Kimball.[1]

Helen Mar Kimball's sealing to the Prophet Joseph Smith was first proposed by her father. Helen recorded:

---

1 Joseph Smith, History, 1838–1856, volume D-1, May 14, 1843, p. 1563, The Joseph Smith Papers.

/ / ... he [Heber C. Kimball] taught me the principle of Celestial marr[i]age, & having a great desire to be connected with the Prophet, Joseph, he offered me to him; this I afterwards learned from the Prophet's own mouth. My father had but one Lamb, but willingly laid her upon the alter ...[2]

Many struggle to reconcile Joseph Smith being a man of integrity and virtue with the fact that Helen Mar Kimball was 14 years old at the time of her marriage. The Prophet Joseph was 37 years old at the time. Is this a 'stain' upon the Prophet's character? Should we be embarrassed, and possibly even apologetic?

Early Sealings

Helen was sealed to the Prophet Joseph Smith in May 1843. The historical record is not clear on whether the marriage was consummated at that time or at any time prior to the Prophet Joseph's death. Celestial marriages were performed for eternity—not merely for time. Consider the following pioneer account of the sealing of Mosiah Hancock at eleven years of age and a young woman named Mary:

/ / Although I was very young, I was on guard many a night, and gladly did I hail with many of the Saints, the completion of the temple. On about January 10, 1846, I was privileged to go in the temple and receive my washings and anointings. I was sealed to a lovely young girl named Mary, who was about my age, but it was with the understanding that we were not to live together as man and wife until we were 16 years of age. The reason that some were sealed so young was because we knew that we would have to go West and wait many a long time for another temple.[3]

This account shows that it was not unheard of for marriages to be performed that would not be consummated or fully recognized until the participants reached an appropriate age.

---

2   Helen M. Kimball Whitney papers, 1881-1882, p. 3, Church History Library, https://catalog.churchofjesuschrist.org/assets/2c0cb6bb-493b-417a-8bd5-dce48180827f/1/2.

3   Mosiah L. Hancock autobiography, p. 30-31, Church History Library, https://catalog.churchofjesuschrist.org/assets/5a733b82-8d36-4d13-b4d9-1ea286414adb/0/32.

Underage marriage?

One of the most difficult—and oft-forgotten—aspects of correctly interpreting history is that of endeavoring to remember the culture and context surrounding every event. Can we truly understand Joseph Smith while 21st-century political correctness and modern tradition distort our interpretation of his day? Have we paused to ask: *Is it the truth, or only a cultural paradigm that causes repulsion with Helen's 'underage marriage'?*

It is a documented fact that, in the past, what we now consider 'under age marriages' were often the norm. Several historians and authors have documented the prevalence of teen, and even pre-teen, brides in the last millennia. Historian Margaret Wade Labarge noted:

// It needs to be remembered that many Medieval widows were not old. Important heiresses were often married between the ages of 5 and 10 and might find themselves widowed while still in their teens.[4]

Researchers Richard Wortley and Stephen Smallbone also commented on this cultural norm of the Medieval age:

---

4 Margaret Wade Labarge, *A Medieval Miscellany* (Canada: Carleton University Press, 1997), 52.

Romeo and Juliet, by Jules Salles (1814-1900)

❝ In Medieval and early modern European societies, the age of marriage remained low, with documented cases of brides as young as seven years, although marriages were typically not consummated until the girl reached puberty (Bullough 2004).[5]

An example of teen brides during the later years of the Renaissance can be seen in the female protagonist of the famous Shakespearean tragedy, *Romeo and Juliet*. Juliet is only 13 years old when she secretly marries Romeo. Wortley and Smallbone comment:

---

5   Richard Wortley and Stephen Smallbone, *Internet Child Pornography: Causes, Investigation, and Prevention* (Santa Barbara: Praeger, 2012), 10.

// Shakespeare's Juliet was just 13, and there is no hint in the play that this was considered to be exceptional.[6]

We've heard many criticize Joseph Smith for his marriage to Helen Mar Kimball, but we've never heard a public outcry demanding the cancellation of theatrical performances of *Romeo and Juliet*. Numerous film adaptations, musical compositions, ballet productions, and educational study courses are consumed without a second thought. Are we creating a double standard in our minds?

Wortley and Smallbone traced the history of teen marriages across the Atlantic, from the Old World to the New:

// The situation was similar on the other side of the Atlantic; Bullough reports the case in 1689 of a nine-year-old bride in Virginia. At the start of the nineteenth century in England, it was legal to have sex with a 10 year-old girl.[7]

For thousands of years, teen marriage was far from shocking.[8] However, this historical record proves nothing more than the fact that our cultural ideology regarding the proper age for marriage is an anomaly when compared to the past. Still, the real question is: *Regardless of what has or has not been culturally acceptable, is this right?* To answer this question, we turn to two of the greatest heroines in recorded history: Mary, the mother of the Son of God, and Rebekah, the mother of Jacob, or Israel.

Mary, mother of the Son of God

Many today are unaware that according to several ancient texts, Mary may have been betrothed to Joseph when she was around the same age as Helen Mar Kimball when Helen was married to Joseph

---

6   Ibid.

7   Ibid.

8   Note the following contemporary examples, as shared on Debunking-CESLetter. com, "Marriages to 14-year-olds were uncommon but not scandalous in the 1840s. For example, Illinois Governor Thomas Ford (1842-1846), the state official who forced the Prophet to appear at Carthage where he was murdered, married Frances Hambaugh when she was 15 and he was 28. Jesse Hale, brother to Emma Hale Smith, the Prophet's wife, married Mary McKune when she was fifteen and he twenty-three. Martin Harris, one of the Three Witnesses of the Book of Mormon, married his wife Lucy when she was only fifteen." "Helen Mar Kimball," Debunking-CESLetter.com, https://debunking-cesletter.com/polygamy-polyandry-1/helen-mar-kimball/.

Smith. The Gospel of James (also referred to as the Infancy Gospel of James, or the Protoevangelium of James), recounts the story of Mary's upbringing. While this text is considered 'apologetic' material, and it's authorship likely occurred no earlier than the 2nd century, this apocryphal text reveals insights into Jewish culture and the 'acceptable' age for marriage. This account claims Mary was consecrated to the Lord and served in the Temple, similar to the ancient prophet, Samuel. When she reached the age of 12 years old, she was betrothed to Joseph:

> And when she was twelve years old there was held a council of the priests, saying: Behold, Mary has reached the age of twelve years in the temple of the Lord. What then shall we do with her, lest perchance she defile the sanctuary of the Lord? . . .
>
> And the priest said to Joseph, You have been chosen by lot to take into your keeping the virgin of the Lord. But Joseph refused, saying: I have children, and I am an old man, and she is a young girl. I am afraid lest I become a laughing-stock to the sons of Israel. And the priest said to Joseph: Fear the Lord your God, and remember what the Lord did to Dathan, and Abiram, and Korah; how the earth opened, and they were swallowed up on account of their contradiction. And now fear, O Joseph, lest the same things happen in your house. And Joseph was afraid, and took her into his keeping.[9]

According to this 'Gnostic gospel,' Mary was two years younger than Helen Mar Kimball at the time of Helen's sealing, and Joseph, her betrothed, was an "old man" who already had children. [10]Whether or not the account is accurate, the story reveals the

---

9   Matthew Brown Riddle, *The Sacred Writings of the Apocrypha the New Testament* (North Charleston: Jazzybee Verlag, 2016), 16.

10   Some have expressed concern with age gaps between the man and woman. Again, historically, this was not considered a serious issue in the past. Edgar Allan Poe was 27 when he married his cousin Virginia Eliza Clemm Poe who was only 13. George Washington's brother, Lawrence, married 15-year-old Anne Fairfax when he was 25. Historic literature also reflects similar traditions. For example, Jane Austen's *Emma* portrays a romantic relationship between George Knightly and Emma Woodhouse, with Mr. Knightly being at least 16 years older than Emma. In Charlotte Bronte's *Jane Eyre*, Jane is only 18, while Edward Rochester is in his late 30's when their relationship begins. These relationships were consummated as marriages—again, a difference that does not correlate to the Prophet Joseph Smith's sealing to Helen Mar Kimball.

Child of Mine, by Jon McNaughton

customary age for marriage in the ancient past. The apocryphal text, *History of Joseph the Carpenter* (likely dating to the late seventh or early eighth centuries), is believed to have been based on material from the Gospel of James. It similarly recounts:

// Now when righteous Joseph became a widower, my mother Mary, blessed, holy, and pure, was already twelve years old. For her parents offered her in the temple when she was three years of age, and she remained in the temple of the Lord nine years. Then when the priests saw that the virgin, holy and God-fearing, was growing up, they spoke to each other, saying: Let us search out a man, righteous and pious, to whom Mary may be entrusted until the time of her marriage; lest, if she remain in the temple, it happen to her as is wont to happen to women, and lest on that account we sin, and God be angry with us.

Therefore they immediately sent out, and assembled twelve old men of the tribe of Judah. And they wrote down the names of the twelve tribes of Israel. And the lot fell upon the pious old man, righteous Joseph. Then the priests answered, and said to my blessed mother: Go with Joseph, and be with him till the time of your marriage. Righteous Joseph therefore received my mother, and led her away to his own house. And Mary found James the Less in his father's house, broken-hearted and sad on account of the loss of his mother, and she brought him up. Hence Mary was called the mother of James. Thereafter Joseph left her at home, and went away to the shop where he wrought at his trade of a carpenter. And after the holy virgin had spent two years in his house her age was exactly fourteen years, including the time at which he received her.[11]

Jewish culture allowed women to embrace the opportunities that came with adulthood and motherhood at a far earlier age. One author sources the Talmud, stating:

> B. Sanh while arguing that a young girl should not be married to an old man or to an infant son, urges that daughters should be married when they reach puberty, and the same position is taken with respect to sons.[12]

Yet another ancient text, the Gospel of Pseudo-Matthew ("pseudo" because scholars do not believe it was written by Matthew, the early apostle), places Mary's age at fourteen years old:

---

11   Matthew Brown Riddle, *The Sacred Writings of the Apocrypha the New Testament* (North Charleston: Jazzybee Verlag, 2016), 49.

12   Harvey McArthur, "Celibacy in Judaism at the Time of Christian Beginnings," *Andrews University Seminary Studies* 25, no. 2 (Summer 1987): 167.

❙❙ Now it came to pass, that when she was fourteen years old . . . Abiathar, the high priest, arose, and ascended to the upper step, so that he could be heard and seen by all the people; and when great silence was made, he said, Hear me, O children of Israel, and receive my words in your ears. Since this temple was built by Solomon, there have been therein virgins, the daughters of kings, and the daughters of prophets, and of high priests, and of priests, and they were great and admirable. But when they came to a lawful age, they were given in marriage to husbands, and have followed the course of their precursors, and have pleased God. . . .

. . . all the people congratulated the old man [Joseph], saying, Thou art become blessed in thy old age, father Joseph, in that God hath shown thee fit to receive Mary. And when the priests had said to him, Take her, for out of all the tribe of Judah thou art elected by God, Joseph began to worship them with modesty, saying, I am old and have sons, and why do ye deliver to me this little child, whose age is less even than that of my grandchildren? Then Abiathar the chief priest said to him, Remember, Joseph, how Dathan and Abiram and Korah perished, because they con[d]emned the will of God. So will it happen to thee if thou con[d]emnest what is commanded thee by God.[13]

In this text, Mary's age is referred to as the "proper age," and it is noted that she must follow "the course of their mothers before them." The Gospel of the Nativity of Mary, a recast of the Pseudo-Matthew, also speaks of Mary's "advancing age":

❙❙ Now the virgin of the Lord, with advancing age, also made progress in virtue . . . She came, therefore, to her fourteenth year, and not only could they devise against her no evil, nor anything worthy of blame, but all good men who knew her judged her life and conversation worthy of admiration. Then the chief priest publicly announced that the virgins who were publicly placed in the temple, and had arrived at this time of

---

13   B. Harris Cowper, *The Apocryphal Gospels and Other Documents Relating to the History of Christ* (London: Williams and Norgate, 1870), 39, 42-43.

life, should return home and seek to be married, according to the custom of the nation, and the maturity of their age.[14]

Notice that Mary's age is referred to as "advancing age," and that it was time for her to be married "according to the custom of the nation, and the maturity of [her] age." Could the repulsion felt by many modernists upon hearing of Helen Mar Kimball's sealing at 14 be merely a matter of cultural tradition and convention?

Rebekah, mother of the House of Israel

According to another apocryphal work, the *Book of Jasher*, Rebekah, the mother of Jacob or Israel (the revered father of the twelve tribes or House of Israel), was only ten years of age when she forsook her homeland to become the wife of the birthright son, Isaac.

> And Eliezer related to them all his concerns, and that he was Abraham's servant . . .
>
> And they all blessed the Lord who brought this thing about, and they gave him Rebecca, the daughter of Bethuel, for a wife for Isaac.
>
> And the young woman was of very comely appearance, she was a virgin, and Rebecca was ten years old in those days.[15]

If we are going to question the legitimacy of Joseph Smith's young wives, we would also need to question the purity of these Biblical marriages. While we agree that such convention or practice would not be wise today, we should not condemn the Prophet Joseph Smith, or consider this event in Church History as being damaging to faith, when it merely parallels the lives of the mother of the House of Israel and the mother of the Son of God.

---

14   Ibid., 91-92.

15   *The Book of Jasher* (Salt Lake City: J. H. Parry & Company, 1887), 67.

INDEX

L. Hannah Stoddard, author

L. Hannah Stoddard is the lead author of *Faith Crisis, Volume 1: We Were NOT Betrayed!*, *Faith Crisis, Volume 2: Behind Closed Doors,* and *Seer Stone v. Urim & Thummim: Book of Mormon Translation on Trial*. She is the executive director of the Joseph Smith Foundation and the producer or director of seven documentary feature films.

- Nephites in Europe (Episodes 1 & 2, Quest for the Nephite Remnant) (2019)
- Hidden Bloodlines: The Grail & the Lost Tribes in the Lands of the North (2017)
- Unlocking the Mystery of the Two Prophets: Revelation 11 (2017)
- The Prophet Joseph: More than we know (2015)
- Statesmen & Symbols: Prelude to the Restoration (2014)
- For Our Day: Divinely Sanctioned Governments (2013)
- For Our Day: Covenant on the Land (2013)

In addition to directing Joseph Smith Foundation projects for over a decade, she is often invited to speak on various radio and video programs. Beginning at age 16, Hannah helped direct her first documentary film. She has worked as a history and literature teacher, graphic design artist, software developer, videographer, project manager, agriculturist, and research assistant. Her work focuses on Church history and doctrine, answers to Latter-day Saint faith crisis questions, educational philosophy, culture, and defending the Prophet Joseph Smith. Hannah's research supports the writings and teachings of ancient and latter-day prophets.

James F. Stoddard III, author

James F. Stoddard was a film producer, author, entrepreneur, and father of 10 children. James was the executive strategist for the Joseph Smith Foundation. He was a direct descendant of Asael and Mary Duty Smith, the Prophet Joseph Smith's grandparents, and other Latter-day Saint Church history figures. James was the co-author of *Faith Crisis, Volume 1: We Were NOT Betrayed!*, *Faith Crisis, Volume 2: Behind Closed Doors*, and *Seer Stone v. Urim & Thummim: Book of Mormon Translation on Trial* and the producer or executive producer of eight documentary films:

- Nephites in Europe (Episodes 1 & 2, Quest for the Nephite Remnant) (2019)
- Hidden Bloodlines: The Grail & the Lost Tribes in the Lands of the North (2017)
- Unlocking the Mystery of the Two Prophets: Revelation 11 (2017)
- The Prophet Joseph: More than we know (2015)
- Statesmen & Symbols: Prelude to the Restoration (2014)
- For Our Day: Divinely Sanctioned Governments (2013)
- For Our Day: Covenant on the Land (2013)
- Creation and Evolution: A Witness of Prophets (2007)

James worked in private, public, religious, corporate and home education as well as engineering, videography, property development, and natural health. He started and helped operate several family businesses and enjoyed working with his kids. James spent any free moments working on Highland Cathedral Estate, a planned family retreat and learning facility with perennial gardens and walking trails specializing in experimental farming techniques and four-season food production. James worked as a release time Seminary teacher and as an instructor at the Provo Missionary Training Center (MTC). His research supports the writings and teachings of ancient and latter-day prophets. James passed away peacefully on September 6, 2021 after a courageous battle with stage 4 lung cancer.

Nephites in Europe Documentary
(Episodes 1 & 2) Quest for the Nephite Remnant
Winner, 2nd Place—LDS Film Festival Feature Documentary—2020

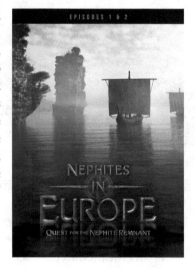

For over a century and a half, we assumed the Nephites struggled to extinction. What if remnants escaped to Europe, Japan, New Zealand, Burma, etc.–to become nations, kindreds, tongues, and people? An ancient Icelandic text records a royal family in Northern Europe descending from a prince by the name of Nefi or Nephi. Another Northern European tribe was known by a name that likely means the "people of Nephi." Did Nephites travel to Europe?

EPISODE 1: NEPHITES IN EUROPE

An ancient Icelandic text records a royal family in Northern Europe descending from a prince by the name of Nefi or Nephi. Another Northern European tribe was known by a name that likely means the "people of Nephi." Did Nephites travel to Europe?

EPISODE 2: NEPHITE SURVIVORS IN PROPHECY

Did righteous Nephite families escape and spread throughout the world? Was Joseph Smith a descendant of Joseph, son of Lehi? Why did the Lord tell Joseph Smith that the Book of Mormon would be given to Latter-day Nephites, Jacobites, Josephites, and Zoramites as well as Lamanites, Lemuelites, and Ishmaelites?

Guest Appearances: John D. Nelson, Scott N. Bradley, Timothy Ballard

RUNTIME: 1 HR 2 MIN

Order now at www.JosephSmithFoundation.org
or watch on Amazon Prime

JOSEPH SMITH FOUNDATION DOCUMENTARIES

www.JosephSmithFoundation.org

Statesmen & Symbols: Prelude to the Restoration

What do LDS temples have in common with the Great Pyramid of Giza, Stonehenge, and the Hopewell mounds in North America? Why are some of the sacred symbols used by the Founding Fathers also found on tapestries in China that date to the time of the flood? What are the details of American Founding Father Benjamin Rush's vision concerning Thomas Jefferson and John Adams?

Unlocking the Mystery of the Two Prophets: Revelation 11

Who are the two prophets in Revelation 11, the two messengers who lie dead in the great city? An assassination by enemies, a forbidden burial by persecutors, and bodies lying in the street for three and a half days are only a few of the clues found in scripture revealing their identity. The two prophets have generally been shrouded in mystery ... until now.

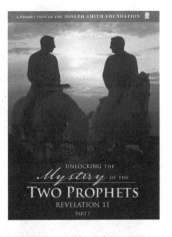

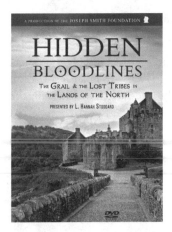

Hidden Bloodlines: The Grail & the Lost Tribes in the Lands of the North

Winner, 3rd Place
LDS Film Festival Feature Documentary—2018

The legendary search for the Holy Grail has resonated with millions for centuries! What is the Holy Grail, and why is this legendary symbol important to the lives of Joseph Smith and the Son of God? Was Jesus Christ married and did He have children? Discover your own heritage, your own royal birthright, in a way you may never have imagined!

Joseph Smith Foundation Documentaries

www.JosephSmithFoundation.org

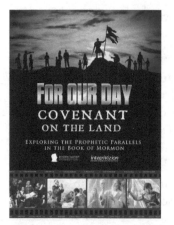

For Our Day: Covenant on the Land

This film discusses the covenant on the Promised Land for both ancient and modern inhabitants, presenting inspiring history from the American colonization, paralleling the Puritans, Pilgrims and other righteous forebears with Lehi, Nephi and the first part of the Book of Mormon. Is latter-day history laid out and foreshadowed in the Book of Mormon?

For Our Day: Divinely Sanctioned Governments

This film compares the Nephite and Latter-day governments of liberty, covering principles of liberty including: Unalienable Rights, Oath of Office, Federalism, the U.S. and Hebrew connection, as well as the Laws of Mosiah. This feature documentary adds an understanding of governmental principles as they are taught in the most correct book, the Book of Mormon.

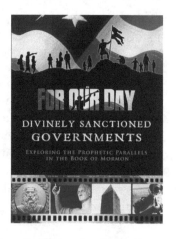

The Prophet Joseph: More than we know

Ground-breaking research on latter-day prophecy! Is the Prophet Joseph the Angel in Revelation 14, the designator of Zion inheritances, the Messenger in Malachi, the Servant in Isaiah, the passport to Celestial glory, the Voice crying in the wilderness? Discover the Prophet Joseph Smith in a way you have never imagined!